The Boringbar War

Being a Tale of the War and the Pieces Left Behind

by Michael Wallace

The Angry Clown
Drawn by the Authors Son
(age five) at Boringbar

A Handbook on How to Survive

- Divorce

- Madmen

- Witches and

- Insane Lovers

Property For Sale

PROPERTY FOR SALE: 250 acres going cheap!
Seaviews, Waterfall, Springs, Creeks.
Bordering National Park and VERY private.
Owner must sell. All offers considered.
Approved for Subdivision.
Close to Bling Bling and Sin City
1/2 Cleared with Rainforest and tall timbers.
Comfortable cottage with pure water

Leuconoe, close the book of fate,
For troubles are in store,
Live today, tomorrow is not.
- Horace (Quintus Horatius)

• • •

We are
sandwiched
between our
reality and our
dreams.
But if we
survive
ourselves and
our self
created
situations we
discover that
our conflicts
are merely the
cutting of the
jewel.
Our abrasions
whittle the
wood of our
being and in
time, with
luck, we may
even become
useful to
ourselves

We may even
come to LIKE
ourselves.

• • •

The world's a stage and most of us are desperately unrehearsed.
Sean O'Casey (1880-1964), Irish playwright

**This Book was written for the 3 Day Novel Race
Queen's Birthday Long Weekend
Start: Friday 9th June 2006 @ 9.20 pm
End: Monday 13th June 2006 @ 7.42 pm**

The Waterfall on the Boringbar Property

**As this book was written in 3 Days
My apologies in advance for those persons I omitted
And whatever the Literary Sins I committed**

THE BORINGBAR WAR

Being a Tale of the War and
the Pieces Left Behind

Copyright © 2015 Michael Wallace

All Rights Reserved

Published by Ladder to the Moon Publications.
ISBN: 978-0-9941798-0-7
Mailing: PO Box 1355 Kingscliff, NSW 2487
WEB: laddertothemoon.com.au
All rights reserved to the copyright holder.

This book is dedicated to Erwin Baudzus
You may not be here, but I still feel you around. Who would want to rest in peace? That would be a waste and I know you prefer to be busy helping people, as always.

INDEX...

The Boringbar War

Being a Tale of the War and the Pieces Left Behind

Today, my son, Ben, broke his collar bone. It all happened just a few hours ago. I get the call, and so Dad (that's me) is once more off to the rescue. We get to the doctor, the hospital nurse straps him up, then come the pain killers, some dinner, and his bed is set up in front of the TV with chocolate, food, an X-box and instructions to take it easy.

The poor little guy. His whole weekend is now ruined. It was planned (as always) to experience the greatest degree of fun possible. Stay over at one friend tonight, (ruined) another friend Saturday night, (gone) then go to the Raceway on Sunday. (kaput) Monday, and there is no school as it is the long holiday weekend, so maybe stay home to recover? Get some friends over, ride motor bikes, tell stories. A mere two days school, then holidays start Thursday. It was all looking good. Brilliant, in fact.

But today, tragedy.

Right now he is in pain, his plans are all in ruin, and it IS tragic. He is in the car, grumpy, everything hurts, and the weekend fun is as broken as his collar bone. "And just before the holidays," he mopes. I admit to laughing to myself, quietly, even as I felt for him. He is just getting a taste of all the broken plans and lost dreams that life will hold for his future, but of course I say nothing.

Ben just wanted sympathy, a bed, and some pain killers. But above all (and this is a secret all parents learn) an unhappy child needs CHOCOLATE. So before we go anywhere, right after the doctors we go to buy CHOCOLATE. Just the sight of it works a treat. Chocolate is the best pain killer of all. Feed em up, roll em out, rawhide. So Ben is fed chocolate, nursed, drugged and watered then left with the remote while Dad ducks off for his appointment with destiny to write this "Instant Novel" you now hold. I check often, but he's good.

It's an odd notion, isn't it? Three days to write a book? Earlier that day I had been in contact with Professor George, the writer of the "Diceman" books (amongst others equally famous yet less notorious novels) looking for advice. It occurs to me in the to and fro of our conversation that "Light, Easy, Snappy, Funny" are concepts that count. All these are important. And whimsy! But also solid stories that smack you between the eyes. SO whimsical stories that have a solid point would be perfect!

Yet where do I start?

I ask myself: Where is the meat in this tossed salad of thought, this ocean of notion? Prof George had already suggested writing about the characters I had met, a sort of real life "Little Prince". Why? It keeps it real, it keeps it to things that HAPPENED, and I don't have to create storylines or plots. This allows me the freedom to just write, no invention needed, just find the connecting thread between all the various strange characters I have encountered. A theme? Maybe the journey from confirmed bachelor to the married man to the divorcee? No, that's not it. Way too dull.

Then the phone rings. Ah yes, I forgot. The fellow I was going to deliver the non-running ride-on mower to is wondering when it will arrive. Bugger. I think to myself as I hear his eager voice: *My God, what drama and travail that Ride On Mower has seen. What paths through jungles it has beaten!* He has NO idea, but he is getting it cheap and he gets it delivered. Let's just say I suffer no remorse letting it go.

I had forgotten him. I was getting ready to deliver it when the call came from Ben "Daaaaaad, I think I broke my collar bone!" I get to the Doc then get him home. THEN a pair of Yahoo's turn up who want to rent a room. Nice enough fellows, but I had only advertised ONE room to help cover the rent. They want TWO. And we all know that two yahoos mean their friends, and weekends full of noise, and cars. It also means I evacuate this writing room.

However, Ben is deeply impressed by their significant body piercings and their utterly cool 20 year old attitude, so he stirs from oblivion and asks questions about the cars they drive. Herein lies flat mates who have the possibility of heaven for a 14 year old lad. One of the chaps (I think of them as boys) brags that he has spent over $200K on cars in the last 7 years. Race Cars, Show Cars, Car Cars. Ben is more than happy, and somehow they arrange to move in next week. I still wonder about some of the things we agree to in the quest to survive.

A curious fact: Strangers and friends all share a common goal - their own interest. They need a place to stay, I need some money. Between these two rocks of compromise we hopefully will find a pillow rather than a hard place. Mind you, these guys were tame compared to the mad freaks that regularly camped out on the property at Boringbar. Or 250 acres of madness, one visitor described it.

And all this is happening right when I am supposed to be getting to this book. I have only ideas, and notion of the thread that connects them. Right now, I sit and scratch my head, and notice that it is already well after 9.00pm on Friday the 9th June, 2006. I have got to get moving! May the Muse strike me.

All I know is that I have survived a war. A small war to be certain, but a war nether-the-less. Was it a tragic comedy or a comic tragedy? Both masks represent life and theatre and I have had BOTH visiting, dressed in full clown outfits during this last decade. This time at Boringbar has been about Divorce, Insane neighbours, Mortgages, Courts, Trials, etc. Is it a divine comedy or merely an improvised kaleidoscope of mayhem? Either way, it was worthy of Warhol and the whole show mirrored a cast of weird, wonderful characters.

I wonder today how on earth it all happened. More to the point, why? Perhaps it is simple. Between the Fields of Mars and the Cupids Arrow we are all just the suffering, plaintive observers of our experience. We are the actors given the script, and though the plot has no sense, we act it anyway. We turn each page, and read our script, hoping it is all going somewhere.

There are some rules in life is seems.

- ONE: Whenever you gain ANYTHING, someone or something will want to take it from you.
- TWO: Whatever joy you find there will be an equal and opposite pain ready and waiting to surprise you. Life is a high wire act between adventure and defeat.

Let me indulge is a moment of platitude. FACT: Our life is our experience. And experience always comes at a cost. We gain an inch, we lose it. We make a gain, we endure a loss, and we suffer from both. Yet we grow. And we grow BECAUSE of the process, not in spite of it. Ideally our process teaches us the wisdom to define our lives and draw clear boundaries. Why would this be important? Well, if we don't know who we are, and if we don't understand our limitations, Clint Eastwood will shoot us. He will, I have seen it in his movies!

1. **Every Gain inevitably has a cost. (Money, Time, Friends, etc.)**

2. **You can call it Karma (Difficulty and Odd Circumstances) but then we choose. And what do we choose?**

3. **Detachment or Stagnation: We get rid of the wrecks, or we drown in them.**

Obviously, I am already writing and the stream of consciousness is flowing down the corridors of memory, and running through the portals of Boringbar experience. Only now do I sit back and realise that I survived a war, a brutal, no holds barred battle with ex-wives, neighbours, erstwhile friends and a variety of hangers on that make the freaks from the local circus look normal.

My greatest enemy, however, was really myself. I learned a lot about how to deal with things over this decade of argument and conflagration. We never learn enough, and I still fuck up, but at least now I know now how badly I can do it. Surely this has a value?

Official Start of Book: Let's call this started, shall we?:

War, and the motivation for war, is very simple: It's all about getting something someone else has, and defending what you have got. More importantly, it's all about that single thing we all share, that thing called the Human Condition.

Boringbar: The Human Condition.

"Human, all too Human"

Wisdom in hindsight is a cliché for a very good reason. When we look back we can easily see how stupid we have been. When we look forward, never. I started out being innocent, naive and truly unaware of human depravity. I had all the baggage or our shared Roman heritage, all those high-flung notions and ideals of our forefathers stamped across my brow. Borringbar cured me of such innocence.

In our society, great ideals such as Nobility and Self-Sacrifice are held up as marvellous things, and they are in small doses. Yet true wisdom tells me that I can't eat an ideal or survive the cross.

Facts are: Nobility looks good in the mirror and sacrifice is good for the Soul, but let's face it, we also need a pot to piss in. Beyond eating, farting and flushing away the remnants of our culinary pleasure as every animal does, the reality of life is about survival. And like any desperate men in desperate times, we often survive a minute longer by drowning someone else.

Children survive by being parasites to their parents. Lovers survive by sucking on the affection of the beloved. Rarely do we find the full glass not being drunk from by an empty one. We tend to live in each other's pockets, and then get busy trying to get into each other's pants. It all tends to be a ritual of "Get get get". We know that in the process someone, or something, has to give, but preferably not US.

And we are deaf to the obvious. Go up to a fat man and tell him he is fat because he eats too much, and he will say "No, I simply don't exercise enough!" Tell him he is fat because he doesn't exercise enough, and he will say "Really, no, I just eat too much." Tell him he is fat because he eats too much and doesn't exercise and he will cry, then eat a cream bun to console himself.

That's the Paradox of the Fat Man. It's our paradox as well, in some way.

As the wise man said "It's complicanated" It is quite extraordinary and you may not presently believe it, but virtually ALL of our beliefs and almost all of our thoughts are all based in horse crap. We have a thousand notions stuffed into our heads, and almost none of them are more than marginally true except those precious few ideals we might class as "Selfless". And most of those I find are suspect.

Herein lies the Human Condition. We suffer a variety of very basic day to day questions: When is enough, enough? What is my fair share? How much do I pay and what do I get?

Well, first let me just say that the human condition tends to tell porkies. We tell lies to get what we want, and most of us want to WIN. Most of us want to do better, get more, and be richer. Modern society has changed natural values: "What will you give me for this?" has become, "What can I get from you?" We run around, usually blind to our natural selves and to others, with the focus on simple survival shifting to becoming a need to WIN! Winning at any cost is called success. It's not a good way to make friends.

The Temple of Apollo gave the advice to all who consulted the Oracle: "Know Thyself". But on the OTHER side of the plinth there was another far less quotable quote: **Nothing Too Much**. This is where the saying "Moderation in Excess" comes from. I see a lot of the opposite. Our entire modern life is closer to Heinlein's reversal of this: *Excess in Moderation*. And generally, we would all get more excess into ourselves if we could, but we usually run out of the money or energy to obtain it.

Let's cut through the philosophy. I will tell you the secret: **It is all horse crap.** Not just the depth of it, Madam, but the sheer quality of the horse crap is what we must appreciate. Just as the Inuit (Eskimo) have thirty six names for SNOW, we have 3000 names for our social Horse crap. Call it "Processing" or "Emotional Release" or "Cultural Difference". Call it what you will, your experience of life in the Western world will be full of it. Even if YOU are pure as the driven snow, someone is throwing Horse Crap over you, somewhere, somehow. So when you next look in the mirror, there you are, covered in crap.

Don't give me "Piety" or "Modesty". These things are invariably skulking sexual predatory behaviours merely painted up to look pretty. Peel back the veneer of respectability and there's someone trying to pull the wool over your eyes in order to get something from you. The Rules are:

- *If it looks nice it is probably expensive.*
- *If the pretty girl is smiling at you, she wants something.*

If you are lucky, you want the same thing as the pretty girl. If not, you have already lost your wallet. Who am I kidding, you already lost your wallet the moment you put eyes on her.

Maybe you will call me jaded, but I prefer to call it realistic. Half full or empty? Who cares. Do you want to drink it, or not? The truth of our society is that many of our so called noble ideals are really just an avoidance of self dressed up in a fluffery of shoulds, woulds and coulds.

How so? If you are scared to chat up the girl on the bus, you may pray to the Gods, and possibly blame them for your sexual starvation, because they do nothing. Going up and directly asking her is she is interested sets off all your fears of rejection, so you pray for salvation. Why? We pray to unknown Gods because we are scared that we are not worthy, and with unanswered prayers ringing in our ears, we fell abandoned. As a consequence, we then work to a position of power in a bureaucracy or office, so we can convince the mirror of our fate that we are "good enough". Basically, we are avoiding our natural selves. That's the start of the horse-shit world we are digging our way through.

What is more, if you revealed the raw truth of the personal social lie most live, they would then reinvent this as a prayer to a higher force, and call the avoidance of self a noble ideal. Example: How wonderful that I struggled under my insecurity to fight the good fight and get that great job. In other words, I crucified myself and I can't tell anyone how stupid this whole process is.

We start out OK. Our initial horse crap smells sweet and undefiled. As children we often imagine ourselves to be Superman defeating the evil ones, or heroes of some drama. We are the ones that protect the frailty of the masses and triumph over adversity. This sort of imagination is horse crap, but it is GOOD horse crap. Noble ideals and kind people can grow from this manure.

However, time usually provides us a downward slope to slide on. The slippery dip of middle age comes on us and the edges of our ideals are worn down to what we call a 'practical' sheen. You might otherwise say we polish the turd. Let me ask you: Are you more content with a good chat and a decent cup of coffee than a great dream? There is nothing wrong with this, if we ARE content with who and what we are, but how many can truthfully claim this? Who is really happy? Who has grown a rose out of their personal allotment of horse crap? Precious few. Most slide the slippery slope to slop and slosh in Slithey Toves of Sloth.

As a direct result of the "slide" most people become liars to themselves. We paint our face with a smile, while inside we hate our life. We are polite when we want to scream. We act "nice" when we want to fornicate and run wild in the woods. We are forgotten of our instincts.

We once were eagles, but after so long hanging with the seagulls, our talons are blunt on the rocks of the day to day. Yet in our minds eye we are undiminished, our dream image remains unglazed and bright. Who wants to hear the truth? No, that is to be avoided while we lie to ourselves, and paint carefully our two faces of inner and outer self, deeply fearful of truth's mirror which will show we are not Cinderella after all, and that the prince is not at the door.

You cannot believe how much pain we cause our life as a result of this habit of lying to ourselves. Read Bukowski if you want to understand this. Yet he missed something profound. In all his hatred of the human condition, and despite his innate wisdom, he missed a simple, simple thing. Love. We are never greater than the love we demonstrate. But at least he spoke his earnest truth to his personal mirror, and did so without blame.

Many come to believe their lies to their personal mirror IS their truth. Inside the thoughts of the most common fool, his imagination is telling him that he is a marvellous chap, deserving of the greatest accolades. Stealing he will call survival, and another person's loss is merely a possibility for personal gain. It is all about "me".

Boringbar, that cruel and harsh teacher of wisdom, showed me all of this, yet it also showed me the opposite. A few of the old farmers in the valley were so up front, so without any form of guile or pretence that you would swear they were made of the Earth itself. And they were. No Lie had ever survived their self-deprecating candour. The soil of ages had ground into their being. Long years of living in the hands of the fates had given these Souls a fortitude and directness that honoured each moment with the truth of what they see and who they are. If you are full of crap, they know it. But to these folk it is OK if you DO something with it.

Horse crap has but one use, to help the roses grow. A spade is a spade, and it's no use unless you are working it,

Even so, most are still run by this simple truth: *We are often made happy enough with our lot simply by seeing someone else suffer more than ourselves.*

You look at news on the TV don't you? If you feel the smallest satisfaction when someone else is doing it tough while you are OK, then the Social Lie of smug self satisfaction has a piece of you. And the paradox is that this smugness will often show as SYMPATHY. Sure!

You may feel bad for them, but quietly, don't you really feel just that little bit superior? It's all part of the subtle self-loathing. The cure? When we LIKE ourselves, we are free.

Self Worth, this is the issue. The Lie is tied to the belief we are in a competition with life, that we are either better than another, or less, according to how THEY value us. This belief causes us to act outside of our true nature, while self worth holds us within. When we use our sense of self worth to define ourselves we find it creates what seem to be our natural boundaries.

But why should I chastise you, or judge myself? I blame no one, and merely seek to observe the obvious. Humans are human and we all share the human condition. Even when we do attain success, and find a degree of achievement or accolade in our lives, we still squabble amongst ourselves.

Why? Seems to me that we live like chickens in the pen, seeking only a pecking order within which to place ourselves in life. We are animals, and I look at the cats around me as I write, and I think "We are largely the same."

The main difference is that animals recognise horse crap, and avoid it.

Or do they?

Of Cats and Men

Two cats: The black one on my lap is glowering at the other cat who is sitting a tad too close for comfort. Perhaps I will pay the "other" cat too much attention? Of course, Lynx, the "other" cat looks up and says to me with her eyes "Why do you pat that miserable little tart? I thought *I* was the one you loved!" So I reach out and pat her, and point out (lovingly) that perhaps she has her faults as well?

Alas she heard! *Forsooth doth brilliant the fangs most nastily protrude with exuberant charm.* The claws I currently feel in my hand are not anger, no! They are merely honest responses to things that upset her.

You see, Lynx the 20 year old cat is telepathic. She KNOWS I like the other cat. Her subsequent stand-off-ishness and turning away when she believes she is being ignored is not jealousy; it is simply keeping her dignity intact.

In fact: How DARE I cater to the whims of her opponent (the other cat) in the realms of affection seeking behaviour! There can be but ONE of importance and that is SHE. The other is a minion to be ignored, chastised and cast out at every possible opportunity. To emphasise this, she turns and hisses in the general direction of the evil sister.

Yet on other days, the pair get on quite well. We humans are like cats.

We are no better than our felines and, in many cases, far worse. Look at the similarities. We kill for the sake of it. We are vain and allow our pretensions to rule our every move, and worse: We go further down the dark corridors of self destruction than any cat would dare. We have developed an extraordinary ability for martyrdom. Even as we immolate ourselves in our desires, we burn for more! We seek to consume, to be consumed and to consummate our consumption with a cry of "MORE!"

The black cat has now moved so Lynx hops up to purr into my lap, and my mind is cast back to the cat fight that has been the Boringbar experience. I am out of it now, safe and secure, closeted in a nice house far away from the maddening crowd. But I ask: Where do I go from here? What exactly is the future away from the blood stained emotional battlefield of Boringbar? I don't have post traumatic stress disorder, I just have a post-trauma disorder! Disorder, as it is hard to keep things tidy when so many things you dreamed and held valuable are trashed and in pieces all around you. I had the war, now I have the pieces. It is a distant memory already, and I ask myself: Did ANY of the entire journey have any redeeming values at all? If so, what, and why is it important?

Such questions are dangerous things. They take us on journeys; often to place you prefer not to go. If I dare travel inside, moving past those Blake inspired Halls of Los where the statues reach out and beg me for their attention, then what is there? What hides behind that door at the end of the locked room?

Without even realising it this book opens up to me. I begin to write. I open the creaking hinges of the recent past, and fall headlong into the waiting arms of the lost dreams, broken promises and the wasted years that represent what Boringbar is to me. I summarize this below. (I do lots of summaries)

Boringbar Equals:
1. **Low-heeled, two-faced bitchery that holds pretence as the ultimate sacrifice.**

2. **High notions of grandeur died black in the slothful bath of human desires.**

3. **Badly repaired emotions sinking into an endless ocean of compromise.**

4. **Flotsam and jetsam of dreams pretending to be Titanic's before the Iceberg**

5. **Paranoia of the fear that we are paranoid of our fear**

A Jewish woman once advised me, "Make paranoia your friend, and you have a friend for life." I thought she was just being paranoid. However it is a truth. The reality we share is generally not the kindly dreams of childhood where friends play easily in the sand pit. No, now they have knives and anger. People backstab our good name, corrupt our good intentions and generally presume we are similar, or at least their equal, in personal vindictiveness. Some at Boringbar are quite possibly their better! So get in FIRST. Like caged animals we roam around the constraints of polite society wanting, wishing, dreaming of raging against the machine, yet in the end, we simply rage against our rage. We become emotive Luddites, carelessly throwing the spanner of self-loathing into the works of our own being.

We destroy ourselves and our relationships because we fear. We fear because we have not experienced enough love. We cannot experience enough love, because we fear. It's a bitch of a circle. We are playing a crap shoot with relationships, and we don't even know the stakes.

An Example: Internet News: June 9 2006.

Teen convicted in dice game killing By Carlos Sadovi: Tribune staff *reporter. Published June 9, 2006*

"A 13-year-old boy was found guilty of first-degree murder Thursday in the fatal shooting a Hazel Crest man during a dice game on the South Side. The boy, who was 12 when the shooting occurred on Nov. 13, is one of the youngest people in Cook County to be convicted of murder."

Have you any idea how many people murder someone after a Dice Game? I looked it up, it's not uncommon and goes all the way back to Roman times. Dicing with death, indeed! People destroy each other in a hundred ways.

How many headlines do we need before the reality is rubbed like salt into our eyes? Yet before I came to Boringbar I knew nothing of the depth of this depth of our human pathology towards destruction. Perhaps I had observed the perimeter, the shape, the texture of the human condition, but nothing prepared me for the little town south of the border.

It looked so charming, benign, sweet and so very 1950's. Yet as I scratched the veneer I was to uncover an extraordinary one-eyed two-face barbarity coming from certain members of the Boringbar tribe.

These ones regard you with singular disregard, and paint your 'out of town' presence with disdain. The most curious form of disregard is the one that has a depth of depressive, single-minded cunning while disguising itself as nature-loving, caring and gentle. It's an act, and at first you believe it. You truly believe the person cares. Yes, well, I grew up. It fooled me, at first. I believed I was moving to the country where neighbour helped neighbour, and the smiles were genuine, but really I was joining the cast of a real life Survivor. False Smiles, False Friends and False Impressions, with the only goal being to WIN!

But to win what? I pull away from the brink, and realise that this dialogue, this mere panache of stitches and dreams and hobnobbed views (Can you hobnobble a view?) is a story meant to entertain!

Forgive me as I stray into the personal worlds of observation. I sincerely would like to think the writing of this journey, from my flourish of fresh faced pre-Boringbar childhood to the after-Boringbar jaded adult, would help me find the signposts back to the childhood that is lost within myself, but in all honesty I don't hold out too much hope in this respect. Some things go on for just too long, and engrave themselves into the consciousness. The dysfunction punctures the surface, and stains itself under the skin like a tattoo.

1: Low-heeled, two-faced bitchery that holds pretence as the ultimate sacrifice.

That curious by-line may seem unintelligible to most, but for you few who do grasp the meaning there is probably little need for you to proceed further. You already hold more than 90 percent of this dialogue inside your bitter heart. I both pity and envy you who have already grasped the above.

An Epiphany of Bitches, Bullshit and Blame

The problem started when I bought in an area of the valley where no one else had bought for some 30 years. Now, in the 18th century this may not have been such a thing, but in the modern society where people are in and out of residences every 2 to 7 years, this is a remarkable thing. Longevity and continuity are not conducive to a society where electronics are replaced every two years, and light bulbs are designed to fail.

I unknowingly committed a grievous crime. Not only was I the first to move into the area in 30 years, I had also bought the largest single acreage in the valley. And as if this wasn't bad enough, I bought it cheap. Now to any of you who understand the gossip-ridden mentality of a small town, you will already understand how I lit a fire, and how quickly it would spread. For the rest of you, just wait, you will get burnt by the understanding sooner or later.

Scientists tell us that, according to our DNA we are all given a "Message Stick" on the day of our birth. But it is not just the genetics we are given, it is what we are going to DO with them that counts.

Despite the trials and tribulations I am to face in the subsequent tales I have to say, at Boringbar I finally came to understand the message stick that was given to me. Of course, I had to be beaten over the head with it to fully realize how simple a message it was, but be that as it may, I survived the lesson. I may not survive the consequences. Even though we might survive the atomic test, the radiation will burn you long after the explosion has died. At best, perhaps I have finally learnt how to open the secret codices that will stop the next bomb from exploding in my face. Maybe the apple fell on my head a little too late, but I have finally come to understand the Law of Gravity.

You have seen the Da Vinci Code, or similar? It is all about solving puzzles. The real problem with puzzles, and puzzle boxes, is that just as you think you have solved it, you realise all you hold is a page from a book. When you turn it over, like the new leaf, you discover to your horror or delight (depending on how you view puzzles) that the next puzzle page is written in Finnish. And it has anagrams from the Scottish Highlands you need to now find to solve it.

It all costs us time and/or money to solve. We incur debts during our sojourn at the University of Hard Knocks. That's not the problem, everything has a cost. The difficulty is with finding the emotional cash flow to pay for it. However, I should not stress over such trivialities. The puzzle of human nature and how much it costs us, is one that even the best Professors at the worlds greatest universities can't seem to answer. I should not feel alone in this space.

So MY solution is something I found on the walls of a café in Subiaco, Western Australia. Simple advice from a graffiti artist who wrote,"When your back is against the wall, turn around and WRITE on it."

Read on sweet reader, travel with me on the journey! If you dare unmask the truths herein, you will never be quite the same again. If you are currently bored with life, or just boring, then stop and catch the ride to Boringbar and, if nothing else, put your problems and woes into a new perspective by relishing the drama and consequence of the far larger problems and more complex woes suffered by someone else. (That would be myself, if you haven't guessed.)

I swear to you, everything you read it is all dreadfully, horrendously true. As I say, the names have been changed NOT to protect the innocent, but the guilty. Ah yes: GUILT. A wonderful experience that everyone seems to avoid, yet which most are (dare I say it?) guilty of.

Much of this tale revolves around the Supreme Court and the seeking of justice. So let us close this chapter with a summary of natural justice.

Ah yes. Natural Justice, the Magna Carta, the Laws of Torts, these are all considered the backbone of the Westminster System of Law. We are taught in school how long and hard we fought against the power of Kings to get some sort of right for ourselves. However, well before our current system of justice, the Romans had things pretty ironed out. And specifically, the concept of a

ROAD, the subsequent right to unimpeded access, and this road being free and clear of encumbrance, is possibly the oldest principle of justice we hold.

This book, can you believe it, is about a road. Or should I say, the space where a road should go, but couldn't. But before we get to all of this, let's review how a judge sees the world.

Every Judge in the world knows the following principles:

- **Rule ONE**: People are the cause of their own problems, whether directly through their actions, or indirectly through their inactions.
- **Rule TWO**: People will blame rather than recognise this.
- **Rule THREE**: People will accuse rather than suffer remorse
- **Rule FOUR**: When proven guilty, people will invariably seek to excuse an action rather than repatriate a mistake.

If you can accept Rule One, the rest become unnecessary. So let's presume you are unwilling on the first, and so we go direct to Rule Two: BLAME!

BLAME

"Fate leads he who follows it, and drags he who resists." **Plutarch**

I blame my 3 year old and an old shed no one wanted.

I was pushing him on the home made swing. Ben was a delightful child, smart, happy and so easy to have around. I had recently subdivided and sold off some land, and was looking at doing the same again. A large block was available at Boringbar, which had subdivision potential, plus it was also a beautiful place to live.

I was thinking about it, but had not said a word, when young Ben stops the swing, gets off, and looks directly at me. "Buy Boringbar, Daddy." he says, and gets back on the swing. I made up my mind right at that point. So now, given the circumstances that followed on from this, I can safely lay the blame for everything at his feet.

Blame is good. It shifts the burden of decisions off your own shoulders and requires another to be your (albeit often unwilling) good Samaritan. Placing blame on a person is like booking a reverse charge call where the person at the other end has no idea who is calling, or what it is for, but has to pay to find out.

Blame is a prevalent state of being in the modern world. Look at the Iraqis! They got blamed for 911 and you saw what happened there, yes? No wonder people are increasingly paranoid. But paranoia does have its uses.

In all honesty, if I had a little more paranoia before I purchased Boringbar I would not be in the predicament that I am today. Which is to say, broke. Poverty is a concern you take with you every where you go. (Did you want fries with that?) It gnaws on you, but never more so than after you have been rich, and watched it all slip away. Perhaps I should also dose up on melancholic despondency and self-inflicted despair?

Paradoxically, if I indulged in the luxury of paranoia prior to buy the land in the valley, the locals of Boringbar would have found my presence a whole lot more to their liking. Paranoia, fear and self-loathing are common currency, and if you have this, you are welcomed. As it was, my then naturally cheery demeanour seemed to create enormous suspicion. Odd, but true.

Paranoia, blame and depression were the patterns of behaviour that represented most of my neighbours. Whether this state of consciousness is fuelled by upbringing, or simply induced by liberal amounts of booze, smoke and/or prescribed medication I cannot say for certain. However, I CAN say for certain that this little farming community at Boringbar is finally emerging from the Stone Age, albiet screaming and howling, and largely because the real estate prices have shot up.

So here the locals are, meeting the new world of doctors and solicitors, and their fat wads of cash, but they all carry this deep suspicion that it's all the con. The new people will one day go away, and everything will go back to how it was. They have not really grasped that their world has died.

You would think this would make people happy? Their land is worth more, they have new faces in town, but no. Emerging from the shadows of the 1950's with many a fully-fledged modern psychosis, the locals regard everything not born there as a threat. I read recently of a Stone Age tribe coming out of the jungles of Columbia, saying that they had chosen to join the modern world. Well, by all appearances, Boringbar seemed intent on doing just the opposite. The shutters were down, and the lights were off, and the sign said "Go Away!" After all, what use is the modern world to a farmer?

However, Boringbar also has delights to experience, such as Old Tom. The old guy from next door was out in the field, working as always. I stopped to say hello. He mentioned in passing that it was his birthday, his 70th birthday as a matter of fact. So I asked him "Where were you 70 years ago, Tom?" He answered without hesitation, "Right fucking here, mate. Right fucking here." Dear old Tom. Truly a colour of the rainbow. He is a piece of gold.

Yes, while the natives were intent on dragging the 21st Century and all it represented (especially TV and Hamburgers) all the way back to the stone age, there were others attempting to reverse this trend, to drag the Stone Age into the present. This is a good way to introduce my neighbour, Doogle "Stonestacker" Fowl. You'll hear a lot more about him.

Take the best cucumber, put it in the pickle jar long enough, and soon all you have left is a pickle. There I was in the middle of Boringbar, getting pickled. Within a few years of my arrival the business suits had mothballs, the city slicker clothes were never worn, and the hair was uncut. I was guilty by association. Screaming and proclaiming innocence of hick-dom won't work. You can be the very best cucumber, but put into that pickle jar, sooner or later, no matter what you do, you too will pickle up.

It wasn't all bad at Boringbar. Not at all. The very archaic nature of the place had a strange magnetism that attracted the most curious people. For example, the German backpackers swimming naked in the waterfall, or the Dutch girls cavorting about the place. And it wasn't just Germans and the Dutch. There was a strange pulling power to the place when it came to nere-do-wells, lay-a-bouts and the looney fringe of ALL types and descriptions. The beauty of it was that when you got tired of someone, all you had to do was ask them to pay their way with a little work, and they were gone that afternoon.

Which proves one thing: Human Nature hasn't changed one iota since the little red hen built her boat.

It was Greenacres meets Deliverance. It was a sit-com tragedy that called up a parade of characters too unbelievable to be real, but real nether-the-less. Yet we need a yardstick here, a point of comparison to fully grasp what I say. Let's wind back the clock to the luxurious and easy pre-Boringbar days. (Raise the soft focus, zoom in with lens, cue violins) It all now seems a Camelot, a dream, a mirage: And it was.

We had a nice house, in a lovely spot. No bills, no mortgage. No problems.

There was I, perhaps a century ago, happily married with a lovely child and an easy life. Things were good, or so I believed.

Zoom forward to the present day, of course, and it would be so easy for you to find me spitting venom and calling down invectives on the people and things that shaped the last 12 years. But I won't. I will let it go, for the present.

Let's be generous and magnanimous to all and we will just get on with the story as it unfolded.

The STORY

I t all started simply enough. You only ever heard of Boringbar as a town you drove past on your way to the very chic, upmarket, funky backpacker's paradise of Bling Bling. For the last 40 years Bling Bling had been the Mecca of every weirdo, freak and wastrel that had ever existed.

How wonderful! A nervous paradise, littered as it would be in any given season with the lithe bodies of the young, and the lewd looks of the focused and committed hedonist. I am certain that the term "Backpacker" is a synonym for hedonist, because as far as I could see, there was but one reason for visiting these fair shores: Getting drunk, stoned, pilled and/or laid. Preferably it was all four, with coffee, and all at the same time if you had the constitution for it.

Bling Bling was the centre of the hedonist universe, but as a cultural marker it was a misnomer. Facing facts, it is really a ratty little firetrap waiting for Gods Gomorrah solution. Considering the amount of Sodomy that went on it was a fair bet that if there really was a self-righteous prig called Yahweh who enjoyed all that mayhem and destruction, as much as the Bible suggests, then surely one day he would direct a large Tsunami to those sun drenched shores.

Or at the very least he/she/it might provide a match and a pyromaniac. Either way, the end would surely come, and people would be chastised, and their suitable and appropriate guilt could be found dripping off every dour face like failed virgins at their bar mitzvah. Guilt? Yeah, sure. The good Christians wished for it, but it would never happen. Guilt was just not a very common emotion in Bling Bling.

This God-fearing cleansing event was not today's, or yesterdays, nor tomorrow's fate I fear. Indeed, even if it were true that God would strike the town down, it is still highly unlikely that anyone in Bling Bling would notice, and even less likely any achieve a state of remorse at any time in the foreseeable future if they did. No matter what shame might befall them, you cannot shame the shameless. People were enjoying themselves too damn much.

Even if you did not personally indulge in the orgy of self-satisfaction that the town excelled in, you would have to admit the restaurants were good, and the Thai food was excellent. No matter the course you charted in the seas of humanity, Bling Bling was there to be enjoyed. To sum up the place, when a friend asked a café owner for a decaffeinated skim milk latte', he said, "You want a 'Why Bother'?"

If you are not going to get your butt kicked and your brain haemorrhaged by the coffee, the prevailing view was that you may as well have stayed home.

In my pre-Boringbar MARRIED existence I visited Bling Bling only on occasions. You might visit to show a tourist the sights, or stop in after a drive in the country, etc. For myself, life was moving along well. The money was coming into the bank, I had a business that looked as if it would allow me to retire in a few years, and I was casting about for Investment Properties. You see, I had discovered the secret. Drawing lines on paper had far more value than my erstwhile habit of using paper to write books.

One 54 acre block I had bought had gotten one of these 2 dimensional black linear constructs (a line) drawn upon it. When this magical line was approved by said Council it meant that I had one 49 acre block, and one five acre one.

The five acres had an old house that I had patched up, and what's more someone wanted to BUY it. The return to the family for this purchase was going to pay out the cost of the whole property. So this meant we now held a free and clear 49 acre block of land. How nice.

Banks love people who walk in the door without a mortgage and owning land. They loved me. Indeed they said "Please, have some money! Buy what you want!" However, at the time I was cruising about in a 20 year old Subaru with a one foot pony tail and a blond wife in hippie clothes while we carted about a young baby. It surely did not look like money to any Real Estate agents.

Consequently said agents largely gave us a map and waved us in the direction of some acreage. This was when I first learned of the extreme laziness of real estate agents, beaten only by their extraordinary stupidity.

To cut the story short, I had the cash in the pocket and the time up my sleeve. We went hunting for property. The agent who introduced us to the place at Boringbar (the same agent who was later to go to jail for threatening to burn up his girlfriend and her de facto daughter-in-law for being too demanding) showed me no sign of either his future propensity to violence OR of his desire to do any work.

He did, however, successfully show us the wrong block of land. After that, it was the usual wave of goodbye, handing us the map and giving us the greatest of well wishing. Given enough tenacity we hopefully would sort it all out.

The land at Boringbar was quite a parcel: 250 acres with sea views, creeks, waterfalls, privacy: In fact it was every single thing I had written down on a piece of paper only weeks before as I described the perfect property I was looking for. I said to the wife when I finally tracked it down, "Looks good!"

She didn't say much. I presumed she was considering things deeply, but then again, she was often thinking deeply about things, so I personally gave her silence no more thought. I have to say, however, that if I had known then what I know now regarding "what" she was thinking deeply about at that point, I may have handled things rather differently.

The real estate agents who showed me the wrong block insisted on maintaining his vigilance with sincere and deep disinterest (indicated by repeated phone calls from myself that were never returned). I tracked down, and contacted the owner direct, and started talking price with her. When we got down to about half the going rate for land in that area, I was both excited and cautious. It happened to be the exact amount of money I had in hand after we sold the 5 acres just up the road, and it seemed just too good a deal.

Now I HAD spoken to a few people about the area, and all had mentioned a curious fellow called "Mad Doogle" and his dysfunctional family, the Fowls.

Not a lot that was positive was said about the man, and that made me curious because as it turns out this very same "Mad Doogle" was the one living with his mother right next door to the Boringbar property. I could have heeded the warning, but I am far too clever by half for recognizing such things as the obvious. I believed firmly that all people had good inside them, and that it simply needed the right conditions and enough non-judgment to bring it out. I considered local gossip to be unreliable, and personal experience to be the only thing that mattered, blah blah blah. I should have listened to the gossip, I really should have, but I didn't.

As it stood, Doogle Fowl came up to me one day when I was looking about the place. He seemed very pleasant, so we got to talking. He showed me his new shed, and some of the bananas he grew. At great length he explained how you grow bananas without sprays, how you set up a lathe to carve wooden bowls, and in general spoke about things in the area. Bananas were everything in Boringbar, and everywhere. The hills were lined with them and these same Hills are alive with the sound of tractors.

In due course I arranged to meet his mum, in order to explain what I was intending to do. She put out (yes) banana cake, cups of tea, and the typical polite conversation. It was a pleasant meeting. I went over what I was planning to do with the property next to them, and they said very little, just nodding as I prattled on. In a word, I explained I was going to subdivide. I even suggested that Doogle might like to buy a piece when it was done? He seemed interested, and overtly friendly. I left thinking how so many people had pegged "Mad Doogle" in a very unattractive light, while in truth he seemed fairly harmless, possibly quite pleasant.

Oh, how wrong I could be. How foolish I was to accept such pleasantry at face value. I could blame myself, but as I mentioned earlier, I prefer to blame my 3 year old. I could have done things SO differently had I the hindsight I have now. But the facts remain, if he had not told me to buy it, perhaps none of this would have happened!

Yet such recrimination provides no answer. The fact is, in the climate of 1995 it all looked pretty good. I took the wife down for another inspection, and curiously on a perfectly sunny day storm clouds gathered and a hail storm came scattering down. An Omen! What is more, I KNEW it was an Omen. But like the Pythoness and her oracular predictions, the two sided nature of Omens tend to cause us to interpret what we WANT to see, rather than what is. All I saw is that we all emerged unscathed after the sudden, surprising downpour.

I said at the time to my beloved wife. "This looks like a really good opportunity for subdivision. What do you think?" In retrospect her answer was somewhat oracular-like as well. (though I did not realize it at the time) She said "You can do what you like as far as your business goes, but I really don't want anything to do with this place."

What I heard was "Go for it!" but many years later, what I realize she was really saying was "I am sick of you, you smart arsed prick and the more time you spend out of my sight in this good forsaken neck of jungle the better."

However, to balance your view, dear reader, anyone who looked at the girl would never have imagined a calculating mind underneath such pie-faced blue-eyed innocence. Not one single Soul would have considered that a nasty streak three miles wide ran between her brain and that soft, sweet tongue. Talk about saboteurs and terrorists in Iraq! I was unknowingly living with one, and now it seems I was destined to move next door to another.

I wonder if a 500 pound bomb might not work effectively on Doogle, now I think of it? Al Zakawi is dead and gone as of yesterday. Or perhaps a large Monty Python hammer, crashing down like the wrath of God? But I get away from myself, falling from the heights of Pythoness Predictions to the absurdity of Pythonesque predications.

Which brings me to the 3 year old and the reason I blame him. It is a bright fateful Autumn morning almost 12 years ago. I am pushing him on his swing in the front yard, thinking about all the above just written, and the distinct possibility of buying Boringbar. It looked good, but something nagged in the back of my mind. Everything had been cleared. The money was arranged, the price had been agreed to, the checks had been done. All that was required was for me to sign the contract, and the wheels would be set into motion.

While I am thinking about all this, the 3 year old stops the swing, hops off, looks me straight in the eye and says "Buy Boringbar, Daddy!" It was as simple as that. I had been clearly instructed by the simple wisdom of my little son, so I thought "Fair enough. We buy it!"

And this is where the fun (and the whole thread of the book) begins. The family is at the Solicitors Office, and I am saying to the wife, "Do you want this place put into your name?" She answers "No, put it in yours." We to and fro over the name business, and finally it is decided that as the remaining subdivided parcel we already owned was going into the wife's name, the new block would go into mine. This was to be the pattern of all future purchases, I might add. One for you, one for me.

We literally organised that in front of the solicitor. Neither of us really wanted blocks of land in our name. At the time, the solicitor is shaking his head and laughing, saying "I only wish there were more couples like you in this office." Only years later do I realize the language was open to interpretation.

Interpretation and Communication.

We all hear the words someone utters, but do we understand what they MEAN? What they MEAN is almost always what they DO NOT say. This is what they call subtext, and for most people, here is where the important communication starts and ends: SUBTEXT. My subtext at the time in the solicitor's office was "We are married forever, so it doesn't matter to me whose name things are in" but I think she was hearing something else.

I am not sure, but I now believe I understand what she was saying. It was, "I just want OUT of this, any way I can. Maybe if he gets his own block of land he will just move there? I hate that shit hole, there's not even a house. The dump where we are at the moment is bad enough, and what the fuck is he going to do with 250 acres? I have the citizenship now, so he can piss off at any time." As I say, I heard none of this. At the time, it all seemed like just another adventure.

Cutting to the chase, we sold the old house and 5 acres, bought Boringbar and subsequently moved to a wonderful playhouse down the road that came up for rent . Soon enough I would sort things out with building a new place, but it was time for a break. To be fair to myself, I was not entirely unaware that there were issues in the air. I could tell that something was not quite right with my then dearest, however, so I rented this extraordinary place where she could be happy. It was a really lavish house with thick carpet, leather furniture, pool, its own private boat harbour, and even a golf course! All of this on 30 acres of private island just outside of Town. It even came with a caretaker who did the gardens and grounds.

Looking back I suspect she already had her new lover by this time, because the house didn't seem to cheer her up all that much. Not that I knew anything, I was busy! It was head down and tail up getting the subdivision through for

Boringbar. To pluck the short straw and kill the suspense: It all came through. Three Blocks were approved, which meant that after costs of development and factoring in bank interest, within 18 months at the very outside, this being a worst case scenario, we should have another free and clear 100 or so acres with sea views. My investment of time and cash should return 400% net within a maximum of 2 years.

How do you make God laugh? Easy, you tell him your plans.

Beware Sheds that No One Wants.

I had been warned what a problem the local Council could be, yet what came through with the subdivision seemed not so bad. It all looked good, the only hiccup was the requirement I had fully expected, which was to move sheds that were on the Crown Road that led to the property, the sheds that were right outside Mad Doogle's house.

Should is a strange word. I "should" have realized that this was going to be the issue, but foolishly I really thought I could just talk with the neighbours, and help everyone by proposing to put the road AROUND the sheds. Council were OK with this, and so I presumed that the Fowl family would be happy for the father's shed to be preserved.

The Fowls needed a meeting, but there were two groups. The oldest brothers were one, with Doogle his Mother, and the sisters being the other. The Brothers were all for it, but I received an odd, dull sense of non-response from the rest. It only appeared that way. You have heard the term "Cat amongst the pigeons"?

Little did I realize what I was walking into. The Fowl Family was at best dysfunctional and, at worst, downright vindictive. The worst option being the far more prevalent scenario. To set the story straight, I was really only there for my own gain. I had no real consideration invested in fixing anything, or getting involved with anything. I just wanted a straightforward business deal, but it seemed that in sorting out this deal, I had to sort out the issue around the shed. However, the Fowl family, who had to decide on this matter, were completely, totally and UTTERLY alienated from each other. They could not agree on ANYTHING, even to save their own skins. This meant that (dare I say it) sorting out the matter of the shed really meant sorting out the Fowls.

It was at this point that a truly powerful ray of sunlight broke through to illuminate the true state of affairs. Sadly for myself I was wearing dark glasses and did not recognize it. Doogle Fowl had apparently desired the property I

---

purchased. So much did he desire it, that, by report, upon hearing of myself signing the contract, he openly and very publicly wept outside his house, screaming to my future informer "The contract is no good. It's going to fall over. He is NOT going to get that land."

Doogle apparently stamped his foot in a very similar way that a 2 year old will when they can't get what they want.

Not that I saw any of this. At the time he had remained courteous when speaking to me, though he got more insistent about asking again and again what I was going to do. I kept saying "After approval for subdivision is granted, I will split the place up and keep one of the back blocks. In the meantime if someone offers me around $240K then maybe I will sell." This was twice what I paid for the place, yet with the approval it was under its real value at the time.

So, as we know the approval came through. Shortly after this and soon after the meeting about the sheds, Doogle Fowl called and DID offer me twice what I paid for the place. Even my solicitor, who knew better than I what the Fowls were like, because he had been in court several times with dear Doogle and other Fowl related issues, even HE looked at me oddly when I said "Well, it is worth more subdivided, and I would like to keep a block in the area. It's only going to go up around there."

"It will go up everywhere!" he said. "Surely you are better out of that place?" I said something along the lines that I wanted to keep one of the back blocks, as I had really grown to like the place a lot.

The unmitigated stupidity I exhibited at that point still astounds me. I have done some dumb things before, but it was my total lack of understanding of just how badly behaved a disgruntled Doogle Fowl could be that determined things. Yet while ignorance is no excuse, it still amazes me that I did not let it go at that point. I mentioned the offer to the wife (we were still married at the time) and she said, as always "Whatever you wish to do".

Again I failed to hear that what she was really saying was "You stupid dog brained git. You miserable low life piece of crap!" In this instance, she was probably correct.

Can you believe that, as I write these words, I am wearing a sweat shirt that is emblazoned with the word "Whatever". Be that as it may well be, at that point in time I declined the offer. In retrospect (whereupon all things are made clear) I believe this is akin to throwing a match onto tinder dry wood that has been soaked in petrol while placing fireworks on the top of the future bonfire.

The wife left 2 months later, without any apparent warning. I suppose in her mind she had been shouting loudly for some years, but I never really noticed. Truth is, I paid less and less attention to her general state of silence because I was far too busy creating assets. I had been completely oblivious to most things of note in my life up to that point, but considered the business of building wealth (so all of us could be secure and stable) was more important than her passing issues.

What a waste of energy THAT was. Anyway, she left without saying why, and in doing so she also left behind my about to sprout, and very large issue with the Fowl's. I suspect her female intuition told her something was up, and to jump ship, like a rat.

Mea Culpa, Mea Culpa, Mea Maxiumus Culpa! It is ALWAYS so obvious in retrospect. I had set sail on a course with the winds of fate blowing in all directions but the open sea where I wanted to go. I retained this blind belief that people would act in their own interests, and I presumed that, despite Doogle not obtaining the property he always wanted, at least the Fowl's on the whole would be quite happy that I wanted to continue the subdivision. After all, the development improved their property as much as it did mine, and at my cost.

I met the brothers (who by now had mentioned that they hated Doogle with a passion bordering on murder) and they urged me to continue. This was all part of my decision to not sell, and to carry on with the project at hand. Part of the decision to hold onto Boringbar was because they had offered to pay for half the upgrade costs of the road that needed to be put in, in order for the subdivision to go through. They wanted to subdivide their own place as a way to solve their own family problems, and this road made that process much easier. I discovered at that point that Doogle owned nothing, and that the brothers and the mother were the only registered owners, with the father's will left unresolved, due to legal issues.

Now surely common sense tells us this simple message. If the OWNERS of the Fowl property wanted to proceed, surely their curious and half-mad brother was not such an obstruction. Surely? I had not at that point realized the depth of spineless jelly-like substance that formed the backbones of all Fowl Men.

Now, the Fowl WOMEN, that was a different story. They were truly heartless vicious creatures who would make despots such as Caligula crawl away in fear.

How so? Well one story is as follows: The oldest of the sisters, Uncouth Fowl who had married Rob Tooth to become Mrs Uncouth Tooth, had been offered twice what their own property down the road was worth. The offer had been made by Buddhist monks. Apparently they wanted the property beside her, but had decided that the ONLY way they could buy it was to not have her as a neighbour. Well, she refused their offer for a curious reason. She wanted her husband and sons to sweat it out cutting the bananas because if they had moved to an opulent condo by the sea, well, it might make he and the sons lazy. Obviously we couldn't have that.

Now there's a TRUE Fowl. Yet she did not stand alone in miserly precognition of selfish designs. Her man-hating sister, generally called Hell Girl, was quite possibly her better when it came to sheer, died in the wool vindictiveness. Now to say she was ugly would be untrue and unkind, however, it IS fair to say that everyone around her was more attractive. The fact that THEY were ugly sons of bitchs speaks for itself. At best we might say Hell Girl was the bitter element in life's sweet and sour.

In a town of gossip like Boringbar, where the witches loved to meet over coffee to compare the men (or women) they were sleeping with, Hell Girl's affair with the wife of her brother "and" her rounding up an all-girl Olympics orgy with a few of the locals: Well, surely it should have been the talk of the town? But no, she was barely talked about in public, and I suppose this was mostly due to sheer fear. Hell Girl could cut glass with her eyes, and had the most awesome arsenal of invective on her side. But more than this, more than anything of value in this town, she possessed the only true coin of dignitas that existed in Boringbar. She was born there.

We should stop and mention this very clearly, because it is part of the caustic chain of causation that exists in most small rural communities.

Boringbar had seven farming families that had been there since the dawn of time. Many families had come and gone, many had run screaming from that place, seeking out civilization, but not the Seven Stalwarts. Not the upstanding MINIMUM 40 year (plus) farming families. Now, the Fowls were the very LAST of the Stalwarts, while the Stalkers up the road, and my other neighbours the Shadbolts were the first. But regardless of whether it was 40 years or 400 in the valley, these Stalwarts held sway over all things.

This gave a certain blind courage to the Fowls. In their day they had arrived as moneyed gentry, with cash borrowed (and never repaid) from the grandparents. The Fowl's could therefore afford luxuries such as a tractor and the construction of a rather large house. They arrived as Lords of the Manor, and though time and tide had turned their position to one that was now somewhat more humble, they still believed they had that aura.

Hell Girl had "the faith" in spades because she ALSO had a university education. (Even though I think the main thing she learned was how to best arrange words to belittle the male species) Added to this she had a sharpened and practiced gaze for the visual cutting of the male genitalia. In the minds of the local village folk, this was a terror to be feared and respected. At any rate, the combined force of the Fowl Sisters was specific and damning.

Meeting them one might think their sole purpose in life was a quest to emasculate their older brothers. You know them already. What you don't know is that, apparently, they were the evil ones who conspired to cut the women out of their fair due with the family property. At least, that was their story.

After all, how dare their father grant those lowly bastards they called older brothers a whole ¼ portion each of the Fowl property. Of course, at the time, that was just a trick to keep the sons from leaving, because he needed cheap labour to run the place. The father didn't want his own kids to get a life or an education because that would leave him with all the work.

Just because the brothers were taken out of school to slave on the family farm for over a decade with no pay, working the farm that fed the sisters for their entire comfortable upbringing, this was no damn reason at all for their bastard father to favour them.

Death was too good for these scum bag curs, these low-life toads. In consequence to the father's unfortunate will and legacy, which we are about to hear of, the sisters hatched a most evil plot, one of the most evil dastardly manipulative plots ever conceived in the history of mankind.

It All Started the Day the Father Died.

To find out how something ends, we must look to the beginning because, as the wise man once said: *The fruit of any situation is found in the cause.* In this case, the father himself is the trigger for much mayhem. So let's look at Jack, the father.

A more cantankerous prick you would never meet. He used to love stopping anyone who was walking on the Crown Road (that ran to what is now my place) on their way to the swimming hole. People were only going down a legal road for a swim at the waterfall. They had every right, but Jack would very aggressively demand they ask him permission to cross HIS property.

If they objected, stating such ridiculous claims that it was a public road, he thoroughly enjoyed stuffing a shot gun under their nose and asking them what on the good God's earth might it be that they had in their mind to walk on HIS road. Few argued, and the waterfall was left to its own devices for quite some time. Yet his attitude was such that the Crown Road that traversed the Fowl Property became a battle ground for all who owned the property I had purchased. It became a lonely place as few wished to argue with a load shotgun.

Jack used to employ casual labour, but always women, and the younger the better. His favourite technique was to send them up the rows to pick the vegetables or fruit, and he would work behind them, watching as they bent over. To be fair, no one ever lodged a formal complaint, but it was widely known he got his hands dirty in more ways than one.

As I say, a more cantankerous prick you would be hard put to find. Hated by neighbours and despised by the tradesmen he refused to pay, the man was not exactly mourned at the time of his passing. However, he had one good point: He despised his son, Doogle, and made sure the boy knew it. In fact, Doogle's mother was always stopping the father from beating up the child he un-affectionately called "The Poof". (slang for homosexual)

It is fair to say that Doogle had a strange habit. He was a pathological liar from birth, but that was not the habit. When Doogle realised he was getting caught out in yet another lie, he LISPED. He went into this baby talk nonsense and lisped. Well, I am told that in childhood Doogle lisped a lot. He still does, which is fair, considering how his every word is a lie.

People say this "poof" label by the father was the cause of Doogle emotional problems. Certainly it caused his mother to flutter around him like a mother hen protecting her child from the fox. Perhaps this was the reason why, when his mother finally passed away, that he got a heroin addict for a girlfriend. He was then aged 46 (note: this was his first and only girlfriend) and the girl thing triggered rather strange emotional outbursts.

I saw him once, sitting outside with his head in his hands, screaming. She left him within 2 weeks of moving in, and naturally took anything of value she could carry with her. They say the father is the real psychological reason he tracked her down in Sydney, paying a lot of money to private investigators to find her. They found her, he followed, and then he begged her to come back, saying "Don't worry about the jewellery and cameras. It was all insured!"

Apparently he was deeply ashamed that it looked like he was gay, and hopefully having a woman around would stop the rumours. Someone really should have told his boyfriend.

So what happened? Who knows: I have long said "Upper Boringbar, complete with Web Feet and Banjos!" Some say the true depth of weirdness in Doogle was too much even for a smack addict, others say she got scared by the curious way his eyes bulged when he got excited. Maybe she could hear the sound of Duelling Banjos in the background? Who knows? What is known for certain is that even a heroin addict had more self-respect than to want to put up with Doogle, and refused his offers. That refusal by his first and only girlfriend I suspect broke him at an elemental level. Even his occasional affair with the town Magistrate no longer gave him enough guilt to make it exciting. But I diverge from the father!

Dear Old Jack. A week before he died, he collapsed and was taken to hospital. Now, in one of those wondrous quirks of fate, his neighbour Cecil Shadbolt also collapsed and was taken to the SAME hospital. The good nurses could not believe it, two neighbours both in critical condition on the same day!

They put the unconscious men in the same room, so they could keep each other company, and as it happened they both woke up at roughly the same time. Cecil saw Jack lying there. Jack saw Cecil. Now you can imagine that two men who had worked the fields side by side for some 20 years might have some sort of thought to share, or a laugh to make, or some word to whisper to cure any ills or misunderstandings there may have been in the past. But no: Jack was the mother of all pricks, and Cecil knew this simple truth in intimate detail, one born of years of experience. In fact, Cecil himself had ended up in court over what was destined to be the SAME ROAD that I eventually took the Fowls to the Supreme Court over a quarter of a century later, and for the same reason.

Cecil opened his eyes, saw Jack, and immediately pressed his buzzer for the nurse. She came in, bright eyed and bushy tailed, saying "My, how are our neighbours doing this morning?"

Cecil didn't flinch, and simply said "I have had to live beside this prick for the last 20 years, and NOW you want me to DIE beside him? Either get my gun from home, and make me really happy, or move me to another room." He was moved, and his brother Tom once said to me "He hated that prick, he would have preferred to have gotten his gun."

Both Jack and Cecil died soon after.

Now in our new world of peace and harmony and United Nations, we would like to think people can patch up their differences, get over their hurdles, make love, not war, etc. Well, that's bullshit. Believe me, I know! I have lived next to the Fowl's. You can wish them well, you can harbour no ill will, and have all good intention. But the fact remains; the very best Fowl is a dead one.

And please understand that I do not criticize! Not at all, I merely make an observation of fact in the same way as a person might observe the temperature while reading a thermometer.

In the hospital, as Cecil was leaving the room, Jack laughed and called out "See you in hell!" Cecil replied "I am an atheist, but I will convert if it means I get to keep THAT promise."

The father died, and the women took over the house. They had all been waiting for him to go, and they all hated him with a passion. The excuse was that they were rallying around their mother, but the truth is, they were organizing dear old Doogle to attack those bastards that owned the other half of the farm. A quarter share was now up for grabs, with half already in the hands of the brothers and the other quarter being owned by the still living mother.

Now they could find out about the father's will, and see what was in it for them. Finally they were to get their ounce of blood and their pound of flesh. Yet the reading of the will had a few surprises in store. It may not just have been the incompetent solicitor, it may well have just been the natural vindictiveness of the father, but he made no clear guidelines at all in regards his property and what was to become of it.

He did say that Doogle, worthless though he was, would get a 5 acre section of property carved off for himself, and that the others could split the rest amongst themselves. Some Uncle got a bit of furniture.

The father made no mention of the difficulty in getting a local council to agree to creating a five acre island of land in the midst of hundreds of acres, nor did he mention exactly where these five acres were to be. Indeed, he failed to mention quite a few things, and I wonder to this day if it wasn't intentional.

Certainly, no mention was made of the caveat over the property by Jack's parents, who had lent him the money to buy it in the first place. He had always faithfully promised to pay them back, and when they died I am told he put the cheque in his mother's grave, just as they threw in the dirt. Generous and kind as this fellow was, he even made it out to cash.

However, the sister's plans were in ruins. The will was impossibility itself. What to do? The Fowl Sisters were somewhat stunned by the verdict, I am told. They all rushed off to their relevant solicitors with a copy in hand to decipher the will, yet the simple truth echoed by all the learned and educated minds was that the property was a shared property, and as such what they had was either the option to sell up the property, which meant selling up their own mother, get it settled in the courts in some way, or live with the hope that the brothers would offer them some money.

Indeed, even if they DID petition the courts to sell up, only an executors of the will could force the sale of the place, and as one of these was the oldest brother, it was considered unlikely he was going to cause himself grief.

That was when the plot thickened into a stew. The sisters mutually agreed to covertly work on a targeted assault on the mother AND their youngest brother, Doogle, in order to get their fair share of the loot. This involved a combination of nagging, cajoling, bitch sessions, and various forms of emotional bribery that culminated in the death of the mother.

In the Fowl Sister's mind, this is what they call success. I saw the mother shortly before she passed away, and naively asked her if her illness had at least brought the family more together. The poor woman visibly paled, and her body shook uncontrollably with that one, pointed question. I was quickly moved outside by the only daughter who actually cared about her.

I was not to know it at the time, because in the Fowl household all was politeness and smiles, yet her looming death had brought out the very worst of avarice in all her children. And, if you know the Fowls, you can believe it when I say the very worst is indeed a blacker shade of dark. We skip the light fandango, and go straight for the jugular.

The Gang of Three had already successfully lobbied the mother to cut the oldest sons out of the will, leaving just Doogle and themselves still in the race for the remaining portion. Then on the mother's deathbed, Uncouth and Hell Girl further urged her to sign a new will that left everything to just themselves.

When THAT particular unsigned (but already witnessed by the two nasty sisters) copy was discovered by the other sister who was 'cast out": Well, I think I heard the screams from a mile away. Third Sister, almost removed. She was, of course, the only nice one.

This was the drama I knew nothing about at the time. If I had realized the sheer depth of depravity and dysfunction that was the very fabric of the ties that bound the Fowls together, I may well have revised my decision not to sell. In fact, had I know the facts, I would have been out of that place at cost! As it stood, however, I had too many fires of my own to put out to deal with any other external issues.

Ah yes. My tattered and sorry life at that point is not worth a lot of effort to describe, but I will outline it for the sake of completeness. Divorce! It is a strange thing when you don't realize you have been divorced. All I knew is that I was no longer living on a private island with a caretaker doing the gardening. No, somehow that had all left, along with any money I possessed. I ended up sharing rooms in a house with two delightful, but extremely fruity, dope smokers. I had just sent three months and a lot of money to renovate the house for my own family to live in, but guess what? No wife!

In between paying bills I was quietly trying to piece my own life together. Yet I remained weirdly convinced that the wife was going to come back. She would wake up, realise things were good, and return. So, sharing the house, which had a spectacular location on the Tweed River, and walking through the dense cloud of marijuana while saying my polite hello's to the drug-riddled sushi-laden new-agers who happened to be sprawled around my lounge: It all seemed just part of a process.

I was by then in somewhat of a depressive spin. Things had appeared to be going so well a mere 2 months earlier, but now the coin had flipped to reveal the other side.

The major stress factors at work in any person's life are well documented. The Top Five are: Death in the Family, Divorce, Moving House, Bankruptcy and Ill Health. I had just gotten the divorce underway, and moved house. As a result of the above two reasons, I was facing Bankruptcy, while also physically very ill because of the previous three. If I had only committed suicide I could have managed to get all five in one basket! Forget statistics here, I had absolutely NO idea what was happening. It was a case of shell shock.

So really the question is: What on earth was I doing trying to make something like a subdivision work in these circumstances? Emotionally, physically and mentally I was just not well enough, nor was I financially equipped enough to handle the naturally callous business of butchery that is needed for such endeavours. And that was in normal circumstances, when you are trying to battle mere mindless government bureaucracy and their swath of regulations.

In retrospect, this was nothing compared to the Fowls.

The Fowls, and those damn sheds that no one actually wanted.

POSITION POSITION POSITION

The Three Rules of Real Estate were drummed into me by my father, a licensed agent for many years. This is why I always looked at position when buying, but I looked at it differently to most people. I followed a rule where I looked for a large acreage, suitable for subdivision, which was just outside the "line" where agents would want to take people.

I figured, in naïve wisdom, that as prices in the city went up, people always looked one step further than they did last year searching for suitable property. If the agents only went as far as 20 Panorama Court on Monday, come Tuesday, they would be looking at number 22.

Boringbar was a watershed moment in 1995. It was in the ideal location for this sort of arrangement. Situated in the very middle ground between Sin City and Bling Bling, two of the most attractive destinations in Australia, it was destined to be "discovered" in the not too distant future. This simply meant property prices were guaranteed to go up, and also that property would be easier to sell. In all of this I have been to be proved to be 100% correct.

What I had not countered on was how the wonderful Position, Position, Position I just happened to in was beside (possibly) the most dysfunctional family in existence. For me to secure the second part of my plan, the subdivision, there was one small obstacle. Just an old shed that no one wanted.

Just an old shed no one wanted, yes, but what a drama it was to become, complete with a cast of characters worthy of the best Hollywood potboiler. The stage for a Shakespearian tragedy had been set. Without me knowing it, the wheels were in motion, the game was afoot, and I was the one who would blithely and unwittingly construct the stage upon which many actors would arrive to play their part. But who erected the guillotine?

You must wait, dear reader, you must wait. The joy in this tale is in the actors, and you my dear, sweet reader will have the great good fortune of visiting one by one the salient personages who graced this small platform of experience, that lay at the end of this curious valley, in the middle of nowhere.

I suppose this story really comes down to is change, and resistance to change. As mentioned, I was the first person in some 30 years to buy land in that neck of the wood. The other end of the valley, just around the corner, was completely different. This area had seen regular trading of properties and everyone got on quite well with each other, but not where I landed.

No, at MY end the Fowls had been there for 40 years, the Shadbolts for 100 years, Cranky John down the road was 35 years into his tenure, The German at the start of the fork (The one no one spoke to or cared about) apparently had been there for over 32 years. This left only Miss Bad Ass Legal Bitch as the most recent buyer at some 30 years earlier.

I once looked at a book that displayed the maps of Europe stretching back for thousands of years. At every 50 year interval a page was presented, and the boundaries of the various countries outlined. There was not a single 50 year period where there was not some major boundary change between countries. In 6000 years, regular as clockwork, every 50 year cycle had seen a major change of some sort. Think about it, this really meant WAR every 50 years. In another perspective, this also meant that every single generation saw violence and mayhem somewhere in Europe.

And so I come to Boringbar in the modern age, and in 30 years nothing much had changed or happened. Doogle (the antagonist of this tale) was 40 at the time. I believe he had been born around the time the family had arrived in the valley. So, in effect, this meant that our dear Doogle Fowl had barely seen one iota of change in his entire life. In retrospect it is little wonder that when I came in talking about new roads, new people, new everything, that it outrightly threatened him. I was the bogey man; I was the one rattling his cage.

And in this instance his "Cage" was wrapped up in the Sheds that no one wanted. In particular, it was the milling shed his father had built, which up till that point had meant nothing to anybody.

And THIS, dear reader, is what the real problem was. Nobody gave a rats arse that Doogle's father was dead, and truth be told, many were happy he was gone. I suspect Doogle instinctively knew this was to be his own fate, and so some part of him believed that by defending the sheds, he was somehow salvaging his own life from complete and total anonymity.

It just struck me as I wrote the above: Isn't it a fascinating and extraordinary irony that the most likely person to save Doogle from oblivion was his greatest foe, myself! I am the one giving his life a modicum of purpose and reality with the writing of this book. Isn't that extraordinary? So I guess his fight for the sheds worked! But Doogle is not a lone star actor in this saga of loss and deprivation of liberty.

Many actors came to visit the drama that was to ensue. The Mad Monk, the Mini Skirt Mum, The Smacked Out Freak, The Psychotic Paranoid Wife of the Mad Monk, and an assortment of back packers and wastrels that meandered up from Bing Bling looking for a new sensation. All of this and more came through the mayhem, and most were quite ignorant of the real story. And as life was to prove, so was I! The focus on surviving, paying bills, raising my little guy, and struggling to keep my emotions above water kept me blind to the obvious for quite some time.

One of the noteworthy things is how, in my fortieth year, I built my son and I a house. I built that house all on my own, hanging off ladders, drilling then nailing the 80 year old hardwood timbers, piece by painstaking piece. This is one of the most grounding things that we can do in life. Seeking to create a new foundation, I literally poured my own foundations, and set upon this new horizon the place for my being. Noteworthy is how my oldest and extremely ADHD child helped mix up the cement for the posts that was the start of the journey. There was something important in the symbology of this, but for the life of me, I can't quite quite put my finger on it.

You cannot imagine the site before I started. It was a slope with 30 foot of lantana growing all over it. It looked like a disaster but instinct told me there was something there. A big dozer came in and levelled the lot, making a house pad onto which I started to insert the various types of sticks that make up the humans nest we call a home.

This all happened soon after the divorce. After selling off property and giving pretty much all the cash to the now ex-wife I looked at the total cash reserve and it stood at $12000. Now, most people would think "What can you do with $12K?" and I have to admit, I thought the same. However, I had some mates in the demo trade, and

The House that $12k Built

they knew the predicament I was in, so they called whenever they had sold what they could off a site, and for $50 I could pick up what I wanted of what was left. I would hire a car trailer and dash up to get what useful sticks I could find. Well, in simple terms, I found quite a few.

In fact, I found everything I needed, including the roof sheets, flooring and various building materials. I collected 6" x 4" beams in 80 year old hardwood for the beams and joists, and found Tulip Oak for the floors. The wall sheeting I picked up at a garage sale. Everything was ready to go, I just needed some power to be able to build the thing.

Fortune smiled on me. I spoke to the former wife of one of the Fowl brothers, a very Christian woman, and she allowed me to run a power cable some 500 meters from her place to where I was building, which allowed me to get moving. I didn't have enough money for running proper power in, so this temporary situation would have to do.

And here was the first symbol of resistance from Doogle. He didn't want me there, and I often discovered that the power cord, my electrical lifeline, had been cut. This happened, generally, in the middle of the night when I was working on computer, writing up whatever it was I was working on at the time. Other times the signals he sent of his displeasure were more malicious: The broken windows, the stolen tools, and the really nasty little things like a pin prick in the water supply to the house.

I had water coming in via a siphon from higher up at the creek, and that small hole meant it no longer worked. It is things like this that really piss you off. I was quickly learning what my neighbour Doogle Fowl was really all about, which was (in a few desultory words) vindictive mischief, cunning deception and petty vendetta.

This was all very annoying and aggravating, so with the other neighbours' approval I trenched the cord into the ground and started locking everything up. I also got a large dog with a very fierce bark. And what a great dog he was, a king amongst beasts. Stimpy was a cross between a Rottweiler and a Labrador, and he was a lion of a dog. Most of those annoying problems stopped when Stimpy arrived, however, this simply propelled Doogle to take another tack.

He called up the power board complaining about the "dangerous" cord that might electrocute him. The Electricity people came out, inspected the line and declared it illegal. I nodded in abeyance, disconnected it, and reconnected it as soon as they left. It would always take them some months before they came back, and this set off a little side game of cat and mouse where through the days I would run over and disconnect the lead, then go back and reconnect at night.

Of course, Doogle would then run in and disconnect the lead at night, and as it was hundreds of meters away and out of sight it was hard to catch him at it. In time I raised the finance and had a power line strung across from the Shadbolts property, which infuriated Doogle no end. So he complained about that as well.

In fact, Doogle lodged numerous complaints with just about every single government Department you could imagine. I had visits from Social Security, National Parks and Wildlife, The Police, the Power Authority, the Creeks and Rivers authority, the Roads authority, the Shire Council, the State Government, and even the weed inspectors. You name it, they turned up.

Most people soon realized that the long litany of letters from Doogle was simply another disgruntled neighbour causing trouble, but what it meant was that I was not able to put my plans into motion as I hoped. The idea at the outset was to build a series of bungalows and rent them out to meet the repayments, but I knew Doogle would cause no end of problems if I started down that road.

Doogle was what is known in Australia as a "dobber". It is somewhat close to the lowest point on the evolutionary scale, and it took me many years to discover WHY he was such a dobber. He dobbed in anyone who was growing hooch, or doing anything illegal. Even someone who bent the rules a little resulted in many letters of indignation from Doogle Fowl to the appropriate authority. Finally it tweaked as to why.

It took many years before it emerged that dear Doogle had himself a healthy home business growing large crops of hydroponic dope. But that little snippet, and the associated nude sun baking on public beaches, is all still to come

Few people who have not experienced it can believe how difficult a bad neighbour can be. Most people on properties bend rules, and do things as needed rather than as instructed. It is not like a city where everyone has to follow the rules, in the country you give yourself some flexibility, some privacy to set up your own world.

This was the hard part, and I found myself getting drawn into a conflict not of my making and not of my desire. It was to take years before I realized that the real problem was not that Doogle was a selfish, pathological liar who only existed to cause trouble, it was simply that he was mad.

You cannot expect common sense or decency from a mad person. What is more, when I let go of the sense of what "should" be, I found I could relax into the madness all around me. Because I could relax, slowly I found a thread to lead myself out of the situation.

Of course, this little Boringbar show, this drama where I was the unwilling star player, provided the entire witch community of Boringbar with an indescribably good source of gossip.

Witches, Bitches, Bwitches and Gossips

"Although the most acute judges of the witches and even the witches themselves, were convinced of the guilt of witchery, the guilt nevertheless was non-existent. It is thus with all guilt". **Friedrich Nietzsche**

No cursory inspection of the village of Boringbar would be complete without a visit to the witches. They are part and parcel of the whole story, and must rate a passing mention . There were 12 in all, with a few hangers on. These were self-styled "Wise Women" would clutch cups of tea during the day, and bottles of beer during the night. They were all avowed to be concerned citizens, and indeed a number were health professionals. On the surface there seemed little to connect them, but underneath they shared one binding trait, GOSSIP. The glue that really held them together was the simple fact they were all rampant gossip mongers.

But more than mere gossips, they held this belief that they somehow had some magical sway over the affairs of the valley. The Fowl Sisters were not invited into this group, which was a pity in one sense, because this meant the only "true" witches in the valley were not invited to the club meetings. This crew (though believing and entirely convinced of their own personal magical powers) were really more "Bwitches" than pure witches. What is a Bwitch you ask? She is a Bitch who aspires to be something more than her natural commonness. This is done via the use of nasty asides and vicious whispering campaigns, whilst living in the glory that only a deeply concealed sense of pretence can give you. In other words, Witches in Britches.

The Witches in Britches used to ride their horses up through my property and into the National Parks behind me. Initially they would look over with heavy stares, as if it were a challenge for them to go past an occupied house.

It is worth noting that my property was the site of first settlement in the valley. But that was a long time ago. Not since the 19th century had anyone actually lived on my place, but if you stir up the ghosts of the past, you discover right where I built used to be the town of Upper Boringbar. I found it curious that they never stopped to ask permission, but I had no reason to stop their horse riding, so I waved to them as they wandered through. Finally, after many months, they came up and introduced themselves, and asked if it were OK to go through.

"Of course!" I said, I thought but obviously didn't say what was really on my mind. "Look, nags on nags!"

Up close for the first time I saw no warts on their noses, nor broomsticks, nor even a semblance to a magic wand. (I suspect they had an eye out for the magic weed as they went along, however) They were not particularly attractive in either appearance or personality, and all fully realised that their flower of youth had long since departed. Yet they were all genuinely happy on their horses, and quite pleasant people, individually.

Apparently the witches believed I was some sort of warlock up the end of the valley, doing magical things that I never spoke about. Surely it wasn't the fantasy of bored women imaging a new man? Be that as it may, it must be equally clear to those who know about these things that warlocks, specifically those who never speak about their magical things, are obviously up to powerful magic, and therefore must be respected. What is more, dark magicians who smile politely, and seem quite charming, are possibly the very worst, darkest most evil creatures you could imagine. So exciting! Such a thought naturally intrigued them, and possible got their juices flowing.

One of them I knew got VERY excited, and left her husband to rent the vacant house near to me. She took to wearing miniskirts and makeup, and giving her rather delightful 16 year old girl the evil eye when the girl looked at me with sexually curious eyes. I guess her daughter was also a little fascinated with what on earth had caused her Mum to act like such an idiot.

Be that as it may be, we two (the daughter and I) got on famously. And didn't THAT cause a waggle or two from the split tongues of the witch brigade.

The witch that moved in, the mother, was called Moigle, and she was a real dominator. She just loved to rule the roost. Of course, at heart she was a sincere and caring person, but I suspect the lack of sex from the estranged husband caused her hormones to go flip flop. The effect was curious, she would literally command people like some high Queen, instructing them of how they could serve her best. I had never known anyone to be so demanding, and yet so pleading, all at the same time.

Moigle turned up one day in yet another mini skirt (really, very few 40 year old plus women can successfully wear a mini) and with makeup shouting from her eyebrows. She was tarted up to the nines, which in the backwater of a backwater valley of Boringbar, proved one thing: Moigle was obviously KEEN! It was at that point that I experienced something rather unique, a thing that stays with me to this very day.

Some women when excited put out a strong scent of sex, but this was entirely different. This was more of musk. I swear I could smell her desire, which was somewhat off putting for myself because I just didn't have an attraction towards her. I have since been told by a Tantric Master that men search their entire lives for such an experience. Apparently this scent comes only to a woman who is genuinely enriched by passion. Sadly, I didn't have the return sensation for Moigle. I really liked her a great deal, but at this point something else had affected me. And it was a remarkable turn-off. This was her bulging eyes. I came to understand in time that whenever she got stressed or excited, her eyes would bulge. I don't know why, but it rang alarm bells.

On this day, she arrived with eyes fully bulged. Apparently Doogle had followed her up the road, trailing her (as he will with his victims) on his 4 wheel farm bike. Did he catch a wisp of that ape-like scent thing? Did he have a nose for desire? According to Moigle he clearly intended a non-platonic experience.

She shook him off, excited yet scared, and came racing over to inform me all about it, and asking that I call the Police. I hesitated for a moment, not only because I knew what the Police would do, which was zero, but because I truly had no idea what to say. If actual harm is not done, it's a civil matter. "How do you know he intended possibly harming you?" I asked.

"It was his EYES!" She explained. "They BULGED OUT. Only mad people and manic's who are lying through their teeth get this/ I know, my Ex-Husband does the SAME THING! Only SERIOUS Bi-polar's, the full on manic-depressives get eyes that BULGE like this!"

Let me pause, dear reader, and consider this circumstance. I realized that providing Moigle with a mirror to see her own bulbs bulging was a possible death sentence for myself, and yet somehow I also had to refrain from laughing. It was far more difficult than you might imagine.

I had failed once before, many years ago when applying for a job at McDonald's. The interview had gone well, the fellow liked me, and then the small talk part of the interview arrived. I politely noted that the McDonald's people were very loyal. At this point, the fellows' eyes BULGED. He slapped his pen on the table and said, like some military commander ruling the fort with his iron will, "My OATH we are loyal. I am McDonalds, my Wife is McDonalds, our whole family is McDonalds!"

I knew that to laugh would mean no job at McDonalds. But try as I would, the irony would not be resisted, and my face contorted to a smirk. I lost the job before it began. I was determined not to do so again. This time, I broke this bulgy eye contact and rushed to get a pen and paper, with the excuse that all important details could thus be written down.

For all the world I looked MOST serious and sincere as I recorded everything she said, and then carefully explained that if anything untoward should happen, I have it all noted. If something should happen. then there is no way such villainy would go unpunished. We even printed it up, duly signed and witnessed the proclamation, thus setting the matter into irrevocable stone.

Moigle slowly settled, her eyes went back into their sockets, and she slowly realized that life was not fated to come to a close on the end of Doogle's dick. The drama slowly faded, and then Moigle, from out the blue, asked me the oddest thing, "Do you want to sell your car?"

It would have been extremely odd, however, as I had a for sale sign clearly written on the back window I guessed that what she was really asking was "How Much". Now this car was an old 4 WD diesel truck. It had a suspension that was as hard as three rocks glued together and believe me, as the driver you felt every bump. It was, by any gender specific definition, a BOY car. This was a car built for hitting huge lumps and climbing hills and carting tools about.

"You don't want the car, Moigle... It is not a girl's car." I said.

Well that was it! I had slapped her in the face with the worst and most insulting gauntlet you could have imagined. All her feminism was outraged and her hormones soared to new heights. She was now going to have that car come hell or high water. I put her off some 4 times, and yet she kept coming back, wanting the car. Eventually I gave in and she bought it. In my heart I knew there would be a problem, but what else can you do? If I didn't sell it, she would nag me until I did.

She was a single minded creature and she wanted that car. Now, of course, in my years of ownership it had never failed me, not once. It was a beast, but it was reliable. There was only one thing, you had to fill up the water every week at the radiator, and not at the overflow tank. I explained this, in careful detail, to Moigle, saying that it must be a little corrosion in the head, because the water does not draw properly from the overflow.

It only took her a month to completely stuff it. She ignored my advice and did not fill at the radiator, and then, when it overheated (because it ran out of water) she panicked that her 16 year old daughter (who was safe in town and not on the highway like herself) would get raped and murdered, so she drove the overheating car all the way to the main shopping town, and was surprised when the engine seized on the way back home.

Then of course she accused me of selling her a dud car. I asked for these details, and offered to pay for the parts she would need. I even put her in touch with a very good diesel mechanic.

Well! The story only blossomed from that point. Suffice to say, she was such an irritating creature that the price from the mechanic went up from the $500 it started at to $2500, and apparently I was STILL to blame. So I tracked her down a deal that would only cost $1500, which pissed off the mechanic who thought he was getting some easy money. But this only annoyed Moigle more, because it meant that HE was a bastard and a cheat as well. But it had a thankful side effect.

Moigle left the house next door. Beyond this the car went off to the wreckers, and I didn't see her very lovely daughter again for years, by which time Moigle realized she loved me again and was giving me that slightly bulgy eye look once more. I finally asked her, "Why on earth did you want to buy that 4WD?" and she said "Well, you built your house with that car, and I wanted to build a house for myself."

That is how life is with bwitches. There is no logic that the mind can fathom, but to the woman in question it was perfectly sound thinking. I was fast coming to the conclusion that absolutely everyone in this entire valley was cursed, insane or completely brain dead. It was possibly a combination of all three. The real problem with this understanding was the realization that I, too, lived in the valley. And like any cucumber in a jar of pickles, was I getting pickled?

Witches in Britches: They all had their roles in the various dramas that unfolded in the valley. Mostly they were simply side bars, minor flares shot up to mark their position in the scheme of things, and no more. But taken as a whole, now that was a different story. All they needed was a leader to focus them, and as such they created a singular attraction to the most venous and vicious witch the valley had ever known.

What is more, it was to be years before I realized it, and it had been dear old Moigle in her panting sexual frustration (prior to the extinguishment of desire via the car) who had sussed it out.

She had said to me once (pre-car self destruction) "You think your ex-wife is your friend, but things are not what they seem to be. She told me that you intimidated her, and physically stood over her. I know you better than that. She is NOT the person you think she is." Well? At the time I immediately thought of how dear Moigle intimidated and stood over people, and thought "Sounds like a reflection in the mirror to me" but I noted the words she claimed my lovely ex-wife had said, and I made sure to ask her about it the next time we met. Zoom forward 2 weeks.

"Oh really?" the ex-wife responded, acting surprised. "No, I would NEVER say anything like that, Believe me, it is just not true." I thought, "Poor Old Moigle, inventing anything to get rid of perceived obstacles."

Yet I have discovered a curious thing. Time almost always tells a different tale from the story we hear in the present. And at that point in time I was entirely unaware of the depth of calculated destruction to my reputation that was being carried out behind the scenes. Surely I knew that my ex-wife had somehow managed to meet, and then visit, and even stay, with every single person I had introduced her to since we arrived in Australia. I was not aware of the coolness that appeared in relations between myself and people I had known for 20 years, but these things happen with divorce. I had just never put two and two together to add it up. But respect where respect is due.

Despite the fact that the knife was getting buried up the hilt in my back, and being done methodically and often, in time I came to grudgingly admire the sheer vicious contempt the woman must have had for me. Forget the Fowl Sisters, forget the Boringbar Witches! Here was a creature who had been contacting every single person I knew, quietly ingratiating herself with them by doing their gardens, their dishes, you name it, all to get back at me!

My ex-wife would even managed to move into their houses and stay for awhile, in the guise of free rent in return for services, but it was really all to plant the seeds of my destruction.

And it worked. She thoroughly destroyed my reputation, and caused me such a degree of financial cost and stress that I still to this day wonder what on earth I had done to make her hate me so. Yet she gave ME no indication at all.

When she saw me all I got was the warmest hug, the biggest smile, and the most heartfelt look that would seem for the all world to be the fine gift of human caring. Moigle may have been a hormone driven fool (as we all can be at times) when we first met, but I have to give her this. She spotted the wolf in the sheep's clothing long before I even guessed at the possibility. She was indeed the wisest woman in the valley, and in all honesty, the best hearted of them all.

But I stray from the literary cut and trust of the point. The point is WITCHES, and specifically the Ex-Wife. She was one that, by all standards, looked frail and innocent, and incapable of speaking a lie. All who met her truly believed that a radiant angel now walked the face of the earth. I believed it myself, and even when all the evidence was pointing to the contrary, I still presumed it must be some misunderstanding within myself. Of course, let us remember that Lucifer is an angel of Light.

The effect of this "angel" was that people I had known for over 20 years grew distant. Yes, I noticed, but I had no idea why it was happening. Apparently, it later emerged, these people were all firmly of the belief that I:

A: Kicked her out

B: Had taken her child from her

C: Robbed her of her money, and

D: Left her stranded, sick and all alone in the world.

I guess the fact that when we divorced she had three properties in her own name, which she sold, then spent the cash, didn't count? Neither did the fact that she was the sole heir to mummy's rather large fortune get considered in all of this? For SEVEN LONG YEARS this woman, who refused to get her own house, had somehow managed to get herself camped down in the home of every single person I knew who lived within 80 miles of me.

Imagine this: Your wife leaves you; she has no friends in the country, so she moves in and lives with each and every one of YOUR friends. What's more not one of them asks WHY. Isn't that just extraordinary? Seriously, she was the witch to make all other witches look like amateurs.

However, from my end it meant that my child was often getting taken to inappropriate houses on his weekends away with her. You see, some of my friends were drug addicts and alcoholics. I love them, and it's fine by me, but when my son is dragged into their world, I have a problem with that. Ben was also getting upset, and I could feel the problem growing inside him.

It got to the point that I offered to find a house to rent for her, and I even offered to PAY for it. Her constant gypsy-like existence was taking a terrible toll on my son, and I told her that it had to stop. Ah HA! The fireworks got cranked up at last. The cat really jumped out of the box when I started insisting she not take him to other people's homes every weekend.

She would not accept a rental house, and gave no reason, as per usual, so I opted for second best. I suggested it was better to let him stay home where he had all his belongings, and she could stay over. Of course, from that point on she moved in every weekend, and as I felt so uncomfortable with her creepy hugs and sweetness (which I now realized to be somewhat of an act) *I* was the one who moved out. I went to stay with friends at Bling Bling.

Isn't that weird? I build a house with my own hands, and I am moved out of it. Years later I realized the trick: **She didn't want me, but she sure as hell didn't want anyone else to have me**. What a perfect way to keep any prospective woman out of my life!

Unlike men, women see things clearly at this level. Imagine the story if I brought a girlfriend to my house? I bring her home after we have been at a party, only to find an ex-wife staring at us. Not only a single parent with a child, but one with an ex-wife hanging about? You can imagine why I just didn't bother, even when the odd luscious hitch hiker or party girl made the possibility obvious. (And there were a few)

As it turned out, this became a challenge to one woman. Sinella was a real witch. She had studied in the Bon Monasteries of Tibet and knew how to REALLY hex someone up, and what is more, she enjoyed it! Sinella was a shit stirrer witch who spotted, in my predicament, a way to have a bit of fun on many levels. She muscled in to my life proclaiming, of all things, everlasting love. I believed her, and gathered her outrageous flirting when she was married was attraction, rather than a technique to get her then husband passionate.

Everlasting love? Wasn't THAT a dance for 6 weeks.

The first wild two weeks, the next two weeks of discussion, and the last two weeks of being pissed off. It was the perfect Bling Bling romance! It ended, obviously, and the best spin I could put on it all was that in the process I came to understand there were some background problems in my life. Sure, I got used and abused for that short period, but what the hell! I was raised a Catholic, so it felt normal.

However, the EX thought differently. She met this new kid on the block, this Sinella, and promptly had a mild heart attack. You see, Sinella KNEW what sort of woman my EX was, and this was part of the attraction to me. It was a game of cat and mouse, and nothing gives a cat more joy than playing with mice. But my ex-wife gave that particular cat no joy. She also knew the game and ducked it by feigning severe distress. She ran away to a cubby hole at some former friends house until the storm passed.

Witches: I promise you, in all the burnings of the reformation of the middle ages not a single true witch was caught. The real ones are always just out of sight, and never advertise their wares to any but the most willingly eager ears and mouths. The real witches are the ones organizing the bonfires.

Six Weeks and a lifetime of emotion. My EX (in one corner) didn't want me but didn't want anyone else to have me. Sinella had me, but after playing with the mouse for a few weeks didn't really want me. I vaguely wanted both and had neither. The tension was magnificent. Spiraling out of control, events took up their own head of steam and I was left like a dead bird, on a wire between two hooks in a butchers shop.

It got complicated. First, Sinella's had her own EX (the Artist who turns up later when talking about Steve Rose) turn up, kick in the door and screams deep hatreds about how events had taken such evil turns for the worse. Now I knew the fellow, and had known him for years. He had not only been married to her, but he had introduced me to this woman I was currently sleeping with. His Macedonian blood got more than a little boiled with the fact that I was now in her bed. And really, you really can't blame him for this.

Well, it didn't take too long for me to realize that *real* reason I was here with Sinella was mostly to provide the fuel to boil her EX. What's more, it became double jeopardy as ANOTHER former EX of this Ex-Husband (The Macedonian one who had been kicking in the door) had been in contact with the woman I was now sleeping with, and they had secretly collaborated in creating a plan that would really cook the poor fellow's goose, the one that they now both equally loathed. I was just the meat in the sandwich to help their plans unfold. My GOD, it was complex!

And on the vice versa, similar things were happening with my side of the fence. Only MY ex-wife was far smarter and did not kick in doors. No, she did the feminine faint manoeuvre. It always works such a treat! You see someone you once genuinely cared for look at you all doe eyed, and then they fade slowly to the floor, and all your chivalrous charms are pulled out as you rush over to say that you love them. I was so dumb back then.

They recover, slowly, saying how much they are grateful for your ongoing concern. Once the bait is taken and the hook placed firmly back in the mouth, then they don't want you again. My GOD! Who needs Soap Operas and professional actors to live out your emotions when you have Boringbar?

I became the meat in the sandwich, as I say. However, things turn in the oddest of ways, and the best lemons makes lemonade with the right twist of fate. This twist came with a friend, Hacksaw Jack. He was visiting at the time and I had asked him to collect my son, Ben, from town because I couldn't get up there. Here was the REAL turning point, something I had never even suspected. Jack discovered to his surprise that when Daddy wasn't around my dear little, sweet boy was an absolute monster.

Hacksaw Jack

Jack could not believe what he saw. He felt odd mentioning it to me, but he felt he had to. I had absolutely NO idea what had been happening when I was not around, yet apparently my sweet, shy son was behaving rather badly when I wasn't there. In simple terms, he had become an absolute brat. By this I mean, pinching, kicking, screaming, stealing, and abusing: A real Bart Simpson.

All I had ever seen was a sweet well-mannered child. So I started asking around, and sure enough, there was a major problem with his behaviour. As a result, for HIS sake I took the reins. The little guy had been with me most of the time, but now he moved in with me full time. Amazingly, right at this point it was discovered that my EX was desperately ill and on death's door. She needed this break and spent a good deal of time and money getting well.

Curious timing. In actual fact now that she was set free from caring for her child, apparently the dear girl was soon off frolicking in Vanuatu with a boyfriend no one ever knew about until some 5 years later. They can be very secretive creatures, women.

My EX was a magnificent hidden witch, yet she met her match with Sinella. Now here we need to separate ourselves from the story for a moment and understand that between women in competition with each other, a secret psychic war erupts. *Secret Women's Business* and the vicious flicks of the callous eye that stabs the heart. Men invariably miss it, unless they are gay.

When my EX realised she had met someone on par, and possibly better, with witchy-ways, she cowered and vanished up her own orifice. Sinella knew it was avoidance, but that is an effective tactic in psychic war. As is the way with cats and mice, when the superior bitch succeeded in her various conquests, Sinella got bored. Once she had gotten her revenge on her former husband by sleeping with one of his best friends, her job was done. Subsequently she moved to Tasmania with some other poor sap (another former friend of the former husband) in tow, seeking new fields to sew her havoc seeds.

I knew none of it at the time, of course. I knew nothing of the "Secret Women's Business", that undercurrent of whispers and surreptitious glances which, when it comes down to it, are simply bitch games. In truth, the world of this type of woman is like a bad Valentino movie from the silent movie era. It is all looks and glances and dramatic dramas unfolding. Now, women don't actually SEE these glances so much as SMELL them. They smell the scent of someone watching, they smell the vibe of sexual desire, of doubt, and indeed of any strong emotion, and this is what excites them. In relationships women simply follow their nose to what smells good to them.

Finally I came to understand why my wife divorced me. Finally I could shut that door and move on.

The main reason a woman will divorce a man is almost never mentioned. It is because she no longer likes his smell. The other senses of sight, taste and feel follow soon after. It is an inevitable tango of death because if she doesn't like the smell of you anymore, the relationship is dead. Of course, it may be that she likes the smell of your money, or your power. This perfume may well cover up your real scent enough to make her want to stay, but take away that perfume and see how long it lasts.

However, a word of advice, should you care to listen. If you have a pretty girl that you know is only with you because of your money, then just be grateful you have your money, and enjoy it.

Yet, in my personal situation, the leverage of relationship had shifted in my favour. No woman can hold her head up when she is revealed as being a poor mother, and more to the point, Ben was very happy to be with Dad.

Let's be clear on this. It was nothing new that he could take or leave his mother. He had chosen by age two that Dad was the one for him. How do I know this? His Mum went away to the US on a trip, and it took him 10 days to even bother to ask about her. And the question was not "When is Mummy coming back?" it was, "Is *she* coming back?" He was seriously not concerned if 'she' did or didn't return. Thick as I was back then, I realized there must be some sort of deep issue between them.

I felt sorry for her, wondering why her own son really had no interest in her. Casting back now, I realize that at an early age I lost interest in my own Mother because I could see she was two-faced. She was saying one thing in public, but acting differently in private. Of course, years after I came to understand that this was the norm. Certainly I remember the shock it was for me to discover my own mother appearing to lie, and this was at two years old. Maybe my little fellow saw and felt the same?

Oh, his Mum still visited, and still stayed the weekends when she wasn't being gypsy girl somewhere else. But the dynamic of things had shifted, a decision had been made and slowly I was becoming aware of what I call the "Witch Dance". This is other people moving and swaying to get your attention, but only in order for you to do as they desire.

Slowly I started to understand how this thing we call "Karma" rolls out and around situations, knitting events up in an embroidery of circumstance, one that, with Boa-like consistency, slowly constricts, and finally suffocates.

"Resolve to be thyself: and know that he who finds himself, loses his misery."

Matthew Arnold

DOWN COMES THE RAIN

*"'**Know thyself**' is a good saying, but not in all situations. In many it is better to say 'know others.'"*   **Menander**

It rained last night, after a month or two of dry. Yesterday the grass outside was parched, and a fine dust was getting into everything. I cast my mind down to the property. Boringbar would be extremely wet today, which meant farmers off to the pub, taking their seats, gossiping their gossip, and drinking their favoured ale.

It echoes across the country. Crusty old men, testosterone fuelled young ones, worn out women, and beer. Lots of beer. Come evening it will be rum and some young stud will shout, "Beam me up Scotty!" (serve me a Jim Beam, bartender) but today in the country, on this rare day of rain, the call will be for BEER. Beer is God, and you KNOW where these people worship.

I guess this is a part of the reason of why I never really fitted into the fabric of Boringbar society. I am not much of a drinker, and certainly Pubs are not high on my social agenda. There were other options at Boringbar, if you cared for them. The so called "Sports Club" had a licence, thus a de facto bar. This was where the family people tended to go. I always found it curious to see the diehard regulars sitting there, talking pub talk while their kids (all ranging from 3 to 13) ran around on the football field outside, occasionally coming up asking for another coke, some food, or chips.

Or else they vanished into the bush with some equally underage child. Mind you, it was probably how their parents met when they were that age.

You could say that such vices as underage sex, drinking, drugs, and even incest were not invented in Boringbar, however let me assure you, they were well rehearsed. Media talks about the degeneration of Aboriginal societies in the West? Well maybe someone will one day look at places like Boringbar, and discover how trashy bored white kids can hold their own in any of the social decay stakes.

In the few years I was there, I can name any number of young adults that started as bright-eyed kids, but through a combination of booze, pills and dope they slowly mushed their brains into a sort of pulverised rhubarb, where the only intelligent conversations was in the singing of ditties from Ads. Raised on a diet of Big Brother, small dreams, low grades and highs from home grown weed, these were human beings who slowly, inexorably aimed their lives towards the scrap heap of the dole and/or other forms of low grade criminality.

One lived down the road. A really decent fellow. He had read Proust, for God's sake. His father was a sculptor, and artist and thief. This is, apparently, a legitimate occupation if you proclaim it to be so. The father reasoned that because everyone knew how he earned his money, he was being more honest about his profession than politicians, policemen and priests. But he had raised his son and gave him the best of the best as far as culture and the classics went.

He also taught him the honourable art of growing "the weed". This was a different sort of cultivation than you might get at Harvard, but I promise you, it pays better. I think I was the only person in the entire valley who was not at least paying off their rates bill with a "Cash Crop".

I suspect this had something to do with the aliens who were going to come through the night sky to get me when I was 21.

I was at Seals Rocks, and stoned off my tree after 90 or more bongs around a friendly campfire. It came to the end of the night, and I struggled back to my tent with but a candle in hand, and some cliffs either side. The Aliens were looking through seven rectangles in the sky, seven definite black rectangles. Then, the candle got blown out! Fear struck hard. I reasoned then that even if I were wrong about the aliens, and that this was indeed the drug induced paranoia that I suspected it may well have been, even so, in an ideal world one should not tempt fate either way.

So I left that particular vice, and took up a rather priest-like notion of spiritual purity. I lived for well over 20 years from that date where no smoke, no alcohol, no nothing of the devil, et al, passed my lips. You can clearly see how I was NEVER going to fit into Boringbar.

Boringbar was cultivated, alrighty. It had the sacred green herb in every nook and cranny. The herb partook of every social gathering, and seeped into every brain and it disseminated its packets of THC. My Proust reading friend was an advocate of the herb, but he hated it as well. How so? "It has ruined me," was all he said. It gave him a good living, why hate it? This sticks like glue in my memory.

Here was the nut of my friends' problem. He wailed and moaned his fate to me some years ago, on just such a wet Saturday morning as today. I had called by to visit because I needed some help with an extension to the house I had built. My friend (we will call him Chubby) was a good carpenter, and he was also interesting company. Here was a rare thing, a young man who THOUGHT. He considered notions of life and his place in the universe, and had something more in his head beside the sexing of some scatty young 14 year old, or arguing the football results.

However, Chubby was depressed that wet day, and it was very obvious it he had been like this for some time. I had asked if he were interested in helping out with an extension to the house, and then he got really, really depressed. I did not want to push things, but I was curious about what set him off. So I asked why.

"I cannot work anymore." He said flatly.

"Your back has given out?" I suggested politely.

"No, it's not that. Even if you were paying me $20 a hour cash in hand, the problem is that I am just completely fucked. I would be there for half a day and all I would be thinking of is how I would have made five times as much just by sitting here, packaging up some mull, and going off to sell it down the pub. The dope has ruined me, it's just too damn easy, and because it is so easy, and I have so much spare time, I smoke the shit myself to fill in the empty spaces.

"Then the paranoia hits, and I know I have to stop. But it is so damn easy to keep going. So I hate myself for being this weak, and I am getting unfit because of it. I am sliding downhill and I hate it, and yet I want it at the same time. I am a complete shit. I am totally fucked up, and useless."

"Well," I said genuinely, "If it helps, you can work on the house at no charge, then you won't have to get depressed at how little you are getting paid. Call it service to the community, and feel better about dealing because you are putting something back in."

I was serious. This was in fact a really good solution for Chubby's dilemma AND it would have helped me out enormously. It was not that long ago that I had fallen from the house I had been building, and was put off work for 3 months. I was still sore and in pain, and needed a helping hand.

Well, Chubby declined the offer, and what's more I never saw him again. He moved out, and in real terms, he loved out.

This is where the real decline appears, in the small gestures of kindness that slowly but surely evaporate between neighbours and friends. Our world slowly turns in on itself, seeking greater internal satisfaction from some drug or habit, and step by step we start the process of disappearing up our own orifice.

Soon after, I discovered by chance, when calling over to see if Chubby was OK, my missing wood lathe at his Dad's place. When I asked the father about that, he simply said he was looking after it for me. "But not the stand?" I questioned. No, it was too awkward and heavy to shift.

Dysfunction: The Mother of all Paranoia's

"we elected the body, the parents, the place, and the circumstances that suited the soul and that, as the myth says, belongs to its necessity."

James Hillman

Have you ever wondered how Dysfunction comes about? The social workers try to tell us it is a lack of communication, and if we can only start talking, it will heal. But that's crap. Dysfunction is more like the wish to continually pick a scab so that it never heals.

Communication is simply connection. I can understand why people who have never suffered deep and lasting dysfunction say it is a cure. It is not merely an excuse to hide the fact they have absolutely no idea, and do not want to appear powerless. But the fact is, if you force dysfunctional people to talk, you increase the blather and decrease the communication. If someone WANTS to talk, different story, but you cannot prescribe communication like it is a pill from the doctor. Let me put it differently. People who blow themselves up for Allah are dysfunctional human beings, but they talk! Genuine dysfunction is actually the function, or purpose, the person exists for. It is completely wrong to any outside it, yet completely right when you are in it.

We like to think of life as ideally being a win-win, but the truth of Dysfunction is most often found in the opposite. It looks for, and generally achieves, a Lose-Lose. But not just ANY Lose-Lose. With a dysfunctional persona, the ideal of winning is that you LOSE less than the object of your hatred. If you think I am wrong, look at every divorce case ever run by lawyers. It is not negotiation; it is simply "No Go" Titillation.

I was determined not to get embroiled in the Fowls' dysfunction, because I knew that, while they all hated each other at this very moment, I was not only NOT family, I was not a 30 year plus Boringbar resident. If I made myself the target they would all line up against me. I knew this, and wanted to avoid solicitors specifically because the Fowls had their dysfunctional family hatreds, with the subsequent motivation to be unreasonable, combined with the money and assets to expend in an extended Lose-Lose scenario.

So I went out of my way with discussions and negotiations and then still more discussions to try and resolve the issue. But it came down to this: Even though ALL the Fowls were happy to put a road around the sheds, none of them could agree with each other on exactly how to do this. I know it sounds absurd, I know it is ridiculous, but even when they all agreed, they could not agree.

I spoke to our mutual neighbour, Miss Hard Nosed Legal Bitch, who was well versed in legal argument (as she worked for one of the leading advocates in the area). She advised "They all hate each other and love their money. We all know how tight they are. Let nothing come between a Fowl and a Dollar! Just start the legal process and they will all soon agree and sort it out. After all it is their OWN skin getting skinned here, and it's a case you simply cannot lose."

I replied, with a morose understanding of dysfunction, with a very old axiom. "Blood is thicker than water."

It turns out that I was, sadly, correct. Supreme Court dates were set, and that very expensive snowball was put on its path down the hill. Soon it would gather moss, snow and whatever crap it could find it its path. This was the sort of case where the really nasty solicitors love to put up their hands.

Why? It is simple. A dysfunctional family with a valuable property fighting a cause they cannot win always means large profits for the firm. Dysfunctional families always need at least two legal opinions on everything, and they always run two sets of solicitors, two sets of barristers, two of EVERYTHING. It is wonderful thing for the bank balance when you are a solicitor with clients like the Fowls. I did warn the brothers, but they ignored me.

Predictably, while the brothers engaged one of the most ruthless, money driven pariahs of the legal profession, the other side (Doogle and his Sisters) found an idiot who was noted mostly for his blind viciousness, but also because of his absurd inability to understand grammar. On one side the brothers legal representative was marked by the number of his (very legal) family members who had been struck from the Bar, as a result of very illegal and indecent circumstances, while the other side was noted for the fact that their solicitors own legal partner was desperately trying to get away from him.

It was all an education on how the legal profession really works. There is no logic, no reason, no ethics as we might like to suppose. However, there is a whole lot of MONEY involved. To be fair, I had a very decent fellow looking after me. He carried the entire case, as he knew I had no money, but also because he knew I could not really lose.

However, the Fowls! My goodness. They contracted Private Investigators, they brought in expert barristers, they called up quotes from the most extraordinary sources, and they refused to answer the most simple questions put to them. In all, common sense was avoided at all costs, because if the dictum of reasonableness were ever to be applied, there would be no case.

What's more fascinating is how the Fowls, dear dysfunctional ones that they were, all thought this was perfectly NORMAL. Take a look through their eyeglass for a moment. All your life you have harboured resentment and ill will to your family members. All your life you had an axe to grind. Now you are elevated to a position where you can finally take all the collected knifing in the back experience and get highly qualified advice on how to do this better.

What is more, you will learn how to do this PROFESSIONALLY and you can do it as a FAMILY. Well, for the Fowls, this was a FAMILY BONDING experience. It was heaven on a stick for a Dysfunctional Fowl.

I had offered the Fowls the most treasured thing, the most deeply satisfying event they had ever experienced. I offered them the ultimate family argument, one that they could all agree on! If you can wrap your head around this degree of dysfunction and paranoia, you are doing well.

All up, the process lasted some 6 years. I remember speaking with my solicitor saying "Well, at least the judge will see how much effort I made to try and avoid the courts." His answer was surprising. "You know, I hate to say this, but this works against you. The system is set up for WAR, not conciliation. If you are conciliatory, most judges see this as a weakness. If you don't believe enough in your cause to go to war, then your cause must be weak.

"But... YOU go to war!" I answered.

"Yes... That is exactly correct. WE are the ones who are supposed to put on the shining armour, not you."

"This makes absolutely no sense at all." I said flatly.

My solicitor, who had much experience in many areas of humanity, not just law, smirked satisfyingly. He looked quite wry as he commented, "Yes. This is exactly right. Now I see you finally understand."

Paul Brown, a simple nurse who made the shift to become a lawyer. You were always the best of them because you remembered to be kind yet truthful.

THE CHIEF JUSTICE of EQUITY

in the Supreme Court of New South Wales

He opened proceedings with a very simple question. *"Please tell me ... Why are we here?"* The wigs on the opposing bench could not actually answer this, but promised that they would, eventually. They never quite managed it and lost the case. The sheds were ordered off the road, with the only noteworthy comment to come out of all being the one made by a Barrister for the Fowls. I had passed by him after proceedings had closed as I made my way out of the Supreme Court. I was curious, so asked, "How often do you see absurd cases of such absolute nonsense that cannot be won taken so far, for so long, for so little?"

He smiled. "All the time" he said, rubbing his index finger and thumb with a covert glee. An ancient sign for Money.

The point of all this? Well, apart from the fact that your solicitor cares far less about winning or losing than he does about his fee, the rule is this:

Dysfunction cannot be negotiated with, nor can it be reasoned with.

Dysfunction only seeks dysfunction, and will only ever be happy when the other person loses more than themselves. I may have won the court case, but we all lost. We lost time, energy, money. But that's MY take on things. The Fowls, remarkably, saw it as a bonding experience.

Of course, within 2 months of the court decision being handed down, they were back to hating each other all over again. That's just the way of things with dysfunction. People can sit at the table to eat the meal, but if they are Fowls they just love to glutton up, and then, like debauched Romans, they vomit all over their neighbour. It's a peculiar form of satisfaction, because it relieves pressure AND sends a message.

More on Vomit Shortly.

Dysfunction: The Rules rarely change. No matter what shifts in the course of our human endeavour, the rules of the Human Condition almost never deviate from the Five Principles of Dysfunction.

Dysfunction has Five Principles

1. **Low-heeled two-faced bitchery that holds pretence as the ultimate sacrifice.**

2. **High notions of grandeur sloshing about in the sloth of human desires.**

3. **Badly repaired emotions sinking in an endless ocean of compromise.**

4. **Flotsam and Jetsam all pretending to be Titanic's before the Iceberg**

5. **Paranoia of the fear that we are paranoid of our fear**

True Dysfunction has a "not negotiable" clause built in. We like to think there is a solution for every problem, and there is. The Courts or a Gun. You want a SOLUTION? Remember, a solution is not an ANSWER, it is simply a situation where elements (read assets) get DISSOLVED. An easy example: Divorce is a solution that a marriage gets dissolved in. If more people realised this, court cases would drop significantly.

Each of the following stories touches on at least one of these five principles, and many touch most of them. Perhaps I may suggest a break from the Fowls for the moment. We need to spread our wings and gain an insight into other forces that were driving the circumstances at Boringbar, so let us pause and take a look at some of the other characters and actors that loom large on the stage of our absurd tragedy.

VOMIT and POO

"One of the best temporary cures for pride and affectation is seasickness; a man who wants to vomit never puts on airs." **Josh Billings**

At Bling Bling I would often visit friends, and one such visit found me at the home of the local Lord and Lady, Skerick and Dealer. Dealer was this elegant high brow type of woman who, despite (or perhaps because of) the reserved exterior, loved to do curious things such as Colonic Cleansing. Indeed, she had opened a business as a Bum Flusher.

For years I had noticed in their bathroom an odd bottle and tube that looked a little like a drip from the hospital. Eventually I got around to asking what it was for, and Skerick explained it was to be filled with warm water, and you placed the "drip" end up your butt. It filled slowly with water, and then you evacuated all the internal remnants of your food orientated desires.

I gather you evacuated in the shower, the same shower I had always used when visiting. I further noted there was no such contraption in their own private en suite. However, this all was of no import to Skerick, who explained to me, in detail, the joys of warm water induced flushing. He did so with a rather self satisfied smile as he drew deeply on his marijuana loaded pipe. You may think such a thing is odd? Clearly, you have never lived in Bling Bling.

However, on this particular night Dealer was enraptured with Vomit. She studied more things than mere Bum Flushing, and she now waxed lyrical on her latest fad. Fresh back from a peculiar cleansing ritual, the Ayurvedic technique of VOMITING for days on end, she positively GLOWED, giving us her report on how much stomach congested mortals could toss up.

Sounds a little bit harsh, doesn't it? Tossing up for days on end? However, I was assured it was effective. People take these herbs that cause them to vomit, and they do so as a group for up to four days. Not quite the pleasant holiday retreat most people would aim for.

For several hours, like forensic scientists we discussed the various forms of vomit. The colour, the shape of the pieces, the texture, the scent, the malleability. All the time I could not help but recalling how someone once told me that the Eskimo had 36 words to describe snow. What ever mere snow is to you and I, to an Eskimo it is a vast world of experience, a delight, an amazement, a conflagration of communicative concepts.

So too it was with Dealer and her discussion on Vomit. Being the perfect guest, and quietly fascinated, I asked all sorts of questions about the true nature of vomit. What other variations might one find? Gooey Texture versus Watery? Do you find undigested carrots in there? Etc. All the while Skerick sat back, smoking pipe after pipe, making odd comments such as "My God, that's just so gross!" and "What about the smell, how could you stay in a room full of vomit smell for 4 days!" Of course, he was as enthralled myself, and right in there with it all, experiencing the horror movie.

Now let me pause: I didn't really have the heart to tell Skerick that the real reason I suspected for his wife's deep interest in Ayurvedic treatments, particularly the ones that took her away for days at a time. These journey's were apparently were more to do with the teacher than the teaching. It was just a guess, but from all I heard who had left the school, it was an accurate one. No, dear Skerick lived in a smoke dream, and I must suppose his wife saw no reason to alter the situation.

Indeed, it would seem she propagated it. One night when we are sitting having Thai at a local restaurant we are talking about relationships, marriage, and the like. Skerick pops up with the most curious comment. "I own my wife, and she is happy about it."

It certainly caught my ears. I looked up at Dealer and asked if she felt the same way. "Of course I do. I appreciate being owned, and I love belonging to this man. He belongs to me, I belong to him. It's perfect."

Try and I would, I could not pry from either of them a thought to the contrary. I suggested what would happen if someone tried to come between them, not necessarily a lover, but perhaps a Mother? (Both had possessive mother's who acted non-possessive)

They laughed, but I was serious. "Really, who can own anything?" I questioned. "Is your marriage license a deed? And what is the real cost of the mortgage you take out to buy it, if it is?"

Speaking as a single man, I was free to ask such question. Had I had a wife beside me, I know the edge would have been blunted by the need we call self preservation. I also had a small awareness that the Ayurvedic lessons which were increasing in frequency were not about ownership, or education, but enjoyment. I was curious if any hint may be dropped? A clue guessed?

But no, the illusion is complete. These two are bonded for life in their security of ownership. Until death do they part, but in the meantime, why waste a good opportunity for pleasure? After all, Skerick had his Hooch.

It may be why he eventually killed himself, though.

Claire Merrin, and the Alien: Merikosh

Now I know from this very word and deed of yours, what free choice is, and what it is capable of, namely, madness.　　Martin Luther King

My natural instinct was to transfer the weight of the mad woman over to Skerick. She, the utterly mad one, had turned up out of the blue a week earlier. My oldest boy had been visiting with his new girlfriend, and she arrived on the doorstep in the same manner that a drowned rat might appear.

Claire Merrin was in the process of escaping her mother. Apparently Mum had been trying to kill her mind with drugs because a sick pathetic devil-controlled psychiatrist had proclaimed that she was schizophrenic.

Well, nothing new there. We all knew Claire Merrin was nuts, but as I had known her for over 20 years, I figured she could stay the week that she implored I give her. And only now do I recall my advice to a friend in New York who had suffered a Claire Merrin invasion: *"Keep her at arms distance and get her out of the house!"* A word to the wise: Never invite mad people to stay. Visit, sure, but never to stay.

Apparently our escapee, had been visiting Brisbane and discovered my address from friends. She subsequently stole her sister's 2 door Mercedes, and driven it down. She only scratched it slightly and was very puzzled as to why it revved so high. She went "OH" when I pointed out she had driven all the way in second gear. Not to mention the brake pads that were down to the metal.

Needless to say, and despite my own best advice to others, the bags got moved in.

Then, like an encyclopaedia salesman with his foot in the door, the girl promptly announced the REAL cause for her visit. Aliens had come to her, and explained that she was the next President of the United States. Her job was to get the Pope and the Archbishop of Canterbury to a meeting, whereupon the aliens would reveal themselves and the true messiah would appear. Which, of course, just happened to be Claire Merrin.

Where are those drugs when you need them? Thinking back to the drug induced haze of my distant past I pondered: Maybe Aliens really DO come through rectangles in the sky?

My oldest son was staying at the farm with his girlfriend, and this girl noted the obvious, that Claire wrote copious notes in her diary. Being a curious creature, as all women are, when I had Claire out the next day the girl peered through her notes to see what was written. (Evil girl, peering into diaries) She discovered, to her delight, that "I" was to be the consort of the new messiah, and if "she" (she being Claire, the new Messiah) cleaned my bathroom this meant that I would willingly sleep with her.

I noted with trepidation that Claire HAD meticulously cleaned the bathroom before we went out. She also asked a lot of question regarding how long my son and his girlfriend were staying. All in all, I soon realized that once IN this was a girl who would not be easy to get OUT. That is when I thought of Skerick and his dear wife and their ownership of each other.

While I was being told that I was the 4th highest living Master in the world (of course, Claire was second, just behind the Alien Merikosh who was the guardian saint that caused the construction of the universe) I saw my exit strategy take shape. I mentioned in passing that I knew another High Master, a very powerful one, and one who seemed to have copious amounts of smoke at his disposal. This was indeed NEWS.

A trance ensued, and I was instructed by the Alien Merikosh to travel to this Skerick fellow, who would have an important message for Claire. Now the thing about Claire is that when not speaking in tongues, and being a channel for aliens, she presented quite well. Like many Schizoid types, she knew how to work a situation to her advantage, and would mould her persona to suit the people in front of her. And she was a good looking girl.

Skerick and Dealer saw a well dressed, quiet and unobtrusive blond who spoke well on any number of issues. They were slowly being drawn into her web, when Claire, who was Merrin just at that moment, announced that Skerick was the 4th Highest Master in the world. Apparently I had quite unfortunately recently been devolved to the fourteenth, for reasons which were not explained.

This mastership ranking business is a very malleable thing, you must understand. I noted that it seemed particularly focused on men, and specifically men who appeared to be in a position to provide something that Claire wanted. However, it became even MORE remarkable. As it turned out, Skerick was not only to be the 4th highest master in the land, it was ALSO his job, nay his very life's purpose, to help her propagate a child.

All this is said with nary a blink of an eye right in front of Dealer, and Skerick, fool that he is for a pretty face, BLUSHED. That was enough for Dealer, she announced that it was late, and that Claire and I were welcome to stay. Here was my perfect out. I said "I would love to, but my son is visiting. Perhaps Claire, sorry, Merrin (She nods sagely at my correction to her true name) might be OK to stay here for a couple of days?"

The poor fools agreed, or should I say Skerick was intrigued enough to want to know more. Six weeks later Skerick was called me up asking "How do I get rid of her? She has found my crop and smoked most of it!" Apparently the idea of propagating a child had fallen by the way, and Claire had moved herself over to another house where she had discovered Skerick had a secret stash growing.

I felt a small pang of guilt, so I agreed to help him out. I called around to the "secret house" to find the fellow who lived there pulling his hair out, entirely unable to deal with Claire who had completely ensconced herself in his lounge, and who was now proceeding to eat everything from the fridge, drink everything from his bar, and smoke everything from his garden.

I kid you not. Claire was a class act! Tiptoe through the tulips dear reader. Walking into that story was like walking on glass.

When pinned on the theft of the dope, she simply said "My goodness. If I had some mull in the back yard, do you really think I would not offer it to you? How can you be so small minded!"

Who needs colonics when you can be given the shits so effectively by one simple human being? In a Ulyssian stroke of insight I arranged for Claire Merrin to be moved on by suggesting to Skerick that if he could find a reasonably attractive fellow who might sex her frequently, then this would be the end of the problem for him. He found one, rather quickly, and despite his ruinous demotion to nineteenth Highest Master, off she went happily airing the fruits of her loins in the direction of a rather cute author's penis.

He was, after all, a published writer. This is a reasonable Everest to conquer. If I ever see Aaron again, I will apologise to him. I hope he was able to cope, particularly as he has probably been demoted himself by now.

A Cafe' in Bling Bling

The Cafes in Bling Bling were the centre of the known universe for many of the town's denizens, as well as a train station for the passer's by to find opportunity, meet people, and get sex. Overall, there are two basic types of Café in town: The Sydney or the Melbourne variations. The classic Bling Bling hippie style café has been diminished to mere juice bars.

The two main cafés were Rash and Unos. Rash had a sort of infectious ability to get under your skin. Of note, the most beautiful girls would work there, and, of course, while this meant that young and old men would be attracted like flies, Café Rash also became a fashion plate for competing girls.

Uno was the classic pseudo-intellectual Melbourne style cafe. To be Uno meant having cropped black hair, pins and piercing of various types, a vaguely punk expression, slightly dirty hair, black clothes and obviously you should be seen reading that expensive magazine about architecture that you found lying beside a copy of yesterdays Melbourne Age. You keep your arm pits down as you talk, because while outwardly you are a rebel, secretly you are ashamed of your "politically correct thumb the establishment" underarm hair. In the heat of Bling Bling, it smells, despite the patchouli oil.

Uno clients tended to have a slight myopic look that seems to match the unshaven zones and pale skin. Invariably the women were slightly fat and highly opinionated. The men who liked this type were art-house freaks and nerds who got scared by beauty as much as they desired it. All were running around confused, hoping for intimacy as they discussed existentialism. Slicked hair was de rigueur, and unisex had never left town. Seriously, the thought of these people having sex, breeding and subsequently raising children was the most frightening thing you could experience in the Melbourne style café.

The Sydney style, such as Rash, was less contrite in regards the destruction of the environment, but all pretty much had the same view of Party Politics and the mistreatment of the indigenous people. No one cared much about any of it, but they all mouthed the appropriate PC comments regarding it all. To be "Rash" meant to be self-indulged, self-absorbed and self-inflicted. To be "Rash" meant that saving the planet from greenhouse gasses was best done by drinking more coffee, because after all, more coffee beans means more coffee plants, which means less CO_2. Rash was not politics or practicality or punctuality, it is all about hanging out, recovering from being strung out, coming out or otherwise just being seen out and about.

In simple terms, Rash was more about posing and being posed upon (is this "im-posing"?) and wat is all about pouncing and being pounced upon. Yes, in Bling Bling the Café is the new pickup palace. Rash (in particular) meant you could sit on environmentally unfriendly wooden chairs and gaze at the human meat walking past on the sidewalks. Stay in Bling Bling and you will quickly see how people cease to be people when sex and hunger come into play. It all becomes meat and eating, and nobody ever gets full.

What's more the waitresses have a code that signalled your degree of acceptance and desirability. These exquisite creatures that lolled about and gently leaned down to place the coffee on your table demonstrated your sexual acceptability with a simple technique that told you if you were meat or leftovers. The degree of eyeful that you got of the waitresses cleavage was an excellent and simple gauge as to your sexual potential on that day. In simple terms, the more tit you saw, the more sex you got.

One of these creatures was known to me (not biblically) through as association with Lucifer Street. (who we shall meet shortly) The rather choice young lady loved to languish her brown eyes all over me, and I sincerely appreciated the attention, even though it was her general habit with all vaguely desirable men. But she showed that she was very low cut, so I felt pretty good.

More to the point, I was intrigued as she embroiled and educated me in the various gossips that ran like a torrent of whispers through the Rash Café.

To Whit: The owners were very gay, and head-trippers of the highest order. Their penchant for mind games and twisting up the emotions of their staff are the very stuff of legend, and, sad to say, as of this present moment they have abused and freaked out so MANY beautiful girls that they are down to second rank beauties and blow-in backpackers.

The basic game was to entice the young things back to situations where many drugs and handsome studs were available. As the elixir of lust grew in the veins, various scenarios unfolded. Soon the girls (and boys) compromised themselves in all types of orgies and sexual deviations. Such experiences were situated in rooms with secret cameras, subsequently videoed, with the film being sold on at high prices to private clients, or onto porn sites. It was a very efficient way to defray staff costs, especially given the cost of continual training, given their exceptionally high rate of staff turnover.

Still, what did this matter? In Bling Bling, if you threw 10 stones into the air 8 of them would land on a pretty girl. You were never short of waitress material. Firm buttocked young men were also in demand, in a ration of 1 to 4 as a rule. They were to pimp about, gazing at the girls, while allowing the gay men to get an eyeful as they rubbed their young supple arms in front of them. Strike a pose, get a tip, and sometimes more than you bargained for.

All were duly instructed in the fact that they were there to LOOK good, not just serve coffee. This is the very Sydney part of the show. Looking good is all important, while in Melbourne looking as if you **matter** is the rage. And for the moment it seemed that looking gay was the best thing of all. You are both a fashionable minority AND expected to be a poseur. How perfect.

Girl gay (but not dyke) is particularly good, and for girls in particular, the appearance of being gay while you are actually sidling up to get the girls boyfriend is even better. This was standard practice in Bling Bling, you pretended to be gay, chatted up the girl, and then suggested the boyfriend you actually wanted in the first place, join you both.

It was all ultimately cool, especially when you got to tell all your friends all about it. This is where the real fun begins, because then THEY try and do the same, and so on. The net result is that relationships in Bling Bling are not known for longevity.

Honestly, when in Uno's I overheard some young things speaking, and it so perfectly underlined the reality of the place: "You know, I mean, you know they have been, you know, going together for, you know, absolutely FOREVER. I mean, like, I really think they are an IT thing, you know."

"Really? Like they are REALLY serious, as in you know, an ITEM?"

"Yeah, you know, I saw that and like, wow, I mean, you know, like they have seriously, and I mean seriously, been going out for like SIX MONTHS."

Silence fell on the table beside me, and a girl said "WOW! Amazing. Six Months! They are like REALLY serious then?"

Six months as an "item" in Bling Bling rates as a relationship somewhat akin to a marriage of 50 years elsewhere in the known universe.

Foolishly, I was intent on finding just one girl. Part of the joy of living at Boringbar was that you got to leave the overheated passion and false emotions of Bling Bling, and got back to normality. But after a while, you start to question: What is normal?

RELATIONSHIPS: Are they Ships without an Ocean?

The epitome of the failed relationship was Mr Stonehenge. This Libertine of Lust was a charming fellow who just happened to know every female in Bling Bling. I suspect he knew every female in Australia! Honest to God, I have walked down streets in capital cities far from Bling Bling, and women have come up to him, smiling warmly as they recognised his face, saying "Remember me?"

Once, after scaling a mountain down South we both went to an isolated town whereupon a girl looks up from where she was working and says "Mr Stonehenge! Fancy meeting you here!" She had the look, that inviting look reserved only for those whom one hopes will become aroused and interested. He always got that look, while I always got a sort of dull glance.

I didn't have the curly brown locks or that glint in the eye that sparkled when any pretty girl walked up. Perhaps I was jaded, but I tended to see trouble where Stonehenge saw only opportunity. Therein lies the difference between myself and all of Bling Bling. I foolishly sought something of substance to fill the empty holes in my life, whereas everyone else was simply seeking another substance.

Mr Stonehenge was so named because he created the Stonehenge that greets you at the roundabout into Bling Bling. This rather harmonious setting of stone was something he had created in a matter of weeks, and came about directly as a result of discarding the original architectural drawings and "free handing" it.

Indeed, Mr Stonehenge had a dream and accordingly just rocked up to the foreman on the road project, and said *"What are you going to do with the round-a-bout?"* The foreman showed him the plans, and Stonehenge told him that they were crap, and gave him good reasons why. Wrong plants, wrong layout, poor safety, blocking of visibility, etc. etc. The foreman, in true Bling Bling style said "Well you do it then!" He did.

In contrast, the edifice that was a small pelican atop a very large pole that marked the next town up the highway took 2 years and three committees to plan, and another 7 years to complete. And it was still crap. But not with our Mr Stonehenge on the job! He was a good man, but also a paradox.

To explain: He was overtly transient in relationships, and yet when he had a girlfriend, he became incredibly jealous at the same time. Indeed, I regularly received the odd text message warning me away when he believed the new girl he had just met was the "IT" girl. Apparently I, who only ever got the dull glance from them, was now competition. If only it were true! (Later I was to discover that a few of his girlfriends had suggested as "extra" dick would be nice, and that apparently I would have sufficed)

However, the relevant girl (fill in any name you can imagine) was only ever "IT" for that month. Some lasted two or more, but they rarely lasted beyond the next fling. (his or hers) There were exceptions, however. Notably, when Mr. Stonehenge got together with Dragon Girl. Yes, well wasn't THAT fire and brimstone. It went for tumultuous tempestuous temperamental MONTHS.

Finally he had lost it and smacked her one. Broke her jaw! I asked him why, because he just wasn't that type. "Well," he said "It wasn't that she slept with this other fellow so much, only that I found out he had AIDS and that she knew it, and didn't tell me, but slept with me again soon after." It was, in simple terms, a very typical Bling Bling affair. Anything goes, and then leaves.

It was at Café Rash (while having coffee with Mr Stonehenge some years ago) that I met Rusty Harris. This wild dread-locked madman came up to me, staring me into the eyes saying "Skerick reckons you can write." I nodded that I did, and asked what it was that he wanted to be written. Of course, he wanted me to write a biography about himself. Why? Because he was not that good at writing. I pay little attention to these things as a rule, but then Rusty said the magic words "I will PAY you to do it!"

"Well! That's what money is for." I said I would think about it, and asked more specifically what he wanted done. It turns out that Rusty had recently been a part of a major environmental protest that effectively shut down a Cyanide Leach gold mine in a highland wetlands area, which also happened to be sacred to the Aboriginal Elders. It became interesting and what could I say: He was paying me!

The book came out "Water: More Precious than Gold" and it was not a bad read. Check it out at laddertothemoon.com.au ... but what was NOT written about in the book is the fun part. You see, because of this meeting I fell in with the Rainbow People, the most extraordinary pack of Woodstock remnants you you are ever likely to meet. The happy hippies, the dread-locked derelicts, the hirsute heretics, those happily hooked on hashish, and all the rest ... They were all there, and all were part of the Rainbow Family. Everyone there was of the firm belief that the Western World was soon to consume itself on the bonfire of greed, and that they would be the vanguard of the new people, the new race that would rule with harmony and in agreement with the natural order. I don't think "they" thought about what would happen if this DID occur, and what it meant when their social security cheque's dried up, but that was not the point. The drama of change is what enticed them forward.

Art Shows and Mr Moore

Truth is so rare that it is delightful to tell it.   Emily Dickinson

At one of the Rainbow People meetings I met Mr. Moore. He reminded me, in his way, of the song by Leonard Cohen's "Bird on a Wire". I felt that Mr Moore, like his name suggested, did indeed want a little more. More of what, I cannot say, but he had that hungry prowling look. Yet at first it was his associates that had me intrigued.

At one particular meeting one of the members of the gathering stood up to make an announcement, and I joke not, this is written VERBATIM:

"I am a Breatharian. For the last two years I have not eaten food, and have lived solely on Coca Cola and Chocolate!" The woman then went on with varying degrees of waffle about the political importance of earthworms in the humus, but the thing is: NOBODY batted an eyelid at the notion of a self-proclaimed breatharian who drank coke and ate chocolate. I thought they were supposed to live on air alone, but what do I know? And this was but one!

These people lived throughout the Bling Bling and Boringbar regions, and the common thing that united them was the uncommonness they shared.

Once I journeyed to a local Art Show where my friend (the Artist you meet in the upcoming section on Steve Rose) had won the People's Choice award. Of course, specifically because his work was so much better than any other pieces at the exhibition, that there was not a snowballs chance in hell that a judge would select anything he did. Art judges and critics invariably support failed art and useless artists. Why? Because they are often failed artists themselves.

Any painting that is significantly superior to the best they could personally manage is generally judged as being worthless, with the comment being made that, "Realism is dead". When you fail at life, you become an artist, and when you fail at THAT you become an art critic.

Inside this alternative world of insane hairdo's and Quasi-New-Age-Hippy accoutrement (that was so remarkably last decade) people apparently existed and must have made money somehow. Probably through growing. But at one truly memorable event, the random madness just seemed exponentially greater in its lunacy. Gathered about were all the usual jaded faded fagots and queens drinking cheap wine and offering cheddar fuelled opinions on the opinion of the opinions others opined. This was all the "norm" in this abnormal society, but the thing that WAS something extraordinary: The DRUMMER.

Now, I know you might think it odd that at an Art Show you would have a drummer, a chanting drummer in fact. You might expect a violin, or a classical guitar or a piano. But this was Bling Bling. Now, the Drummer I found to be extraordinary for a number of reasons. Not only because he was a drummer who could not drum, but also because of the way he "Om'ed".

He chanted, if this is at all possible, off key. He OM'ed his little heart out, and here I admit to learning something. It must be hard enough to chant the OM out of key. Let's face it, how can you? He was drumming and chanting. There is no person to harmonise with, no instrument to match tones against. Yet he was fervently out of key in a way I really cannot explain. It was a remarkable achievement, one that I presume that was attributed to large amounts of alcohol and smoke.

But he managed something even MORE remarkable, he was able to drum out of time to himself. With his off-key OM and the random, erratic beat, I personally was amazed, and found he was quite unique and absolutely remarkable. But seriously, more remarkable was the fact that others seemed completely obvious to this fact. Yet it somehow worked! The dysfunction was so even applied across the board, that it seemed normal in some way.

The people there were so totally embracing of everything, that it all seemed part of the ridiculously bad art show. Apart from the piece the judges hated by my friend, everything else there was utter crap. Of course, the crap sold well.

The Rainbow People were there in force, and in between ducking out onto the back porch to smoke the sacred weed then coming to the front porch to drink the free cheap wine, they all successfully and completely ignored the art that was present in order to discuss the evils of a government that forced them to put in forms saying they were looking for work.

Yes, they complained about being forced to put in a little piece of paper that gave them the money they lived on. You know it is a degenerate system when even the free lunch meant putting in a little effort.

After the show, there was a general movement to pursue more drinking, smoking and madness at the fable Bling Bling edifice, the Rainbow Temple.

The Rainbow Temple

All the prior art show madness was nothing compared to visiting Gus at his remarkable hangout called the Rainbow Temple. Gus was the creator of this Bling Bling edifice, and despite his fetish for 14 year old girls (again, no one batted an eyelid) he was a very jovial sort of fellow.

Maybe it was BECAUSE of the 14 year olds he was so jovial? No matter, the important point is the temple itself. This wonderful structure soared 70 feet into the sky, supported by massive telegraph poles, and apart from its roof, it was entirely open to the elements. And it was always ready to morph and transition into something else.

As an example: I had some left over cypress pine from a building job, and mentioned it to Gus in passing. He showed significant and real interest, finally asking if I would like to donate it to the Temple. "What on earth would you use it for?" I asked "I was thinking of another floor!" but his mind trailed off to another notion, even as he spoke. I didn't have to answer, because both he and I knew he would never get around to it.

But what a joy to visit that wonderful Temple and look all the back packers and hippies it brought out of the woodwork. It was just THE place to be in through the summer. In winter, well, Gus had less visitors. The communal shower and toilets (open and in full view of the passers-by) were invariably interesting, and the communal kitchen was to be noted for the lack of food. Overall you would denote the term "primitive" to the accommodation and be called generous.

You stayed at the temple and contributed $70 a week, and this meant food was provided. It was! Every second Monday bread, apples and rice were placed like jewels into the open shelves. Come Tuesday, there was nothing.

The great and salient point to the Rainbow Temple is that it represented an important element in mankind's collective unconscious: The leisure industry. Honestly, no one worked there that I ever saw. The odd hippie chick went off to pick dope, but that was about it. I am not sure how or even when the place was cleaned. I suspect at random times some German could not stand it anymore, and that on such occasions a working bee would ensue. The Rainbow Temple was the ultimate Hang Out, the place to go to do nothing, and see everyone. It was, in effect, the ultimate Bling Bling Café where you brought your own coffee, but at least the water was free.

Down the road Mr Paul Smart lived in his manor made from mud brick. He was my legal advisor with the Fowls and their arguments. My regular top ups on legal advice regarding the latest manoeuvrings by Doogle Fowl allowed me to often drop into to see Gus more often than otherwise. And what he didn't have on hand as juicy whispers and murmurings was not worth knowing!

Being privy to goings on at the Temple was akin to knowing the heart of Byron, because all gossip flowed through it open decks, guided there no doubt by some mysterious, unseen force. It was also a gathering point for the Rainbow People.

At one of these gatherings the good Mr Moore took me into his confidence. He said, when I was mentioning some of the difficulties with neighbours and council, that "If you are still paying rates or a mortgage come September, then you will know we have failed" This was spoken to me in August 2001. The Twin Towers came down within the month.

Now retrospect is a funny thing. I knew some of the Rainbow people had been making regular visits to New Guinea, and that they were excited for some reason, genuinely believing that the end of the Western Civilization was upon us. But were they privy to the plans of Al Qaeda and 9/11? It beggars the imagination to think so, and looking at that rabble, it seems utterly impossible they would be capable of such an action. Yet I had clearly been told SOMETHING was up.

Perhaps it was the wind in the leaves, and perhaps no one knew that any specific thing was happening beyond rumours, but I cast my mind back a few months earlier when I found someone checking out the vacant houses in the failed Multiple Occupancy behind the Boringbar property. I asked him what he was up to. He said, simply "I am looking for safe houses for our people." I had recognised the fellow from a Rainbow People meeting.

At the time, I gathered he was looking for drug growing areas, but who knows? Maybe under the cover of our very noses huge plots were being formed to take over the country. Maybe 9/11 was supposed to bring down the world by bankrupting the Stock market and as everyone fled to the hills in droves, the Rainbow People would step into the breach? Maybe they all just smoked too much Hooch and imagined it all? I suspect it was the latter.

Months afterwards Mr Moore and I are out on ski boards in a decent swell, with the dolphins coming up around us. It's a beautiful day, no mention is made of the fact I am still paying rates, and then Mr Moore says out the blue: "I have real problem. The women at home, they want me to decide."

"Decide? Decide what?" I ask.

"They want me to choose one or the other. They say it can't be both of them any more, and I have to pick which one."

"THAT's a problem?" I said "I would have thought it was a great ride while it lasted. But the real fact is, it's not YOUR problem. Go over it: They were happy with the arrangement, you were happy with the arrangement. Let THEM make the choice of what they want to do."

"Yeah, you are right!" he said as if a revelation hit him. "It's not MY fucking problem. I am happy enough. Thanks for sorting that out for me."

I hesitated to go further, but I did. "Now, if you want the whole arrangement to continue on exactly as it has, you must do things a little bit differently. When you go back home, you tell your wives that you HAVE made a decision, and they are right. Things could not continue the way they have been going.

"They will expect to hear one of their names, but invent a third one, and say: 'I have chosen to move in with Susan. Sorry, but it just makes things way less complicated.' You will find they will band together against this third, invisible foe, and ask you to chose THEM instead. And your problem is solved."

Mr Moore laughed a huge laugh, and did exactly this. The girls begged him to reconsider, and please, can they just keep their household together. It was a case of happy every after, at least until the next drama struck.

Life, in all its complexity, can be so simple on rare occasions.

The upshot of all of this was not visible at the time. I was experiencing the end of an era. Bling Bling and the associated collection of misfits was slowly shifting into a different stage, and this was largely due to the incredible increase in property values.

Inside the next couple of years, Rusty got his book written, my journey with the Rainbow People faded out, and slowly but surely the hippies themselves were priced out of Bling Bling. In the ensuing few years, as the Yuppie Invasion became a flood, the entire place morphed into a new-age banking paradise where money was the new God, and rich single divorcees escaping capital cities (with their former husbands cash) flooded into, and became, part of the new social status.

The Hippies, Yippies, Dropouts and Environmental Faggots all moved to cheaper horizons where the dole went further. Perhaps you want to find out more? "Water, More Precious than Gold" is up at the laddertothemoon.com.au website. In my humble opinion the book it is worth a read if you have the time.

Sunshine came softly through my window today

Donovan sang this song many years ago, and today it is a truth I literally wear. This was the best part of Boringbar, the simple, relaxed appreciation of the sun, wind and rain that you experienced every day. It was a joy to be there when the issues and problem were not shouting from the sidelines.

Not everyone of the Alternative society were useless scammers and bludgers. A couple came to stay at the caravan near the house for a few months, and they were two genuinely kind people. They had a sense of joy in each others presence, and this made them some of the most memorable people I met in my time at Boringbar.

He was studying to become a Naturopath, and I don't know if she was planning on anything but breathing in the present moment, but all in all, here were two love children from the 60's who had somehow managed to reincarnate in the present day.

Jah and Xochitl (Pronounced Sotchel) were a delight. He was the long haired be-speckled thinker, she the soft warm woman-soul that any man would instantly adore if he had any sense of value for what a female should be.

Dark eyed and wistful, deeply immersed in her thoughts. The name Xochitl (flower) is derived from the Aztec Goddess Xochiquetzal and represents the fifteenth day. (the "Ides" in Roman Times) The South Americans belied:

Xochitl is a day for creating beauty and truth. She especially speaks to the heart who knows it will one day cease to beat. Xochitl reminds us that life, like the flower, is beautiful but quickly fades. It is a good day for reflection, companionship and poignancy; it is a bad day for repressing deep-seated wishes, desires and passions.

Well, perhaps I had a deep-seated desire there for a bit, but when you see such a love between two people it tends to evaporate thoughts of your own. These two were simply a delight to have around, and it wasn't that they did anything, they just carried that "something" that made everything OK.

Jah is one of the sacred names of God, and who is to say that God did not live there? Certainly, their space radiated a calm and a peace that was an oasis for the brief few months they were about. It also gave dear Doogle a message, because he liked to "accidentally" stroll down to the waterfall when they were swimming. Needless to say, Xotchitl was extraordinarily beautiful and they both swam naked.

Well, they also had a red kelpie dog with them. One day, when Doogle's little rat dogs came down to the waterfall, these incredibly stupid little creatures decided they would take on this Kelpie. At odds of three to one, they must have thought they had a chance. Well, they didn't. Have you ever seen a full blood Kelpie at work? They are a working dog trained to round up little pests like that. Without a moment's thought, the Kelpie snapped up on of Doogle's dogs and was about to rip it to pieces when Jah managed to call him back.

The look of horror on poor Doogle's face as he came down, seeing his beloved dog about to become supper for the Kelpie! Well it was enough to stop him ever going near them again.

They were vegetarian, peace loving, thoughtful and the absolute epitome of what the 1960's were supposed to be about. But like the Sixties themselves, they didn't survive as a couple. I asked Jah about it years after, and it seemed that there was a growing apart on one hand, but he had also had a dream, of change. He saw that the right one for him was about to turn up. He ended it, with a degree of recrimination on both sides. But the woman he saw in his dreams DID actually arrive.

He is now happily married and a father to a really beautiful Soul.

But Xochitl? She seemed to go somewhere not so good after this. Some spark vanished from her eyes and I can't explain this, but it hurt me. I think it may have had something to do with recognising a spark vanishing from my own heart. We all floated in our own directions after that, the time we shared moved on, and by us, like a river separating before flowing to the sea. We like to think that the rivers join, but as Soul it often goes the other way. We distil. We gather experience, and from this form as rain to fall down. But at each stage of the journey we must distil again to discover purpose. Therefore, discovering purpose means we must evaporate our past.

It tweaked me a little. My own dreams of domestic bliss were in ruins, and I guess I had really wanted to see someone else live out the dream. But Jah taught me the simplest little message. It is about what is truly and genuinely right for YOU in this moment. If it is truly right for YOU it is right for ALL.

Following your bliss can sometimes mean ending it.

INSERT: As the most remarkable chance would have it, not long after the writing of this book I was catching a plane out of Sydney and, of all people, Xotchitl walked by. I called out to her, and we chatted for a bit. She was going back to the country of her namesake, Mexico. We passed thoughts to each other, like ships flashing signals at sea, for but a few minutes. Then our mutual connecting flights took us once more in separate directions. But you know what, that special softness was back in her eyes.

It all worked out for the best.

SURVEYING

That is the exploration that awaits you! Not mapping stars and
studying nebula, but charting the unknown possibilities of existence.

Leonard Nimoy

T his may seem like the oddest little thing to drop into the middle of a book, but it occurs to me, purely on impulse, that there is a person that most of the world never thinks about. Think about it, what profession has shaped Western Civilization more than any other?

Our entire civilization is based on BOUNDARIES. Countries are defined by them, properties are sold according to them. Inheritance occurs directly because defined boundaries have been set. My entire problem with the Powell's has been wrapped around their lack of boundaries, their inability to grasp that they did NOT own the road that ran through their property.

The person who SETS and DEFINES the boundaries in our civilization is called a SURVEYOR. In Latin he was called a MENSOR (or Agrimensor). It means, in effect, the "One who Measures". The Survey places marks on the ground, pegs that are situated through accurate measurement of terrain. Not many understand this, but these pegs become their OWN legal reality, and these are what determine the boundaries of property. Such a thing was central to all Roman Law and all inheritance. The Surveyor defined the path of the roads, the placement of the walls to defend cities, and as much as the law of the day, the SURVEY gave order to Roman Society. It is the same today.

Surveying an area defines it. The lines on the map which appears on your title deeds were all surveyed by people who were physically on the ground, slogging through hard bush and making incredibly meticulous calculations as they went. In Australia this work meant surviving in the bush in cold winters, ridiculously hot summers, and coping with intense isolation from society. Surveyors are very tough people.

Today, the Surveyor remains just about the only professional who still does it hard. To measure the land, he/she must slog away in the rain and heat. They march through the bush, fighting through the undergrowth in the same way as their kindred spirits did hundreds and thousands of years ago. The really remarkable thing? Even with the best of modern technology and the best of instruments, rarely are the old survey marks out by more than a few inches.

Can you imagine any other profession so consistently accurate? I can't. In 1938, when Mussolini wanted to make more land fertile, an Italian Surveyor translated ancient Etruscan Maps. Based on these it was determined where the old sink holes for the draining of swamps once were. The Surveyor went to the place indicated on the ancient maps and can you believe it? He found the sink holes within 24 inches of where they were recorded some 3000 years ago.

My surveyor was Peter Hurcombe, and though I had absolutely no money for his bill, he laughed, did the work, and said "Pay me when you can". It took 18 months. Then, I needed his help again, and he was there, doing the work, saying "Pay me when you can." That took another 18 months.

Without his assistance on these occasions I would not have been able to define the boundaries that were very important in dealing with the Fowls and getting the subdivision organised. So this is a brief thank you to all those people like Peter, who just help out because it is needed. They are rare in this world, and sadly, getting rarer.

The Fowls had no sense of boundaries. (other than the fact that their "boundary" was based on the fact they had lived there longer than myself) The Surveyor helped to correct that notion, and prove to them that their sheds were on roads, that their roads crossed over onto MY place on occasions, and that many of their beliefs about who owned what were essentially wrong. Did it make a difference to the Fowls? Of course not. But it helped me!

PISS

"He who joyfully marches in rank and file has already earned my contempt. He has been given a large brain by mistake, since for him the spinal cord would suffice."

Einstein

Was it the apex, or the nadir? The High Road, or the Low Road? As a sort of ultimate finale to the experience of Bling Bling and the entire café set it espoused, I met my old mate, Steve Rose, outside Rash one bright sunny day.

I came across Steve in town purely by chance. I didn't even realise he was still here. He usually left after one of his many arguments against whoever he was arguing with at the time, and as he had recently had one, I had presumed he had packed up and left for Melbourne yet again. Steve is an incredible artist, yet also quite mad. I am not to know at the time we chat on the Main Street but he is destined to be murdered in 2 years time.

Steve was, without too fine a point being made of it, dirty. Wherever he moves it instantly turns into a pile of crap. Considering this, it was just extraordinary to me that he moved in with the most meticulous and fussy-about-personal-hygiene creatures I knew, the Artist. (The ex-husband of the former lover who had kicked in the door when he found out who she was sleeping with) We had patched up our differences by now, and shortly before my chance meeting in town he had been bemoaning his conundrum regarding our mutual friend Steve.

"Well, you knew he was a pig when you let him move in." I said quite simply. We both knew and accepted Steve for what he was, but you just do not bring him in to live with you.

"I know" my friend answered. "That's why I put him in the room above the fire stairs, away from the house. But he keeps coming into the flat, and whenever he leaves there is just shit everywhere."

"Then keep him out. Put in a burner into the loft room for him, so he can make coffee!"

"Then he will end up burning the whole place down. Some loose piece of paper will fall on the flame he forgot to turn off, and the whole place will come down and I will lose all my art, and my father will be pissed." And so it went. My repaired friendship with he-who-shall-remain-nameless was a good thing. He was a truly extraordinary artist, with a calibre and execution far above the petty and obnoxious avant guard nonsense that passes for art now-a-days.

However, my friend has a very significant concern. His father happened to be extremely rich, which was a rather curious curse in a sense, because it stole something essential from him. Now the Artist had no compulsion to succeed beyond the fear of dying unrecognised.

No matter what he did, no matter where he went, he would one day be rich. But would he ever be recognized? Being the son of a wealthy man can be one of the oddest sufferings to befall a sincere soul, but of course in the meantime it provided many home comforts, including a flat to be comfortable in.

But what to do with Steve? We both loved him as a brother, but he was so full of venom and spite and hatred of the world that in his cloud of anger he insisted on destroying all relationships and all kindness that were offered to him. I suppose in his mind it was all a test of people's sincerity, but to give a small example, he visited once and left a pair of sunglasses behind. I called him, and said I would post them down, which caused him HUGE anger. "I visited you, you bastard. Why post them? Am I not good enough to visit?"

I should have just kept the sun glasses. However, the storm eventually blew over the teacup, and peace was restored in a few months. My dear friend the Artist, whilst agonizing over Steve and what to do with him, realized as we spoke that he would just have to boot him out, and suffer the outrageous accusations of betrayal and cowardice that he knew would be forthcoming.

Needless to say, we were both fully agreed on Steve's remarkable talent as an artist. This was just the start of Steve Rose. Here was a man who could tap dance AND play the bagpipes at the same time. He was one of the most talented blues harp players I had ever met, but he refused to play one ever again after the record he cut did not make gold. It should have, and would have, if Steve had any notion of how to market himself. And he had to do it himself, because he abused the people interested in marketing him. He just did not seem to want to have anything to do with this world. But at the very least you might have thought he could have learned the skills of how to freeload properly without being kicked out all the time.

However, at this point I had just met him in town. He was sitting at Cafe' Rash and I went up to ask him about the extraordinary report about him, that I had heard the other day. Steve had apparently accomplished the impossible, which was to get himself escorted out of town by the local constabulary. (The Bling Bling piggies rarely leave the station, unless it is to walk outside with a breathalyser to pick up a few fines from passing motorists)

"Sure" he said nonchalantly. "Those pigs are fuckwits, just because I choose to express myself in ways they don't understand, they piss on me, and cart me out of town."

"It was a shop keeper that complained, wasn't it?" I baited, wanting the juice of the full story. "It was something to do with you flashing a brown eye to the female customers, saying to them that if they wanted to buy shit, buy this?"

"Yeah, well, I was very fucking high." Steve laughs at his own antics. "Those stupid bitches piss me off, coming down to look good and not giving a fuck about anything but themselves. Stupid fucked-up prick teasers who flash their tits, but never the nipples, living in a dream of getting some rich bastard to pay for the new Roller while they are fucking his chauffeur." Invectives like this are a wonderful thing, when you are not the target.

However, I had already seen the photo. Steve was demonstrating his rather striking physical anatomy with only the briefest of hot pink leather G-strings to cover the body. This if you don't count the genuine Indian head dress, replete with eagle feathers, trailing down his back. So I ask, "And the outfit? Where did you get the full Indian head-dress? And where on EARTH did you find a hot pink leather G-string?"

"I've had that head dress for years. It needed airing. I stole the G-string from the Wicked shop the day before. Felt good wearing it." That was that, and after a little more drawing down of the curses of both heaven and hell on the bitch's who put the coppers onto him, we settled we got into the real business of the day, which was about doing exactly nothing.

I sat opposite him on the sidewalk tables outside of Rash, and offered to buy him a Latte'. "Sure" he said, then asked "What have you been up to?" Well, clearly it was not much compared to Steve. We had small chat about this and that. And soon enough, as is the way in Bling Bling, a couple of people who he knew rocked up, said hello and chatted. Then someone I knew came along, said their piece, and left. We drank another coffee and the sun continued to shine. I had noted that the whole time he had also been swigging on a curious bottle.

"What are you drinking there?" I asked.

"Some odd sort of Moo Tea. I have been trying to figure out just what it was. Here, have a taste and tell me what you reckon." I brought the bottle to my lips, and sampled the wares. The flavour was genuinely different. I can't quite put my finger on it, but it has a dull, vaguely herbal sensation to it. Very yang, soft, flat tone to the aroma. Mildly salty. Obviously home made, but possibly quite sellable in the open market.

The sun is shining, old friends are chatting, and before us is a puzzle. Some unique, interesting beverage that has a jig saw of aromas equal to the finest of wines has completely enraptured our attention. It has separated us from the trials of the world, and the difficulties of our lives.

We could not quite figure out what it was, or even if we really liked it, but soon the liquid conundrum was to be solved. A fellow Steve had chatted to earlier then came up, looked at the bottle he had left behind shortly before I had arrived, and said "Hey… You haven't been drinking **that** have you?"

Steve looks at me, I look at him, we both look at the fellow knowing something is up, and Steve asks, "What's in that tea you are drinking, we can't figure it out." The fellow shakes his head, laughs, and says, "Ah, I am doing Urine Therapy at the moment!" and walks away, shaking with serious glee.

People talk about taking the piss out of someone, well I just had put it INTO to me. I just kissed Piss! We had just discussed PISS as if it were fine fucking wine. But what can you do? The milk was spilt, the piss was drunk. Holy Fuck, I said to myself. Then something dawned on me. Internally I moved away from revulsion, and into a pure, child-like fascination. As I sat there, I started to think "How very Bling Bling" Some part of me deep inside recognized that I had reached a type of reverse Zenith, a place for which there was no going beyond or below. So high you can't get over it, so wide you can't get round it, so low you can't go under it. So did it rock my Soul? THAT's what the song was about! It was not a nadir, but something else. This was a place beyond which no one can go. This was no low point. It was an achievement!

I had reached an ultimate of some sort, something that precious few others would ever attain. Drinking someone else's piss at a very expensive Café in downtown Bling Bling is not exactly a common place event, is it? Even then I knew it would end up in a book some day.

And that is exactly when it just popped into my head. Something stirred in me to ask a question I had always wondered about, but had never before directly asked of Steve. "Steve, why do you hate authority and society?"

The reply shocked me with its vehemence and anger. Steve's whole body convulsed with tension, and the muscles on his neck pulsed with fierce hatred.

"Fuckin' authority! Fuck you! I had to sit there while that pissed fuck-head pig would beat the shit out me. Call it a fucking father, he was a fucking dog.

Beating the shit out of a helpless eight year old kid for no reason other than he just fucking loved it. He felt powerful, it turned him on to shit on me and I hate the prick. I spit on his grave, and if he ever reincarnates out of hell, I will spit on his face, kick him in the balls and cut off his dick so he never does it to another living creature.

"SO I run away. I run to Melbourne, and find an aunt. I tell her what happened, but she doesn't fucking believe me, and calls in the social workers, who fucking take me BACK to the miserable turd, who half kills me.

"Society never fucking well helped me. I was shat on, spat on, ground into the crap every day, and no one did nothing. Police did nothing. I tell them what happened, they fucking laugh and say I need to grow up. And then when I stole to eat, I get stuffed into a prison cell with disgusting foul-breathed pissheads and rapers. Magistrates just packed me off to boys homes, where the authority there fucked me up the arse. Fuck them all, those miserable scum who think themselves so fucking important. They are not even fucking human."

Then: Silence. A beautiful, anguished silence caught that unleashed demon in a gentle understanding. Have you heard of Green Tara? This Heart of Compassion? I felt it awaken in myself; it seemed to flow in from somewhere I will never comprehend. But it flowed strongly, and it freed me from myself.

That was when it occurred to me, some deep oracular pronouncement just came up from inside. I just knew that if Steve survived the next 2 years, he would get over this incredible hatred that was destroying his life, and be discovered as a truly great artist. I saw it clearly, and what is more, I told him as best I could. "Just survive the next 2 years, Steve. Everything will turn around, just survive."

I never saw him again. 2 years, almost to the day, almost to that very day, he was found dead. His life was extinguished by the man people had thought to be his close friend. As it turns out, Steve was actually his murderers' paid carer. That was when we realised the fellow was mentally unstable, with a history of violence. Steve was the only person in the world who had ever cared for the him. He was his murderers' only family, his only friend.

Now Steve is gone, killed by the one he was paid to look after. No reason was given by this man for WHY he ended Steve's life, other than the most absurd rational you could imagine. Apparently Steve didn't want the fellow smoking in the car as they drove. He pulled over to let the guy have a cigarette, and that is when the madman did him in. Steve was found by the roadside strangled to death. Dead because he didn't like cigarette smoke.

No attempt was made to remove the body. The fellow just killed him, and left Steve where he fell. He destroyed the life that had been Mr Steve Rose, artist extraordinaire, and then just hopped back into the car, and drove himself to Melbourne as if nothing had happened.

I weep not for Steve, but for what he was not allowed to become. I weep for the painting that will never be painted, and the incredible art that will never be discovered. A life cut short is one thing, but a talent with such genius extinguished for no reason is a desperate loss. We are all in the same boat, to some degree or another. We are all trying to survive until that doorway opens, until that Mudra (opening force) awakens to set us free.

I come back to the present: Outside where I live right now the night is falling. It is Saturday evening and I still sit here writing this DAMN book. Then it strikes: Softly it wells up. The bitterness of the last decade is swelling in my heart, and I weep for Steve, and for myself. Tears just fall, years are worn away even as they come into sharp focus. Steve suffered the ancient curse of the Muse: So much talent, yet so little joy from it.

Then it another awareness opens: A part of Steve Rose was happy to die. I seemed to fly back to that time and place, and I see it! He let it happen. Why? Because he was so desperately tired of fighting against the current. Just like Van Gogh killed himself, he gave no resistance, no argument. He just accepted the inevitable.

Just as how, in a thousand ways, our choices are killing ourselves; piece by jig-saw piece. Just as surely as a rock falls after flying high in the sky, the mood that takes you up brings you down.

The rain still falls outside. I have already taken my young son to the X-Ray people and sure enough, the clavicle is broken. The doctors have strapped it up a little better, but for the nonce there is little to do but wait until life mends the break. He is set up in front of the TV with his X-Box and his remote control. He will survive it. The knocks and scrapes of life are normal, and it could so easily have been worse.

The two young fellows I mentioned at the opening of the book? They came today to see about moving into the spare rooms, and maybe it will be good for Ben to have them around. He needs an older brother, especially while his actual older brother is busy propping up a bar up in North Queensland, either serving someone from behind it, or being served in front of one.

However, you hope for the best. You hope and trust that each Soul will not become another lost opportunity in life, another wasted existence. You know that the statistics prove you wrong, but when it comes to family, you hope anyway. Even so, no matter where we are right now, for all of us there is a simple question: Where does life go from here?

Who can say? In the meantime, we have our memories and our experiences. Some memories we will take to our graves. There was I, drinking someone else's Piss in the Main Street of the backpackers paradise of Bling Bling.

It was all a strange, yet ultimate proof, that I had arrived.

But where?

PART TWO

"And there stalks Discord, delighted with her torn mantle." **Virgil**

Doogle Fowl and the Three Ugly Sisters had no Cinderella in the back room, and there was no Prince on their doorstep with a glass slipper. They were utterly bereft of any such redeeming features, and what is more, they all knew it. As a result, the Fowls would always carefully put on their second face before being seen in public. Why did they go out into the public eye? I was not sure, but probably to gather information so they could back stab everyone in private. They knew their lives served no great purpose.

That is part of what puzzled me. They knew what they were doing was horse shit, but they did it anyway. I had no specific issue with them, and had caused them no harm, but because I entered their world I was therefore a target.

All I had ever requested from them was that the problem with the sheds over the Crown Road be sorted out, for access reasons. That was IT. Yet from that request years and years of angst ensued. The mind numbing stupidity of it all still grates me when I go back there, and the ONLY word that explains it is dysfunction, and the subsequent rules we have already discussed.

However, the remnants of their argument are still very much here with me. I have to carry the costs, and they are significant. Tragedy is incremental. It creeps up on us a piece at a time. Steve Rose was a tragedy, a loss, a piece missing from my life. If we hold to the view that Soul simply comes for experience, and is gone, it lessens the pain. But it does not lessen the tragedy.

At 17, when selling encyclopaedia door to door, I was taught a powerful technique. It is called "reduce to the ridiculous". By making the repayments on a set of books seem insignificant compared to the value you get from them, it encourages people to buy. Well, all our concerns and problems can be treated this way as well. We can take any trouble that besets us, and compare it to another worse off, and our difficulty becomes smaller, more manageable.

Now, I look at the situation, and the potential loss of properties I had fought so hard for, then I go inside with a sort of "shrug power" that makes me feel invulnerable. Part of me says "What of it?" You play the game as best you can, and if you lose, what of it? The other part is screaming in pain for the cost and the waste and the suffering it has caused. But really, what of that as well?

I have this thought in mind: Everything is a set up, and the only question is whether it is divine or devilish.

The script is often written well before we arrive on the scene, yet we can still IMPROVISE! More to the truth the WAY we improvise determines the applause we receive. Life is meant to be improvisation, this is the reality of our so-called free will. I wonder some days about the variations to the script that I might have employed, and there are so many possibilities I missed. One thing is certain, I am not hearing any applause from my Boringbar performance.

One option was that I could have offered to pay for the road deviation up front, and not expected anything from the Fowls. Perhaps this would have avoided a whole lot of bloodshed, but it was the PRINCIPLE that drove my actions at the time. My view was that it was wrong, in principle, that anyone but the Fowl's pay for the problems they themselves had created. How expensive are these damn principles!

Another option was to be vicious and bloodthirsty and drive the matter to the courts regardless of the fact that the mother was ill. No Fowl appreciates the fact that I put things off as I did, and it gained me no help at all when it came down to it. That really is a preferred option in our modern world. However, my foolish principles said otherwise.

Finally I have arrived at the realization that ALL our principles are simply a standard we hold up, a flag we wave that marks a position. We fight for the flag, but the flag of itself will not win the war. Worse than this, I was waving a flag from an unknown country called mutual respect and kindness. That was a place not recognised by the Fowls.

Perhaps waving high ideals works in university lectures, but the fact remains there were no "Boringbar" stars and stripes on my personal standard, therefore all I was doing was to advertise my strangeness to the locals. And here is the simplicity of it: Strangers coming in waving THEIR flags on YOUR turf clearly can only be seen as a sign of war.

This is how things go in all of human endeavour. The only difference between Boringbar and everywhere else was that I had neighbours who loved WAR. They grew up at war with each other, and their neighbours, and they understood the principle of attrition. Suffer the bastards to death, and you win.

The Fowls knew that wars are won by survivors. People who allow life to take its toll (literally) on the roadway, and continue to carry the weight are the ones who win out in the end. Like some personal Battle of the Somme, Fowls would send in money, like soldiers, and watch it get mown down in costs.

The weird thing is that the Fowls were fighting for THEIR principles as well. And here is the long and short of it: It really does not matter if the principles are right or wrong, or even if they make sense. Principles are like flags, they are a summation of what we BELIEVE in. They are your faith in an unknown, invisible God and have little, if anything, to do with any reality apart from your own.

Terrorists and car bombers, they believe causing the death and destruction of the infidel will lead them to an eternal heaven. Forget your 20 or more virgins in the hereafter, just causing enough trouble right now brings a Fowl to orgasm.

But while I think of it: *Car Bombers for Allah*, a good name for a band.

In the process of the Boringbar War I discovered some dreadful truths. One of them will shock you if you are a male, and make you laugh if you are a female. We think the male is the aggressor, the warmonger, the destroyer of the worlds, but the truth is that the Goddess Kali is the one to blame.

The feminine nature is the one that creates and sustains. and yet when her cat claws come out, she is also the one who destroys.

I write these next words with a sense of caution, because I know how some will take deep offence. Perhaps I can mollify the story in advance by clarifying that I speak of the feminine NATURE as the ruthless one. The nurturer and protector that will kill to save her children.

You may speak of Genghis Khan, and how he killed not just his enemies, but the relatives of his enemies in case one of them took offence and sought revenge. It IS true! Men can certainly be ruthless and women can be caring, but it is the FEMININE in man that causes him to kill the relatives and children of his competitor.

The female part of him sees what will arise in the coming years if his enemy is allowed to survive, and perhaps prosper enough to challenge him again. The male part enjoys the war, welcomes the challenge, the feminine aspect protects the kingdom. Like a mother guarding her future children, the feminine aspect in man drives his ruthless and vindictive nature.

And conversely, it is the male aspect in woman that allows her to rise above the hurts. To go beyond the slurs and indignation she suffers, it is the male aspect within that says "I will grow past this. I am bigger than this."

It is the Yin Yang, the balance that we seek. But in the meantime, let's take a walk on the Yin side.

Women can be Vicious

Veni, Vidi, Vici - I came, I saw, I conquered.
Said Julius Caesar.

Women took the lesson on board and it became:
Veni Vidi Duci - I came, I saw, I calculated

When the Prophet of Profit became the egalitarian milestone for the capitalist:
Veni, Vidi, Visa - I Came, I Saw, I Shopped

And now the Men say:
Veni, Vidi, Volo in domum redire - I came, I saw, I want to go home

Vicious, Viscous, Visceral: The feminine within is a tiger who prowls the corridors of the home it will protect.

The male tends to start it, or at least he believes this. I have never seen a man be able to go more than one step with a woman who has already decided against him, though. Man sees a beauty he desires, and he seeks to conquer it.

He does not ask if the beauty wants to be conquered or otherwise, the truth is that here and now is where the game begins. Courtship is really a war between external desire and internal issues of unworthiness. But should we survive this, and find some sort of mutual attraction with another, the real argument begins.

The battle of relationship is ever the same, one of mostly taking and occasionally giving. We start with the sweet love-light in the eyes, but as that burns low, the embers of anger and unfulfilled wishes starts to etch into the Soul. This is where all our faults are contrasted in black, which leave very few white patches left at the end of a decade.

Marriage often boils down to a simple thing: One tends to give while the other is happy to take, and it is usually due to this imbalance that creates divorce. Defy the giving nature at your peril, because it will turn, and bite.

Let us stray to a brief and fragile inspection of the feminine force. It augers well for us to be familiar with the pattern of behaviour behind the female instinct, because then we can learn to hear the rattling of the snakes tail, that warning that rises up when we cross that invisible line.

First, a woman will start with a glow of expectation. She longs to unite, to be a partner, to be the helper. But time wears her expectations down like sand paper on ice and her ideal male becomes a hodgepodge of wearied, wasted wandering. He gets as tired of her as she of him, and finally his furtive looks at younger women cement the death of the ideal.

Marriage, once held to be sacred and holy, becomes a testament pit for anger and resentment. Marriage and romance are the colour of relationships, but Divorce is the truth. Divorce is the dangerous creature that arises from the ashes of despair, and it is a dragon, not a phoenix.

Not all is as cut and dried. Women burn slowly over a longer period and bide their time, waiting like the cobra for the moment to strike. If you do not see the flattened hood, if you do not hear the rattlers rattle, more fool you. The nature of most women who have decided on divorce is that they will organize things to get out of the relationship in the best way possible. The cat chooses its exit, hunts it prey, while men are like dogs. They just bolt outside because there is someone to play with.

My story was simple, or so it seemed: I met a woman, I wanted to marry her. We do, we have a child, it should and could end happily ever after. It does not. Done. End of story.

Fact One: The connection was never really there from her side. I offered it, looked for a a deeper state where the energy could rest between us, but you know something, after years of beating myself up over the loss of this "thing" I called a marriage I finally came to understand that it was all one way.

I was giving the love, she was taking it, and pretending to hand it back.

Oh I DO sound self-righteous I know. I am aware of the prejudice that mutters in your heart about the sanctity and essentially purity of woman, and the evil slothful desires of man. But read on dear reader. Read on to the sunset of this story, and the array of light displayed therein will show you a different understanding of the world as I know it.

For myself, and I slip between tenses I know, forgive me when I escape the present and talk of the past, but I am just knocking this out as a stream of consciousness: so please allow me some slippage here.

For myself I was puzzled. She always seemed so caring, yet I kept feeling this emptiness. She seemed so close, yet always so distant. She seemed to be so careless, yet so worried. She was happy when she was painting, but she began to find every excuse not to paint. Now I know she had decided within the first year of our marriage that she wanted out, and I can see how it was all doomed to fail, how it was not to be. But at the time I was simply confused.

The truth is simple. The woman was just looking to find an excuse to end it. In fact, call me blind Freddy. I should have twigged when she suggested I get another girlfriend because she was too tired for sex. However, the suggestion had the reverse effect! How could I stray from a woman who was so considerate? How could I look at another when this one was so kind? Yet she wasn't interested in sex, either. As the Dutch girl was to say many years later: What to do?

It was years, many years later, before I discovered she already had HER boyfriend on the side. That was why she was too tired, she had already had her workout. (or work 'in' as the case may be in such things) That was why she was being so generous and kind when suggesting I find someone to console my passions with. All the time when she was saying "Why not find someone else?" she was meaning "Fuck off, I want to play with something more interesting."

I had been a puritan sort of Soul, starving myself in a variety of ways, but not all through choice. For many years I was not capable of eating normal foods, and for two years I ate almost nothing. In truth, doctors had said I should have been dead. I had picked up a dreadful virus when I was seventeen, what they called the "Hong Kong Flu" and to clarify what that meant, it was an early form of the SARS virus.

I had gone from a 19 year old with a strapping 44 inch chest and 22" thighs, a solid little 12 stone of muscle, down to 7 ¼ stone of skin and bone by the time I turned 23. I was wearing girls 24" jeans. Simple fact was, I could not eat. More correctly, I could eat but if I did the food turned to acid and I invariably ended up vomiting this pure fire that burnt my throat. It was 2 years before a Naturopath would give me a diet that I could work with. Simple and effective: It was fresh watermelon every day, just watermelon, and it worked. Obviously I survived to write this tale.

You know how you forget things that are disagreeable? Well, the memory of this was triggered off just the other month when I gave a suit I had worn during that period to my 14 year old (whom most would consider skinny) and I thought it would be a bag on him. Well, it fitted him perfectly. I was wearing that suit when I was 25, when my health had picked UP. It was a bit of a shock, because quite honestly when I looked in the mirror back then I did not see a skinny little boy. I saw a deep thinking spiritual warrior who was going to take on the world. Mirrors would lie, so it seems.

Now here is the reason for the diversion. The basic problem with the Fowls, the Ex Wife, and even myself is always this very thing. We look in the mirror and see something that no one else sees. We see what we imagine, not what is.

Oh what gift the givee give us, to see ourselves as others see us.

Back then, I was starved and emaciated yet oddly emancipated. In my marriage I was starved and emaciated, but emancipated? My then wife was purposefully starving me, giving warm hugs, then pulling back the hips as if to say "No no no , not there!" It wore me down, and one day when I was out doing the odd jobs I did to try and bring home the cash for food and living expenses I saw a Playboy Magazine sitting on a shelf. It was opened at the most extraordinary pair of boobs I had ever seen.

How can anyone express this? It was like drinking fine wine after sitting in a desert for three years without so much as a drop of water. There was a deep ringing inside, a connection of sorts, and I had to have this image. Now, for most men it was a nothing to buy a Playboy or Penthouse, but I was the shy, faithful type who saw such a move as a betrayal. But I could not help myself.

My eyes just soaked up these perfect breasts, wondering what they were like in real life. How would they feel, how was this woman, really? Passions became questions, and my starvation had taken over the rational mind. What is more, anyone with half a brain would have just looked, enjoyed and tossed the mag. But I couldn't. Weird I know, but I took it home, and put my new paper lover in the office.

Now the wife obviously saw the magazine when cleaning up one day, but she said nothing. However, the next weekend she brings home a Penthouse she picked up at the local fair, a magazine that is far more lewd than Playboy. The next weekend, another one, and then another one. Every weekend for many weeks she would bring home another set of beautiful naked women for my eyes to enjoy, as she said. I could not understand her odd kindness, but she had already made it clear that she wanted no more sex, at least for the time being.

Now I understand the message stick. In her language finding the Playboy was me saying to her "You are not good enough" so she gets more mags to say "Hey, you want physical perfection! Here, enjoy!"

However the REAL message was one she would never deliver openly. Fact is, she was looking for a good excuse to get me out the door. I had given her the chink in the armour she needed, and there was no stopping her now. What she was REALLY saying is "I am tired of this marriage. I was tired of it within the first year. Now you are providing me with the perfect excuse to get out."

What is more, she knew something would have to crack. Starve a man, and sooner or later the world explodes. It was just a matter of time before she could find a weak point. All I really wanted was the weak point in her love pot but she wanted the fight, I guess, not the love. One might say, I was left Agape' !!

What women understand about men is quite simple: Men are fools. Like a hunting cat, women prowl a man's stuttering actions and generally equate our mentality to that of a dog. When begging affection we are vulnerable, and if they can starve us, we simply beg some more.

So: All this is wrapped around the decision to buy Boringbar. She is saying "Whatever you want dear" while she is meaning "I hope you fall on your fucking face in that god forsaken wilderness of troglodytes". When it comes to solving problems, she offers no support, just a quiet hum to herself of "Good, he is busy with that crap so I am free to enjoy myself". But somehow I wore her down with my (doglike) devotion to duty.

Finally SHE is the one who cannot take it anymore, and so she walks out. I guess in retrospect the now obvious avoidance of any sort of confrontation was the warning, though I can honestly say I saw none of it. I was caught totally by surprise. Regardless, within days she was gone, vamoose, out the door.

So, we part our ways, and I try to make the best of what is left. And while I am struggling, building a house, trying to make something of the place, she is quietly saying to all the people she has made friends with at Boringbar, who ask about why she is on her own, NOTHING. She says nothing, and just looks away, and sighs.

If you want to control a situation, and paint a picture, the trick is to NOT say anything bad about the other, but to breath in deeply, look hurt, and say "I can't speak about it." Every single person she stayed with was of the opinion that she had to leave me because I was beating her up. When they are becoming totally convinced I am evil, they demand an answer from her, and she then says, as if they pried it out of her "Well, he was very dominating. I really can't say more.

Obviously, to the local minds, I was STILL threatening to beat her up! This somewhat affects your standing in a town fulls of gossips like Boringbar.

In what way you ask? In many ways, covert and overt. For one example: Even a simple repair to a motor car now takes 2 weeks, and in the end I find I am having to collect the car and do it myself.

A few well placed whispers and a tornado of consequence develops. To the experienced witch, EVERYONE is a fool, and that gullibility is all you need. A brush of paint here, a touch up there, and soon enough the picture before your eyes is clear as the mud she is slowly pasting over your good name. Not a word need be said, just a wounded look, given sincerely. This is enough to tip the scales of favour away from the object of your derision.

This is the secret to TRUE witchcraft. You never say a thing against anyone. This makes people curious. Then you draw the curious person out with a look of hurt, a sense of pain, and they reach out thinking they will help the suffering bird with the broken wing in front of them. Right at that moment of their most heartfelt kindness you apply a particular, carefully crafted dab of paint.

Their heart is open, and the smallest smudge of colour goes right to the core. You just need a nick of red over their eyeball, and everything about that subject you hint at will look red. What is more, BECAUSE you only see the red, every action that person takes is in the red spectrum. What is even more insidious is the fact that every other colour of their nature will appear BLACK or GREY. That is the nature of filters; that is how they work. The real witch learns to colour the filter and not the person. They know that the WAY someone sees is far more powerful than WHAT they see.

And WHY? Why would someone do this? Well, it is the same reason that motivated the Fowls, the simple vexatious sin we call pride. My EX found her PRIDE lessened, and yet this begs another question we need to ask. Perhaps she believed I was somehow better than her, perhaps all her quiet passive manipulation was not working on me the way she hoped. Perhaps she secretly wanted me to kill myself like her former husband did, the former husband whose name she still bore as her surname. I don't know WHY. Nor do I NEED to know, because I have left it behind.

My question is this: Why did I battle on trying to make it work for so long?

Finally as I write this, the answer comes through. This was MY pride at work. I could not accept that I had been so wrong. I wanted to MAKE this mismatched marriage work. I believed I could do it, and I wanted to prove it.

But this gets dull and boring, just like the town I was battling with as I tried to get a simple subdivision done and out of the way. So why do people cause problems and create obstacles? My good friend Paul Smart said it very well in a court case where he was acting for me against Doogle, "Your honour, this matter makes little sense, so I suggest that the reason for all these proceedings are very old fashioned ones. Things like Jealousy, Pride, Anger. Those old fashioned, yet perfectly workable, irrational reasons."

People accuse Paul Smart of being arrogant. He isn't. His real problem is that he sees the lowest common denominator without varnish, and he sees that it is in everybody. He seems the lowest in himself, the client, and the judge, and he accepts that we are all human, all too human.

Yet by ACCEPTING this, he loses his second and third face, and what happens is the different aspects of the man become one, and now it is ONE against the crowd. He becomes powerful in the way we are MEANT to be. Only powerless people call him arrogant, I simply call him a friend.

Why? Because he helped me.

And he slashed poor Doogle to pieces in the courtroom.

LAW: It is no real mystery. It is an instrument designed to pay Lawyers. My first introduction to the reality of the law was when a fellow who had rear-ended my motor bike, and dragged my unconscious body across the road until a passing nurse stopped him. He then took his alcohol soaked breath back to his car and disappeared. I tracked him down and brought him to court. I said to the judge in the middle of the legal waffle, "Your Honour, all I am looking for is some common sense!" The judge simply replied "If common sense were the issue, no one would ever be here!"

I hate to admit it, bet he had a point.

COURTS and LAW

Iniquissimam pacem justissimo bello antefero.

I prefer the most unfair peace to the most righteous war.

Cicero

C OURT Rooms and assorted legal paraphernalia appear to prove that Justice is a fallacy. Many see the Justice System is an auction where more cash = a better result. But not always.

I have learned an awful lot about Court Rooms in the last few years. Doogle made sure of that. He started with harassment, cutting power cords, stealing tools, and breaking windows and when that did not work he went to backstabbing and character assassination. However, no one really took Doogle seriously because he was well known as the local village nutter.

Things proceeded on in their negative pattern for a number of years, as I have already mentioned earlier on in this dialogue, and finally the line of demarcation was crossed. In order to get the Boringbar subdivision sorted, I had to take the Fowls to court. I had access issues, and you need to have clear access before you are able to sell a property or complete a subdivision. It was a matter for the Supreme Court and thus it was also a matter of years before any headway could be made. Something called "Due Process".

But when it comes to the day in court, it can be brutally swift. The matter was closed in a single day with the only decision a judge could possibly make, to remove the offending sheds. It was a court case that was to cost the Fowls $100,000 for those DAMN sheds that no one wanted. Yet shortly before the court case a very fascinating creature turned up, one from my past and from the time immediately after the divorce when I had ended up in a room in a house in the little town of Uki.

This creature was called Josiah, the Monk. He had arrived in town, bald head, robes with a follower in tow, and I considered him somewhat fascination. I invited him in for tea, and we got talking. He mentioned that he had a printer for sale. Coincidence! Just what I was looking for. I arranged to take a look at it, liked it, and gave him a substantial deposit. He said he would call in a week or two when he sorted out a few little problems with the machine.

Well he called, but it was to say that he had to leave the house for reasons he could not go into, but that he would look after the printer as soon as possible, if that were OK with me, He happened to mention that he had already spent the deposit, so he sincerely hoped it was OK with me to wait a little bit longer.

I said "Sure, call me when you have things sorted out." Well, all things being equal I would have normally have just kissed the money goodbye and if anything came back, all to the better. But then I saw a notice in the local shopping centre that my printer was up for sale.

I immediately went around to the house where Sharma had been living, and asked the woman who answered the door if my printer was there. She seemed quite affable, and said it was fine for me to hold it, because Josiah had vanished. And by the way, did I know where he was? I mentioned he had called, but that I did not have a return number.

I turned up the next day with a one armed man and a utility. Have you ever tried to move a heavy printer with a one armed man? Well, we got it down the steps and into the house at Uki. It was difficult, but it was done. That was when weird stuff began. That woman, who had always looked a little mad as far as I was concerned, began to call me every day, asking where Josiah was. I kept saying "I don't know!" Finally I started saying "I don't WANT to know woman. Stop calling." But it didn't stop her.

She started screaming down the phone, "The LORD can see what you are doing. The LORD wants Josiah. I need to talk to him, to bring him to the LORD, and together he will decide who is right and who is wrong!" I hung up the phone, and decided that this woman was stark raving mad, but that perhaps I needed to follow up Josiah and tell him.

A couple of weeks later, the newspapers are blazoned with the headlines "Woman Kills her baby. Other baby and child found sitting car, with dead baby in boot."

It turns out that a woman had tried to kill her own children by poisoning them, but only one had died. She put the dead one in the boot, and had driven around for a couple of weeks before a policeman noticed the smell. He asked the woman to open the boot, and found the dead child's remains, half decayed. Josiah called a week or so after that, and said he was happy I managed to get the printer out. He explained to me that he had to go into hiding because his then wife was mad, and wanted to kill him and the children so they could all go to heaven, and have the Lord tell them who was right and who was wrong. Yes. It was his child that was found dead in the boot.

Naturally, I was called up to the inquest, and I was shocked to find that the legal counsel seemed intent on proving the guilty party was Josiah. He said "I hardly imagine that a loving father would have allowed his own child to be killed by a madwoman, unless he had some part to play in the matter?"

Apparently the words Josiah had mentioned to me, and which I had passed onto the policeman who had prepared some of the matters for the coroner's court, had been taken somewhat out of context. He had said to me, "What difference will a kangaroo court make to a dead child?" The court officers had taken it to mean he either didn't care, or worse, was part of the planning of this "sacrifice".

Now Josiah had a bald head, tattoos all over his body, and he wore robes. That was enough to make him guilty, but when it was discovered that his grandfather was the head of the infamous Toe Cutters Gang, from the docks in Melbourne. Well that proved it.

Needless to say, the woman got put in a psychiatric home for a couple of years before being released. The children were not given to the father; they were given to the mothers' brother. And the other brother? The one just who happened to have a long history as a paedophile? Well, he lived just down the road. I guess that the kangaroo court made a lot of difference to the living children, if not the dead one.

But that was the first incarnation of Josiah. The ties that bind can be many and curious, and as it turns out, he in due course arrived on my doorstep at Boringbar and had his own significant input into the process of the war. In fact, he moved in and stayed on the property with his new wife and child.

I never did get that printer to work.

JOSIAH JOASH

There is no great genius without a mixture of madness.

Aristotle

This is not his real name, but as the bard wrote: What's in a name? Joisah Joash, or whatever his name might be in coming years, was surely the sanest madman I had ever met. He truly believed that at age seventeen he had been spoken to by God while working a backhoe for the local Melbourne Council. And who is to say this is incorrect?

It's the paradox of truth that only you can know your truth.

It worked. He went from being a street "sharpie" (razor blade gang member) to Man of God, reading the Bible, and studying to become a minister. He was destined to go far, because he had such zeal and commitment to his goal. The only thing was that his extreme laziness caused him to drop off things early. Like dropping out of becoming a minister before he gets his Bible College education finished.

He later explained "Who really cares? Not God, surely? Does God want a piece of paper flashed before him when you get to heaven, does the devil claim you because you don't have one? The God business is pretty simple. You just say you are a minister of the Baptist 923rd Congregation. Provide them with a forged certificate, and Bob's your uncle. There are so many Baptist churches and no one talks to each other. so If you look the part, say the right words, they give you the gig because they are desperately short of ministers"

Need drives reality. Necessity is the mother of invention. Josiah was the grandson of one of Australian's most notorious killers, one of the members of the infamous Toe Cutters Gang who terrorized the docks or Melbourne for many years. He just didn't have the same blinkers on as the rest of us.

He had a rough start, in a rough neighbourhood. When the Police called him from the roof because he was shooting some of the immigrant Italians families with a BB gun, he said "They are just Wogs. what's the problem?"

The good officers said "Yes, we know they are just Wogs, but you can't go around shooting them, ok?"

Josiah's way of expressing Gods love was largely (and preferably) found in blessing young nubiles with his (ahem) spiritual favours. Budding young sixteen year olds, (amen) and preferably a few of them at the same time, were his ideal of God on Earth. Eventually he got driven out of the Baptists, who started to ask too many questions.

So he shaved his head, and joined the Basilian Monks. According to Josiah the Basilians were the ones who looked after the Bible until Vatican Two. At this point the order refused to condone the perceived treachery of the Pope in altering the textual content of the Bible, and were thus relegated to the ecclesiastical backwaters of Tasmania.

Josiah the Monk

Who knows … It may even be true!

The truth is that Josiah would attract people like flies. He had tattoos from head to foot, or should I say face to foot, because right across his face he had tattooed a lightning bolt. He did it himself, free hand, in front of a mirror. In fact, he did them ALL himself, sitting up at night with tattoo gun and ink in hand, running random patterns all over his body.

It all started with him covering up the violent tatts from his mis-spent youth, inking over them night after night with curves and shapes. He was making his body more pleasing to God, in his words.

Then it, literally, took over. Every part of him (and I mean EVERY PART) was tattooed. Instead of asking girls up to see his etchings, he asked them in to see his tatts. What is more, they loved it.

More than this, women loved to be abused by him. He picked up a Japanese girl one night, took her home, and in the middle of the evening decided she was prudish and that God was telling him to piss on her. So he did! He got out of bed and pissed all over her.

She screamed and shouted, so he left the room and she ran to the shower. But the next morning, she is bowing before him, pulling down his pants to provide what he said was some of the best oral sex imaginable. She demonstrated incredible enthusiasm, praying, as it were, between breaths "You have shown me how to be humble, thank you Lord." Marvellous what sheer gall when allied to robes can get away with. Just ask the Catholics!

At one point Josiah hated names, considering them confining and artificial. So when people asked him his name, he said "I don't have one." This always caught people unaware, because EVERYONE has a name. "Well," people stammered "What will we call you?"

"Give me a name! Any name. I will be that for you but only because you need it." So Josiah became known for a time as, wait for it: NO NAME.

Seriously, that was his accepted name in town. I could go on, but you get the message. Josiah was a real life Diceman without the Dice. Who needed artificial encumbrances? He had God's Voice. What more did he want?

In fact, he used it to his advantage. When a really freaky guy was staying at the farm years ago, and he just wasn't leaving, I spoke to Josiah about it. "We will have to clear him out, he's just way to strange. But I don't want him coming back and causing trouble."

"Not a problem," said Josiah. 'His mind is weak from drugs. I will sort it out, and you will never see him again."

Josiah went up to him and said "I have to tell you, God is giving me a really strange message. I don't want to shock you, but he said you are too messy (He stayed in a caravan and made a complete mess out of it) and unfortunately he also says that because of this I have to kill you. I am genuinely sorry, but it's God asking me to do this. I hope you will understand." Now, Josiah was a big man. Broad shoulders, well over six foot, an ex-boxer, and he could look at you in such a way that you just believed.

The guy actually managed to reply! Through his state of shock he asked a single, rather tremulous question, "Ahh, did he say when, exactly?"

"Well, no" replied Josiah, seeing the message had been received. "And that's a little unusual with God. It may be the mess that offends him, I don't know. But I have clearly been told that I do have to kill you. But look, you are not a bad fellow. I will give you some time to atone for sins, and be back soon. OK?"

Can you believe it? The guy not only packed up his stuff but he ALSO cleaned the place out and was gone within the hour. One dirty pot was all that he left. I think it was his sign of defiance. A way to not completely give into the Gods of Cleanliness. Or maybe it was too dirty, would take too much time, and his life was more important.

One thing is certain, I don't think he would have ever been able to leave a mess ever again without thinking of Josiah

KNIGHT RIDER

Up behind the property at Boringbar was a defunct Multiple Occupancy that was once called "Money Mountain". It had been christened this by locals who knew that the sole purpose that most of the residents pursued was the growing of dope.

Curiously enough, the very fellow who in the last page had been sent packing by Josiah's information that he was to be killed, shared the same last name as one of the Money Mountain people. The who had disappeared a few years earlier. I had wondered if our dirty caravan man was a relative of Keith Knight but it appears he wasn't.

Keith Knight owed me money, and as he had disappeared around the time I had purchased at Boringbar I gathered the two facts were connected. But now, many years later he STILL had not appeared, it was generally accepted he had been murdered. What is more, all the residents of the MO (Multiple Occupancy) had pretty much all moved out, so it was presumed they had organised it. The net result is that the place has gone from a paradise to an overgrown weed dump.

Josiah said we should go through his empty cottage to see what we could find out, so we did. Soon enough it was pretty clear that he was dead. His passport was still there, and all his papers. Included in these was a list of receipts that advertised the type of business Keith was in. The main receipts were a list of one night stays at the various hotels in and around the district.

Now, this only means three things. Either you are a hooker, a commercial traveller or you are in the drug trade. Obviously Keith was not a hooker or commercial traveller. The standard trick is take a few pound with you, put it out of the way, but with easy access when needed, and take only a few ounces with you to a room at a local pub. You book in, then sit in the bar and casually meet your potential clients.

When you find an interested party, you pop upstairs to conduct business, then you are back down for the next buyer. You never have more than three ounces in the room at any given time, which has several advantages. It stops you being rolled for the lot, and if you bump into a copper, you are not charged as a dealer, but a user. At over $4000 a pound, and given that you can easily move 2 or 3 pounds a night, you can see that it's a very profitable business.

You are gone the next day, and you remain invisible to the Police. The drug squad looks for patterns, and need to establish one if they are to trap a person in a bust. And in simple terms, a person selling an ounce at a pub is not consequential enough for a serious effort, so it is a fairly safe way to conduct business. When you are constantly moving, and always under the radar, you are rarely caught.

Of course, the real risk you face is the same as every hooker. One day, the client you take upstairs may well kill you. Or, as it was possibly the case, the people who share your life at the MO, and who collectively hate your guts, may one day simply follow you out from the property, and do the same.

All I know if that Keith was hated. He was a complete prick to the other three people in the MO where he lived, and made their life misery with legal arguments and by never paying his fair share of anything.

Did they organise his removal? I can't say, but when he vanished, everyone else mysteriously left the place. And we are talking really substantial houses and a stunning property, just left to ruin. This story has been repeated with a thousand variations in a hundred MO's around the State, and it is always to do with issues from drugs, and the money they bring in.

Which reminds me. I never did see that money from Keith.

CHRISTIANS that Will DIE For You

Once at a "Mardi Grass" festival in Nimbin, NSW (Home of Australia's Aquarius Movement and the natural habitat of hippies and wastrels) Josiah saw a Christian tent. He called for me to follow, saying "Watch this, let's have a little fun." We go in. Clearly, a bald man in robes attracts attention. "Are you a Buddhist?" he is asked. Josiah points out that he is a Christian Monk who has come in for a little brotherly connection and to refresh himself in the light of the Lord. Eventually he gets past the small chat, and asks people what they are doing . They are here, saving Souls.

"So, you think God needs your help to save their (the people outside at the festival) souls?" He said, knowing it was a leading question. To those practicing the art of the humbly arrogant, it was all too obvious that God needed their help. But they muttered between themselves a little before declaring that they were merely the assistants of God's will.

It got the conversation moving in the right direction. "Well," Josiah went on, "How did the Lord save YOU? How did he come into your life?" For more it was some event that now seemed a miracle.

"So," he said, "What will you DO to save their Souls. I mean, sitting here in a nice tent is pretty safe. But it's not going to actually do anything as serious as saving a Soul, is it?"

Finally one took the bait, and declared "I would DIE for those people. I would DIE for them if it meant they would get to heaven."

"Those useless bums out there, living on social security, who never do anything that is for any purpose other then get high or get laid. These are the people you will DIE for?" He asked incredulously

The fellow firms up. "Yes," he says "I would sacrifice myself in order for them to find a higher calling."

"Oh," said Josiah. 'But really, they are just hippies and drug smokers. Surely YOU are worth more. You are more use to God alive rather than dead, surely?" The fellow was adamant, his desire to die for them was strong, so Josiah plugged on, "Well, tell me, would you die for ME if it meant saving my Soul?"

The Fellow hesitated, and said "Well, I (er) suppose so."

Josiah had the advantage now. "Really, seriously, I don't want you to die for me. I don't need you to die for me, but would you do SOMETHING for me?"

"I (er) guess so… I mean… ah… what is it ??"

"I want you to wash my car, can you do that for me? (The fellow was looking most obviously nonplussed at the notion, and hesitated before responding) "No seriously, it is a hell of a lot easier than dying, surely? Would you do it for me, would you wash my car?"

Finally the fellow caved in and said "Alright, I will wash your car."

"It's OK," said Josiah, still being quite serious. "I left it up at Uki. You are off the hook." The young man was obviously relieved, and now could get back to the imagination of dying for someone to save their soul.

He was certainly an interesting character to have around.

The part where Josiah connects with the Boringbar War is interesting. He made me an offer I could not refuse. He suggested that if he could solve the problem of the Fowls, would I give him a contract to buy the property. He said he had backers, and interested parties who wanted to build a monastery in these parts, and he felt my place was the perfect situation.

I said "OK, you are welcome to see what you can do." Now here is where I started to really learn about how to do business with the Fowls. I asked him how he was going to get on with sorting things out with Doogle, and he said "There is an ancient and simple principle: Keep your friends close, and your enemy even closer."

He then explained that he would need to say a few things, run me down, etc. in order to get in good with Doogle. He said that the key to the Fowls is

Doogle. Get him on side, and they turn to putty. So he went up, cap in hand, asking about milling some timber.

You see, the whole point of the sheds that were causing all the grief and court action was that one of them was the old milling shed of the Fowl's father. For Doogle, this was a symbol of all that MUST remain and so it MUST be defended. Josiah reckoned the place to start was the milling shed, and obviously this had only one use, milling timber.

So he went up and said hello to Doogle Fowl, cap in hand, asking for advice. He was planning on buying the property, to set up a monastery, if no one objected. But he needed to get an idea of costs for his backers.

He asked about how much it should cost, if he provided the wood, to mill up 2000 meters of beams? If fact, what would Doogle charge if HE were doing the job? And so, slowly he allowed the subject he really wanted brought up to arrive. He knew Doogle would have to ask it, and he did not disappoint; "But I thought you were friends with Wallace?"

Here was the opening. "Oh sure, I want to buy his place, so I try to stay on good terms. But really, can anyone like someone like that? I mean, country people like yourself I can trust. I know where I stand. But him, he's just another damn city slicker and you just never know where they are coming from, no matter what they say or promise." (All this from Josiah, the fellow raised in inner city Melbourne with dockworkers, mafia and thugs!)

That was IT. The gloss worked its charm, and Doogle had found himself a friend for life. Josiah was now camped right on the Crown Road by the creek, with a power cord from my place, living there with his wife and baby. Now Doogle started bringing him bananas, singing his praises in town, and never a bad word could be said about his new best friend.

Then Josiah strung the bow the OTHER way. He got some strips of wood, and asked if he could put up some "sacred signs" on the shed. He put up his moniker, three triangles in a triangle and also a six pointed Jewish Star.

To make it really interesting, I also suggested creating a geometric 3D star, made with triangles. So we did this and hung that from a tree at the entrance to the property.

Doogle, of course, had to ask him what it was all for. Josiah said "They are powerful religious symbols, designed to drive this bastard from the land, and you know the real irony of it? I got him to help me put them up! That is part of the powerful magic in this, particularly the symbol of the Siah Monks, of which I am the head monk. These three triangles in a triangle sculpture is a sign that the heavens will soon fall upon you and your sins will be brought home to roost as you are taken before the Lord."

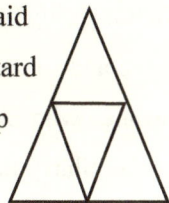

Doogle was mightily impressed, and because the court proceedings were well under by now, he made sure he told his oldest brother, who still had a tenuous connection with him. So then Josiah contacts a friend of his from England, and gets him to mail the "3 in 3" triangle sign off to the oldest brother. He says to make sure he buys obvious and clear stamps that have UK written on them. No letter, nothing but "the Sign" is to be posted in a plain envelope

The cat was put firmly amongst the pigeons.

Not ONE person ever commented that the "three in three" triangles was actually four small triangles linked to form a large one. All they saw was the powerful magic and intent behind it all.

Within the week the oldest brother was on my doorstep, looking very concerned. Now we have not really introduced the two oldest lads of the Fowl Family, have we? Slurry and Prance were tall, (Like all Fowls) blond and really quite impressive looking men. They had a lifetime of hard work in their veins. They were born for the land, and were tough as nails farmers. Doogle on the other hand, while of equal size, was limp and soft in his features, and he had a very gay lisp. Some called Doogle "Baby Face."

Slurry was one of the best machine operators in the valley, and a genuinely decent fellow. His brother Prance was suffering under the weight of a bitch he called his wife, and to say she was a bad tempered evil-minded lesbian slut was possibly not too far from the truth.

Curiously enough, when I first turned up in the valley, she occasionally said hello, giving me the sense that she was angling for sex. She was all muscle and fibre and sinew. Some men love that sort of thing. I know there were a lot of women who liked it. I gathered she, herself, just liked it,

So Slurry turns up looking very concerned, asking about this Josiah fellow. I tell him the truth, and say that Josiah is not his real name. The Truth? His grandfather was a member of the toe cutters gang. He wanted to buy this place, and he was not happy with the obstructions placed in the way of the subdivision going ahead. "What does he want from us?" he asked. I said I was really not sure, but that he had offered to act as a mediator in discussing a compromise in sorting out the matter of the sheds.

Well, that was all it took for the Fowls to come to the table. Slurry, Prance and the Ugly Sisters all turned up at a neutral house down the road where a series of discussions were convened. The greatest surprise of all was seeing the oldest sister in the flesh close up. Uncouth Fowl was a mirror image of Doogle, and quite scarily so. The discussions ranged over a few meetings, and finally all were agreed on an action plan to stop this matter proceeding to the courts. The Fowls all shook hands (Doogle was not present of course) and agreed to a very clear, very specific outline of a legal agreement.

Josiah was chuffed. "See how easy it is?" he said, mightily pleased with himself. Oh that it were so easy! Even the great and wonderful Josiah had been fooled by the Fowls and their incredible dysfunction that would fuck up even things that were in their favour. This most basic and simple of agreements was simply beyond them, because it was beyond them to agree on anything. At the time I was reserved, waiting to see what actually turned up, and when it did (to my non-surprise) there was virtually nothing in their agreement that we had previously agreed to.

I showed it to Josiah, and he shook his head. "There is absolutely nothing in this that we discussed and agreed to! Nothing. Not a single thing. They completely flipped their agreement!" Then it dawned on us. The real villain of this story that we ALL had missed. Sometimes it comes as simple inspiration, but I realized, as did Josiah "UNCOUTH!"

We had spent all this time thinking Doogle was behind all these problems, but in truth, it was the oldest sister. No wonder our plans had failed us.

I expressed my thanks for his efforts, but it seemed now to be inevitable that the matter ended up in the courts. He packed up his tent, and moved down the road to the very same neutral house where the discussions had ensued, and spent his ensuing time eyeballing every single Fowl that drove by.

I think they embarrassed him, and he wanted to make sure they knew it. Indeed, they all had an extraordinary fear of the fellow. But they still could not come to an agreement that worked.

There is no end to the Josiah Story. In truth it just rolls on and moves like an endless tide from one story to the next, and often from the incredible to the more incredible, from absurdity to even greater absurdity. The last time I saw him, I pointed out that he had failed to do a small thing he had faithfully promised. Well, he said "Sorry." I knew it was a hollow phrase, more of a courtesy than a sincerity.

I answered, laughing because I knew him quite well by now. "No. You are not sorry. That is simply not your character." I enjoyed that very small piece of truth. We remain friends.

The Supreme Court: La Nom de Plume a la Pretence

All our efforts at discussion, all the letters of compromise, all the promises that went to and fro: all counted for absolutely nothing. The time and date for the Supreme Court rolled up and I knew that, while the decision was a foregone conclusion, there is always a sting in the tail with these things.

In my case, it was the barrister we installed at the last moment. He arrived late, stoned and tripping off his face in tattered clothes that he was busy trying to pin into place in order to look respectable. The Fowls were in such disagreement over the whole show that two of them refused to show up, so the other Fowls arranged proxy bodies in their place to make it look as if they had.

What a charade. The opposition was trying to quote an incident with a PIE CART in Tauranga, New Zealand where the courts there allowed the pie cart owner permission to leave his registered vehicle on the side of the road in order to sell his legally licensed pies from his legally and licensed pie van. Council had wanted an order to move the van, but the courts refused, saying it was registered and had the same right as any car or registered vehicle on a New Zealand Road.

Now, as chance would have it, I knew the real story of the pie cart. I happened to live in Tauranga, New Zealand at that very time and quietly pointed out to my solicitor (the one who was able to function) that the Pie Van was eventually moved when the Local Council simply changed the parking restrictions in that area. They made his "spot" a loading zone, and he had to move on. And what the hell did it have to do with sheds on a Crown Road?

They talked up the right to have a shed on a Crown Road as much as they could, but in simple terms, the judge would have none of it. The sheds got ordered off, but equally so, he felt such a matter should never have wasted the Supreme Courts time, so he ordered everyone to pay their own costs.

Doogle went about the town proclaiming he had WON. His Brother Slurry turned up a few weeks later, apologising and saying he didn't know what on Earth had gotten into them all, and that he was sorry for the trouble and expense caused. I now know what caused it. Woman stuff. Possession and property. Not wanting to lose face.

Yet also there was simple-minded vindictiveness. The Fowls wanted to extract vengeance on the upstart telling them what they should do. More to the point, it was a game of chess for the women. The Fowl sisters had used this argument specifically to COST the Fowl property money. Quite simply, because their brothers were the main owners THEY had to pay. And so the sisters won THEIR side of the game quite handsomely, and paradoxically because they lost.

The brothers moved the sheds, and I tidied up the road, which inadvertently created the second round of the courts which started soon after. Why? A machine operator had accidentally knocked over a tree that was one metre off the Crown Road reserve. Without going into too many details, even though Doogle was not even an owner of the property, he started court proceedings that went on for another 2.5 years.

Finally my solicitor said "Look, even if he is only awarded a dollar, the legal bill will hit $25K. Just settle and be done with it."

This was all over a worthless tree that Doogle had insisted was valued at $150,000. It was a nonsense from the outset, and it was obviously a nonsense, but with solicitors in the picture the drama unfolded to ever increasing circles until it became a mighty soap opera. It all up cost me $10K, for no reason other than pure simple minded SPITE. Welcome to the reality of so called Justice.

The Barrister supporting the Fowls knew it, of course. While I stood there defending myself on this occasion I managed to toss in a few pithy words to him. "Do you know the fate of those who dwell in, and eat so voraciously, the never ending pieces that are the minutiae of existence, Mr Ghastly?" I asked of him outside the courtroom. He said no, but did so hesitantly. (I presumed that he was unaccustomed to dealing with people who could speak English) I smiled with a thin, vampirish joy, "Well: Their fate is to become it?"

I semi-stole this line from Pythagoras. Curiously enough for an educated man he didn't seem to quite grasp the words. We become the song we sing, people, so be careful what tune you play.

Anyway, the matter was settled and on my way out of court I said to Doogle: "Well, you have won. You are the better man, Doogle. What is more, you have won so convincingly, that I am leaving the valley. You have won, and with me leaving your goal is accomplished, so you have won again! Congratulations."

Mind you, I had always planned to leave when Ben had finished Primary School. Buses to high school took 1.5 hours each way, which meant 3 hours commuting every day for my little guy. And the local schools were crap. I had already been casting about for a suitable place to move to, which is where I am writing this book. Through chance and circumstance I had recently found the ideal school, which he is currently going to.

But I did not mention this to Doogle. I felt it was best to leave him on a high note, and I must say he did seem mightily pleased with himself. Oddly enough, his bitch of a sister Mrs Uncouth Tooth, who was also there, looked guilty. That surprised me as I didn't know this was an emotion that any Fowl possessed!

This is, of course, only a small smattering of some of the insanities in the courts that Doogle attempted. I will add that he has sued every single one of his neighbours, which you might imagine would be a red flag to all judges? But not at all! We have a court system that allows, and dare I say, ENCOURAGES abuse. If you can raise the money to pay solicitors, you can have any argument you choose to argue heard by a judge.

You may not win, but that is not the point. If you are a Fowl the very sustaining breath of life is to be found in the creation of an argument. So, even if you lose, you win.

Sunday Morning Comin' Down

On a Sunday morning sidewalk,

I'm wishing, Lord, that I was stoned.

'Cos there's something in a Sunday,

That makes a body feel alone.

And there's nothin' short of dyin',

That's half as lonesome as the sound,

Of a sleepin' city sidewalk,

And Sunday mornin' comin' down.

Kris Kristoffersen is one of those wonderful musicians, writers and performers that I wish I could be more like. It is so easy to relate to what he sings about, because it touches on something within us all. What the great musicians sing about is OUR pain, OUR story and I wake this morning hearing this song in my thoughts. Why? What's the connection with this book?

Is there anything in this song that relates to MY Sunday? The song is about an alcoholic looking at the loss of the past through the eyes of the present. Well, maybe this is the connection.

This is day three. I am physically very tired, and it's not the three hours sleep, or the two days of writing. It is the simple fact that I have been dragging myself through the last decade of a what I now see as a war

What occurs to me are the following simple home truths:

FACT ONE: We all Fuck Up.

FACT TWO: We do this a few times before we get the message, then:

FACT THREE: Go back to Fact One.

Sunday has arrived, the tyranny of the cats and their competition for affection continues in its own subtle way. One just walked in, looks up, meows. She wants attention, demands it, and if she is ignored, she will go outside as if to say "You miserable toad!" She is up and onto my belly now, treading it with her claws. Now she is down, and lying to the right of me on the chair, becoming a warm and cuddly arm rest. They can be so cute.

When I walked out to see how Ben was doing a few moments ago, the two of them had looked up, and their meow meant "Food". I walk past the laundry and get the ammonia smell of cat crap up my nose. So I stop, collect it, and put it outside. Throwing the crap out the back paddock, I look at the dead ride on mower that I bought at auction, which only ran for a few weeks before dying.

I was going to take it to the tip, thinking: it is broken, throw it away. But something said "Put it on Ebay!" Can you believe that it went for $300? The fellow who bid for it just called to say he will be over this morning. Yesterday someone gave me $162 for the old fridge. A couple of days earlier I sold the old Range Rover for $1350 and at the start of the book I describe how I sold another dead old ride on to a fellow right at the time Ben broke his collar bone.

Was that a lifetime or two days ago? Now my most sacred joy is up for grabs, my old Porsche. Not to put it too bluntly, but I need the cash.

I really do not want to sell the Porsche. It is my one piece of sheer delight, a moment of refinement that defines enjoyment in the most simple of ways; that is to say, hurtling boy-like through the corners, slipping and sliding with wheels spinning in abandon. This car is also a meeting point between father and son, a joy we both share. The classic shape and beautiful lines contain both form and function that is a perfect architecture.

It is not just a car, it is a home for ideals and a temple for the spirit, but sadly, the reality of large bills is knocking on the door and this small gift from the heavens may soon have to go.

After my long battle to hold onto Boringbar and keep my head about water, borrowing money to pay the solicitors and various contractors, then borrowing money to pay back the borrowed money. Well can you believe that after all of this the NSW Government has decided new laws are needed. Because Canberra burnt down at the edges, apparently this proves that the entire State is a fire risk. The collective wisdom of myopic politicians has determined a whole new set of fire laws are required, as if a law will stop a fire. The issue is that these new laws make forested properties, such as Boringbar, a liability of litigation.

In one stroke of a Politically Correct Legal Pen some $300K has been knocked off the street value of the property, which means that all the battles will be for the princely result of Zero Return. Possibly a loss. Through it all "Sunday Morning Coming Down" does seem more and more like something that fits the bill. All I need now is to become an alcoholic.

Boringbar has worn down a good deal of my expectations with life and subsequently my belief in human nature has somewhat dimmed. I certainly have learned a few things. For example: I no longer refuse a port when offered, and indeed have come to enjoy immensely the odd sip. Indeed, there is a bottle of Chartreuse up there on the bar and the way I feel this morning may well mean that when the aches and pains of writing creep in, by the afternoon you will see me supping on its delights.

Chartreuse is like no other. You do not splurge into its delights by knocking it back in an abhorrent lack of self-discipline and neither dshould you find your mind scattered as you pursue the liberties of pleasure that are running through your head. No, Chartreuse is a quality you suffice upon. It is like a classic Porsche of a bygone era that beckons and calls unto the present day. Hear Ye Hear Ye, the bell has tolled, so lift up thy glass and worship the coming of the night. The Mad Parade of Bacchus is your friend!

Chartreuse, the same secret combination of herbs and spices for over 400 years, has comforted many a weary soul after a long arduous trek. It is still made by the very same Carthusian Monks in the same district of France.

Chartreuse has been a backstop against the ages, is a sign that quality survives. Light the lighthouse, defy the wearing effects of centuries, be the beacon of stone that calls out and defies the pounding of the waves. When you sip Chartreuse you are here, not there. Chartreuse is in your blood, and in your olfactory sense, and in your spirit and it heals wounds that ache in the heart.

Extracted from Wikipedia

According to tradition, in 1605 a marshal of artillery to French king Henri IV, François Hannibal d'Estrées, presented the Carthusian monks at Vauvert, near Paris, with a manuscript that contained a complicated recipe for an "elixir of long life".

The recipe eventually reached the religious order's headquarters at the Grande Chartreuse monastery, in Voiron, near Grenoble. It has since then been used to produce the "Elixir Végétal de la Grande Chartreuse". The formula is said to call for 130 herbs, flowers, and secret ingredients combined in a wine alcohol base. The monks intended their liqueur to be used as medicine. The recipe was further enhanced in 1737 by Brother Gérome Maubec.

My thanks to the Good Brothers. Chartreuse fits the modern age as perfectly as a well worn glove. Just think: 130 Herbs and secret recipes, a huge multi-national, and most of all, a pleasing designer colour.

In fact the colour was named after the drink! How did some medieval monks in the (obviously) far distant past manage to create such a perfect indulgence? I don't know, but I can say for certain that quality somehow shines through, and survives, but only if we defend it against the marauding natives that wish to steal, corrupt and/or plagiarize our best intentions and efforts.

I was re-introduced to Chartreuse by Dave, my insane but rather brilliant friend who designs magnificent furniture. At the depths of despair in the midst of unceasing battles to do with roads, banks, and surviving the day (forget about seizing it, I was hard put to stay alive) Dave called up one night and asked if I wanted to come to a Dinner Party.

Here we need to pause and observe a very simple thing. As humans, we really do not need much. We want a whole lot, but what we need is fairly simple: Someone to love us, someone to love, a place to stay and a purpose that makes it all worthwhile. Neither Dave nor I had any of the above, though we were both trying hard to get there. I welcomed the invite, and went along to see the bevy of beautiful girls and interesting madmen that assembled around Dave's banner.

Dave had only recently decided against continuing his career as a drug dealer and pill popper. He had awoken to the fact that while it was all fun, it was going nowhere. Inside he had determined that he had to cement his life into something more worthwhile, and calling a party to farewell the past was a small piece of the new jig saw puzzle he was sorting out.

Everyone arrives, and we are seated around this HUGE slab table with bench seats that Dave had made. Feeling the solid texture of the Camphor under your elbows as Dave pours Chartreuse into your glass is a comforting thing, a noble thing, and after the fifth glass of Chartreuse, it's a beautiful thing.

Everyone is beautiful, life shines, and more than anything your natural brilliance simply flows out to reach all those gorgeous young things that are flitting about.

I amaze myself with the fluid quick wit, the dry humour, the subtle innuendo. Then I realise that everyone else is as high on Chartreuse as myself, and I recall the far distant past when 30 school friends got off their faces on bongs and had this incredible jam. We played for hours and it was just amazing. Fortunately someone had the foresight to record the proceedings, and so the next day we awoke and went to listen to our ready made HIT.

Oddly enough, the incredibly astounding performance of the night before was not quite as brilliant that next day. What a shock! It had mysteriously turned into absolute, abject crap. Therefore I surmised that what I believed to be brilliant in that particular moment would probably, if recorded, also sound like absolute crap the next morning.

But who cares! I was loving this brief respite from the dull monotony that had become the day to day grind of Boringbar. My life to date had been arguments over nothing, and thus occasioned my escape each evening into a world of pixels. Ah yes! Pixel Land, where all the good pixels go before they end up in the infamous and mysterious, pixel graveyard.

Digital Slime (Seek Every Atrocious Nightmare)

I have noted Digital Slime oozing through cyber space. Cold Shoulders will not freeze it, ignoring it will not improve its ignorance.

Look up in the sky!

Is it a Spam?

Is it a Sham?

Is it just the American Trailer Trash Way?

As subtle as a bare foot in bullshit the digital slime creeps over the brain, soaking itself into each corner until it absolves itself of responsibility, and gets you dancing like a puppet to its whim. Digital Slime and his cohort, Cyber Slut lurk in the far reaches on inner space looking for a purpose through verbiage and innuendo but finding only the dull thud of the echo of common sense as it falls to floor like an overtly flogged dead horse.

Beaten to death by its own incessant argument, Digital Slime slobbers over Cyber Slut, crooning "Eat me bitch! Eat me!"

Cyber Slut is deeply pretend horrified, saying "Oh my GOD, you have stained my size eight Ballroom Dress!" She is the moniker of indecent impersonal indefatigable intellectualism parading as truth. Sad, sad truth, a Cinderella left behind to wash the dishes and peel the potatoes while the world spins madly out of control.

Where is the Fairy Godmother when you need her? She is out the back with Peter Peter Pumpkin Eater.

Yours Fruitfully

Mr Potato Head

ON LINE

During the entire time I had been battling the Fowls, surviving the courts, the ex-wives, and everything else I found respite in the world of Cyber Space. Yes, I had discovered the Internet and chat lists, and as a consequence of this, I encountered the remarkable things that people will choose to believe to be true. Somehow that inane muttering of nonsensical rhubarb was a balm to my Soul.

It was avoidance therapy to be sure, but it was effective. You see, when you live at the end of a valley, and every night you have to stay home looking after a young lad who is in bed by 8.00 and there are only 2 channels on TV which are not worth watching anyway: Well, you have to find SOMETHING to keep your brain alive.

Writing was one thing, but some days, you just wanted to blot out.

For me it was Newsgroups and Net Lists. I poured my creative Soul into entertaining people all over the world, and in my first year I had received no less than 5 marriage proposals from women who had never met me. I had charmed their little pixels off, apparently. This is an entirely different chapter of the Boringbar Experience, and it is an extraordinary thing to discover, but can you believe that people on line lie about who and what they are?

You are not all that shocked, I am sure. The Cyber World is full of deeply dysfunctional individuals. But then again, who cares! At least their lies and stories were entertaining. Even if they were fictitious in the extreme, I got to meet some fascinating characters that danced and pranced through the script of each day's moments. It's no different from reading a book. Better in some respects, because it is live to air.

Can anyone describe the joy, the ravenous insatiable joy of simple communication? On the flip side, there is the pain of the simplest things you write not being understood. I suspect we all suffer more of the latter than we enjoy of the former. Think about it. Would Jesus have spread his Gospels On Line? More to the point: Would he set up a You Tube account and sent out parables in accordance with the modern Politically Correct standards?

What I discovered in Cyber Space was that SOME people believed it was real. Over the course of a the next few years I met some of the denizens of the deep, empty space I was exploring, and the extraordinary thing was that many of them somehow became fixed on the notion that the Net World was a greater reality than their own miserable existences. Simply put, those I met who incessantly lurked in the shadow of the pixel were ALL people lacking in what we might term a "real" life.

One fellow in particular became a personal acquaintance, and yet when he visited he talked not about his life, the weather or events he had encountered that day. He spoke about what someone said on a newsgroup, and what they really meant, and who they thought they were, and what sort of trap they were laying for him. I started to distance myself, but by now I was "IT": The friend who UNDERSTOOD.

I understood alright. I understood I had a complete freak on my hands. THEN he started talking about the orgies he used to go to, and how he was actually an alcoholic and addicted to dope and porn as well, and on and on it went. His frequent turning up unannounced, eating the food in the fridge, and rabbiting on with this utter crap that had become his reality. This was not my idea of fun. I had enough dysfunction with my neighbours, so I snipped him. I then discovered the meaning of the term "A woman scorned".

The fellow did what my ex-wife did! He contacted everyone I knew, and created these extraordinary stories about what a huge bastard I was. Herein we discover the paradox of denial: If you deny an accusation, you are in denial. If you do NOT deny it, you are guilty. The point is that I discovered that the net has it dangerous side, the part where people forget where the boundaries are.

Vicious flame wars, sweet sexy whispers, agonising loneliness. On Line had become a Peyton Place of lost souls washed up onto an indecent mirage. Yet, for all its failings, the net gave me a connection to others and, as it turned out, to a greater purpose. It only proves that truth is approached through illusion.

For years I had run a course on Numerology via the magazines. From an early age I had this fascination with all things Pythagorean, and in the isolation of Boringbar I was left with little else to do but to find something useful to do. My attention turned to a puzzle I had nursed for a decade or more, the puzzle of Pythagorean Tone Healing.

In his book, **The Therapeutic Value Of Music,** Manly P Hall gives the background to how the ancients discovered the cure for the ills which we suffer today. He shows us how music protects present-day tribal people all over the world from ailments (specifically the stress-related) that are now most common in modern society.

There is a record in the Pythagorean texts of how musicians from one of their schools had gone to the house of a man with a fatal illness. They played him music, and the next day the man was up and about. Now as a musician playing in bars and night spots in my early 20's this was something that fascinated me. For years I had secretly toyed with the audience when they were not watching, using different tones, timbres and qualities of sound to see what effect it had on them as a group. Sometimes I would insert certain Vedic words that were "Words of Power" and on occasions when using these I would see someone jerk about like they had been struck with a hammer.

There was something in it, but where was the key? What was the secret pattern in all of this? In the journey to understand this, well before Boringbar, I had seen a friend some 500 meters away walking down Oxford Street in Darlinghurst. I felt something tug from within, and a quality came into my voice as I WHISPERED her name.

She pulled her head up, like someone had just attacked her. I felt her shock. I ran to catch her up, and said hello, not saying what I had just seen.

Her eyes narrowed, she looked at me with suspicion. Somehow she had heard my voice, and it had pierced a part of her that was not to be touched. I never saw this girl again, and I was told she left soon after for a trip overseas.

I had experienced this some years earlier in a different way, trying to modulate the voice to project the words to the song. It is an old orator's trick, to modulate the voice so that you can be heard un-amplified in a large room. All old Vaudevillians used it, and all opera singers are taught the trick. Well, something weird happened. My voice stepped away from me, and I could hear my song singing itself from about three feet in front of me.

My mouth was moving, and I was singing, but the actual song was coming back to me from a point three feet distant. It was the ultimate in ventriloquism. It lasted but a moment, and was gone. Try as I would that extraordinary experience would not reoccur.

Now despite the pain and suffering of being the single parent with no money in the midst of a battleground, or perhaps BECAUSE of this, I turned once more to this notion of Sound being a powerful force for healing. The Pythagoreans based all of their discoveries in Music and Mathematics. They proved the two were inextricably bound, and they proved the principles of Harmonics were as true in physical form as they were in aesthetic realization.

Pythagoras himself reputedly started the journey that led to the school of wisdom at Crotona by listening to the sound of blacksmiths beating a forge.

Four of the hammers rang true in harmony, while a fifth sounded out of tune. He got curious, bought the hammers off the blacksmiths, and made careful note of WHERE on the musical scale these harmonious and non-harmonious tones were place. Then he went back, asking the blacksmiths to beat out the metal in the hammers to form a tongue of metal.

When struck, each piece of metal created the SAME tone as it did when a solid hammer. This meant that the density and weight of metal had a quality of SOUND. A physical form related directly to tone and music. Given that his entire teaching was based on the Music of the Spheres, that high pitched sound you hear occasionally in our around your ears, Pythagoras began to look into how each of us was a song, a tone that was emanating from the divine.

He discovered the art of determining exactly what tones a person related to, and by playing these back he could trigger the healing of the sick body and the rejuvenation of the diseased mind. His famous quote regarding this: *The price the Gods demand for the gift of Song? To become what you sing!"*

I spent some years working out the various parameters that might have led him to his discovery, seeking to walk the same path and reinvent that system he had given to the world, but which had been lost to the ages. The more I got into it, the more complex and convoluted it all seemed, and in simple terms, this was not how the Pythagoreans worked.

I realised that as Pythagoras also gave the world a form of Numerology that was still intact, perhaps in the patterns of Number in that process a clue might be found. This is when I decided to keep it all incredible simple, and simply draw a straight line between the numbers in a person's numerical chart and notes in music.

My friend from New York was visiting at the time. I sat down and told him about what I was doing and he said "Give it a go... Tell me what noted relate to my chart" The principle is very simple, any date is a representation of a series of Cycles. Using Vedic Math, it is easy to compile a date down to a distillation of cycles that are at work within it. Given a series of dates, you can see if any cycles or patterns of cycles repeat.

I looked at Greg's date of birth, date of marriage, Parents dates of birth, and I worked a thread of number patterns that correlated and matched and repeated themselves. I read out the sequence of notes that these patterns related to: Chords, melodies and harmonies were evoked by the various combinations of music that Greg's own chart determined.

After an hour of this, he was amazed. This is a professional musician, who may well play a thousand different songs a week, but as he explained to me, when he WROTE music it was different. What I had done was to tell him

EXACTLY the patterns and combinations he invariably was drawn to when he was writing his own music.

He was stunned, because it had never been so clear to him. He saw every single song he wrote was wrapped around a series of harmonics that had been read out to him by a person who had never heard all his songs. That was the "AH HA!" moment when I realised the nut had been cracked. This was the birth of what we now call Number Harmonics.

This is possibly the sole and simple purpose behind ALL the pain and suffering of Boringbar, to force me into such a corner that I had to do something to invent myself out of this deep hole into which my life had been falling. I had discovered a purpose that promised to be both satisfying and financially viable.

Soon I was out at the local festivals doing "Sound Tapes" for the people, testing out the new theories in real life situations. I would take my high end tape deck and a set of Vibraphones, and set up at the various New Age fairs that littered the district around Bling Bling. One of the first customers was the Step-Father of Dealer, Skerick's wife.

He had come to Australia to die. His doctors had said he had but weeks to live, and he decided that one place he always wanted to see was Australia, so he left Germany and when Dealer came up to say hello, he said "Let's get a tape done, what the hell!" So I did the tape, all 20 minutes of it, and suggested he play it every night for the next few months.

He smiled an ironic smile I did not understand, but of course, he was thinking "3 Months? I have not 3 weeks my friend".

The very next day he became very ill. Keep in mind that he had told no one of his impending demise, but Dealer knew this was serious. His step-daughter took him straight to the hospital. And it was here that an extraordinary thing occurred. He happened to meet a young doctor who had done a thesis on the very disease that was killing him.

This bright young spark said "You know, in rare cases the matter is complicated by a blood disorder. Do you mind if I check?"

Sure enough, this was the complication. A simple transfusion ensued and in hours our man, who came to die, was feeling 40 years younger. The doctor explained to him that this transfusion will simply prolong his life a little, and not stop the disease. But offering a dead man a few more years of life it is like offering him the very earth itself.

He lived three more years, arranged all his finances, organised his will, made amends to all, and passed from this life a happy, content man. Did the harmonics participate in any of this? Again and again, I had people turn up, request a tape, and find that their entire life would change.

The website at www. numberharmonics.org was raised on the 01/01/01: According to the Number patterns this was the most auspicious date to raise the standard, and for the last six years hundreds of people have sworn that the CD's they receive have improved their life immeasurably, but the fact is: I know it is just music.

Why it works, I really cannot explain. I suspect it is something that tricks the subconscious into action. There is a music we are born to hear, and I discovered the pattern that unlocks the key to this Harmonic Secret. It is similar to reinstalling the operating system on a computer. When things are not working properly on a computer, the first thing you do is reinstall everything, and most of the time the problem goes away.

Somehow the CD's seem to work like this. I think it gives the inner mind a reference point and somehow it all sets up a pattern of synchronicity. Time and again, when people receive their CD something turns up. A doctor with the right answer, a dentist who points out that mercury is affecting the nervous system, or a chiropractor that clicks the right bone into place.

But did any of this work means anything to the denizens of Boringbar? Certainly, not to my neighbours! If you couldn't shoot it for supper, or if it didn't grow in the ground, it was of no great use to anyone. However, I did happen to meet an attractive young lady called Yoghurt. She lived down the road. She was dropping of her kids at the school bus stop.

The woman was just out from NZ, extremely pregnant and waiting for her husband to come over. She was also curious as to what a person like myself was doing in the godforsaken hillbilly world of Upper Boringbar. I started speaking of Number Harmonics and the work I was doing, and she became fascinated. As I was running a seminar, and as she was not well, I suggested she might want to come up and be a guinea pig for a sound training session.

Like a cat that had been stroked exactly the right way, she agreed. I swear she was purring, now I think about it.

The workshop arrives and an assorted bunch of hopefuls turn up, expecting to find something interesting to fill out the empty spaces of their lives. I talk, I demonstrate, I give them the principles, and finally, I hand over the sound mallets and one by one they play out their OWN music that we have worked out over the last 24 hours.

One by one, the stars come to the eyes, and one by one they sit down utterly amazed. A classically trained fellow, a beautiful singer and one of those pure souls you occasionally meet, had been trying to wrap his head around the mathematics without success all weekend. I said "It is music by numbers. Just work out the pattern, and follow the interval structure."

Finally he let go, and just followed the numbers. Then the magic happened. His hands took on a life of their own, and he found himself flying.

The music had entered his Soul and awakened his spirit. It was a truly beautiful thing to watch, and his eyes grew bright with the experience. This is what all musicians aim for, the moment when improvisation becomes pure inspiration. So, when all is said and done, even though the whole process of Boringbar may have left the bank roll bereft and the credit cards maxed out, at least SOMETHING good has come of it all.

Isn't it odd how we have to be driven into a corner before we invent our way out of it? It's a cliché but in times of war, because of necessity, great progress is made in the field of invention.

The young lady I had met at the bus stop was to turn up at odd moments from that point, usually with boyfriend in tow. I suspect I was slightly Guru-like to her, and while I preferred the company of her man (who I taught guitar to for a while) she was OK. Yet it all changed when Miss Buzz arrived. That was when I realised her interest was not entirely platonic. Further, like so many individuals, they seem to decide that, based on the reason they met me first, this meant that they had a right to be in my life over the person who met me second.

Isn't that a weird way to think? Kids call it "Dibs". Dibs on him means "I own him".

Why do people believe they can own a person by association? Every girl with a Pop Idol likes to think she owns a little part of him, because she bought his album and put his photo on the wall. People seem to think that because they feel a connection that the other person feels the same. Like the teenager who believes they "know" the pop star because they have all his albums, people take ownership stakes in their favourites. Is it their own insecurity that drives them?

Probably, the reality is that people seek to position themselves in life by putting mental and emotional hooks into those around them.

All the problems with the ex-wife, the madman from the newsgroup, and the woman from the bus stop, these really all boil down to an ownership issue. All the problems with Doogle were really an ownership issue. He wanted my place. Everyone wants to OWN what they survey, and like little Hitler's we organise an army of thought to achieve that end. If someone dies in the battle, well, that's the cost of war.

In all of the Boringbar Wars that I fought, won, lost and suffered, I came finally to understand one simple thing. **The only thing I can own is this moment**. It is the most transitory thing in existence, and yet it is the only thing of true permanence in all the heavens and universes of the Gods.

SELF INTEREST RULES

The Paphian Queen to Cnidos made repair
Across the tide to see her image there:
Then looking up and round the prospect wide,
When did Praxiteles see me thus? she cried.

Plato

There are very few people with anything even approaching a noble aspiration in Boringbar. When I drive North from my farm I see the great expanse of the Plaid Valley. One day as I drove into the redneck centre called Murmurbah, I looked out to all the cane fields, the houses, and all the buildings. Then it struck me! Everything I see is due to self-interest.

Civilization and growth is in the interest of every member of the civilization. Of course, a couple of hundred years ago there was nothing in this valley but rainforest and swamp. There are some that curse the change, of course, but they usually have a comfy job in an office. Today we value such things as forests and look back longingly on how things might have been if this ancient place had been preserved. But 100 years ago it was just timber to harvest and land to make arable. If you didn't, you starved.

Murmurbah, once the "Amazon" of Australia, was now flat cane fields.

These cane fields had for years produced the money for the valley, but now they evicted acid sulphate from the soils each flood, the same acids that killed the fish in the river, and which also needed vast amounts of calcium each year to counter it, in order to keep the soil productive.

Yet at the start of the journey to civilization and profit, wood and farming was everything. All the useful wood was taken, and houses, furniture and paraphernalia was created with it. The rest was burned. Yet wood was also worthless because wooden houses burned down. The only "real" house to the local farmer was a good solid double brick box with a red tile roof. Yes, it looked like an inflamed wart and forget the fact that it was entirely unsuited to the climate. Brick meant you were here to stay. Just ask the three little piggies!

I look down the Valley and see how, lifetime after lifetime, the people had pursued one single goal, their own interest. In the area of self-interest came the joys of sex, the security of clear title, and the power of religion. The bargain was a simple one: The women wanted a house of their own, and the men wanted sex. Men would get what they wanted by providing the women with what they wanted. Therein lays the basic trade off with much of human experience. Sadly, once the house was secured the woman's interest in sex seemed to fade. Like the rape of nature, the pursuit of sex often turned out to be a self-defeating circle.

On this day I was travelling with Josiah and one of his disciples to the disciples' parents' house. They were home, and clearly the wife was happy she owned the home. The father looked forlorn, dejected and beaten down by life. (or maybe his lack of it) What is more, to this father's dismay, Josiah had dropped by to say hello.

Clearly, he could not stand this monk character, the one who had stolen his son. I wanted to allay his fears and assure his misery-laden face that his son, the disciple, was no great catch. If he were a fish, you really would have thrown him back. Indeed, this is what Josiah did within the year, but not before making him a bishop! I guess if you are going to get rid of someone, at least make them happy to go.

Of course, I said nothing, and merely observed the mute level of dissatisfaction that ruled every nook and cranny inside that little wooden house he had provided for his sexually disinterested wife. Perhaps if he gotten her a brick one it may have been different? We are out of there as soon as possible.

The Monks disciple gathered up some odds and ends, after which I dropped the Monk and his dutiful follower off to where they had some trade plates to collect in town. The purpose of this exercise was to get a Mercedes that had

---

been stolen from Josiah a month earlier. Here I once more wondered at the remarkable powers of persuasion the Mad Monk possessed. A car dealer in town had not only loaned him a car, he then also loaned him his dealer plates to go collect the Merc!

No dealer lets his trade plates out of his sight, because any accident or circumstance that involves a car carrying them goes straight back onto his insurance. What it means, however, is that ANY car can be driven with these plates strapped onto it. Some months ago Josiah had left his Mercedes on the side of the road while he went down to Sydney. At this point someone had thoughtfully collected the car from said resting place and put in their garage.

It had taken some time to track the fellow down and confirm the car was in his garage. And so it was that, trade plates in hand, we surprised him. We informed the fellow we were here to pick up the car. However, despite the fact that he had been caught red handed he was not willing to part with it. Why? He had spent money getting the car towed to his house, and he wanted the money back. Josiah said "Bullshit. You stole my car from the side of the road. Would you prefer we report you to the Police?"

The fellow shut the door, and said "Go ahead." so we did. The Police that turned up I suspect were personal friends of our car thief, and the subsequent conversation was extraordinary. They stated that the fellow had claimed to them that the car was salvage. Even though the plates were still on the car, because it had sat for so long in the one spot, he had claimed it was salvage and brought it home. We could have the car, but we had to pay his towing costs.

I laughed and said to the officer, "Well, take a look at that late model Range Rover up there. It has been parked there for over 6 months. What you are saying is that I can get a truck, and cart that car off to my place and simply say it was salvage?"

The officer said this was indeed the Law. "But even if this were the law, Officer. If I choose to collect the car, and the owner rings up the police claiming the car is stolen, and then I say that he can have it back but that he has to pay the towing fees I incurred, then you would say he should pay me?"

Finally the officer admitted that the fellow was out of line asking for his towing fees to be refunded, but by the time we got back to get the Mercedes (with Police in tow) the fellow had magically vanished. We said we would just open his garage and get the car, but the good officer then informed us that this would be breaking and entering. Well to cut the story short, the fellow eventually put the car out on the road, but it was missing a whole batch of parts and it was no longer drivable. Of course, he said he collected it like that. If we wanted to take it further, wait for it, this was a Civil Matter.

Everything the Police are disinterested in pursuing is, apparently, a civil matter. In other words, piss off.

Here is where I believe that bribery pays huge dividends, and should be enshrined in law. All life is motivated by self-interest, and we really need to have a suitable bribery gauge set in place that allocates what is an appropriate bribe at appropriate times. For example, if there were a $50 bribe for an officer to open up a garage door searching for drugs, and thus just happen to find a car in there that doesn't belong to the resident, then it is no longer breaking and entering to remove the car.

Making bribery illegal clearly infringes of the rights to Natural Justice with people such as ourselves in these situations.

Indeed, though I would shock you to say it, there are OTHER failings within our system of Law. For instance within our entire legal system we have only two pleas, Guilty or Not Guilty. I feel this is a significant fault, and that we need a third option. As evidence for this view I give the following example.

I was once booked getting towed in a car that was not registered, and I was charged with unregistered driving. I wasn't driving, I was being TOWED!! When it came to court, somehow I had the time wrong, and arrived late, and as a result my guilt was already enshrined on the books.

However, the magistrate was curious what I WOULD have pleaded. I said "Your honour, in reference to the Lindy Chamberlain case, I would have entered a different plea. I would enter a plea of DINGOES!"

He looked at me surprised, but amused, and he asked what a plea of Dingoes meant. I said "Well, we really don't know if someone is truly guilty or not guilty in this matter, so I propose we blame a third party, the Dingo. In my case, your Honour, I was not DRIVING this car, I was getting towed.

"How can I be DRIVING an unregistered car when I was being pulled along in it? Driving, by definition, requires me to be in charge of the vehicle. I was not. In my home State, being towed is the right and proper thing to do when moving a car. Even so, I admit that if the law states I am guilty in this then I am guilty, even though I thought I was obeying the law. If I realized being towed in a car that was not registered was an offence, I would not have done so."

The Magistrate, the hanging judge of minutes before, apologized for dragging me into the court, and explained that in the circumstances he had to find me guilty, but imposed the lowest possible fine and gave me time to pay.

Now contrast this to the fellow who was towing me. He decided to get very serious and make a song and a dance about it. He turned up with solicitors and legal advice coming out of his ears. The Magistrate listened to his arguments, fined him $2000, and suspended his license for 6 months.

Why the big difference? Simple, I appealed to the self-interest of the Magistrate. How? I lightened up his day with a little bit of fun, and this was valuable to him.

Every day he sees people who are the lowest common denominator of our society, and it is a very boring job having to deal with them. Occasionally someone comes along with an argument and solicitors, and the magistrate loves it, but only because it is either entertaining, or he can prove his power.

However, when someone comes along who is entertaining, and has a curious viewpoint, this activates his SELF Interest. The magistrate naturally wants to reward the clown who brightens his day.

The courts and society in general creates laws and principle essentially to maintain the status quo. We all know that Laws exist mainly to feed the law makers. There is no CSI or Perry Mason who week after week defeats the odds and saves the innocent from the guilty. The truth is, the guilty often walk, the innocent generally suffer and everyone accepts this as a sad fact of life.

The whole legal system is merely a game for the paid players who strut its stage, and we foolish ones who wish to argue are the ones who pay them.

As an example: One day Doogle decided to have me charged as a civil nuisance, and sought an order called an AVO, or Apprehended Violence Order. This was where I met Paul Smart, former lead singer for Idle Minds but now a fully registered Barrister in the NSW court system. His parents had insisted on him getting a legal education, but as soon as he got his ticket, he was off with the rock and roll band singing his heart out.

Now probably because Paul had not followed the path of conservative huffery, but travelled the lowly drug stained road of Rock and Roll, this gave him an innate understanding of the most miserable and lowest aspects of any person. Suffice to say, in any given event he would look for the motivation for WHY it occurred, and invariably this would be found with some sort of low emotion such as jealousy, anger, lust, etc.

What is more, Paul Smart had remarkable success in dealing with magistrates because he pointed out this observation in simple language.

Classic Paul Smart dialogue went like this "And so Mr Jones, you are saying to me that everything you have said here today is completely true, 100% correct, and totally unbiased?" Mr. Jones either says "Yes" or he admits he is a liar. They always say "Yes!" So then Paul slides in with the obvious. "Mr Jones, really? Are we not perhaps GILDING THE LILY? Perhaps just a little bit in order to make things look a little better for ourselves? You wouldn't be gilding the lily would you Mr Jones?"

When Mr Jones says the inevitable "No" the judge knows he is a liar. But how can the fellow say "yes" and admit he is a liar? It is the reverse Catch 22.

Courts and law pretend to be about right or wrong, but in the mind of every judge, the courts and the people who appear in them are really about a balance of probability. How do you sway this balance in the judges mind? THAT is all about suggestion, implication, innuendo, and inflammation.

Paul had this down pat. All he need do was to simply brush the opponent's testimony with the allure of falsehood, and the judge would fill in the blanks. He 'was' smart, as his name implied. He always bowed low and allowed the judge to make up his own mind, but not before pointing out the low emotions that were possibly what were motivating the opponent's actions, and implying this as the REAL reason everyone was in court.

Judges will always believe in the lowest common denominator as a cause for evil. Why? That's an easy one: Because they see it every day.

In the case of Doogle Fowl versus Michael Wallace we were appealing an AVO that had been placed against me. Paul opened with the explanation that Mr. Fowl had suffered a significant loss of face, and loss of finance in the Supreme Court. It had cost him a lot of money and now he wanted revenge.

More importantly, his client (myself) was fully prepared to meet all the terms of the AVO and abide by them, however we wanted the matter lifted from the record because Mr. Wallace may well want to go into public service and such a conviction could play against him in such circumstances.

The Magistrate laughed, saying all he asked for was an opening, not the substance of his court appearance, but agreed it was best to cut to the chase. He pointed out that he was obliged to put Mr. Fowl on the stand to hear why he wished the court order maintained, or if he wished to let it go. So up goes Doogle, and now he has to say why he wants to maintain the AVO against me.

Well, poor old Doogle really did not know what to say. It wasn't what he had expected at all, and the expensive barrister he had with him offered no support what-so-ever.

Paul saw the advantage and jumped up before Doogle could speak and added "We are prepared to not pursue costs if the matter is simply dropped, your Honour."

Doogle was even more lost for words, so the judge had to prompt him. "Mr Fowl, you need to tell us WHY you wish this matter to be maintained, especially since, in Mr Smart's opening dialogue, he indicated that his client was prepared to give an undertaking that the restrictions from the AVO would still be obeyed."

Doogle did not know what to say. He knew it was looking bad for him, and the process had not even started yet. He had imagined, I am sure, another drag down fight to the death. He finally stammered his reason for maintaining the order! "Well: He MOWS. He MOWS outside his front gate!"

Now to the uninitiated this utterly absurd comment seemed completely insane, and accordingly the judge directed Doogle to speak with his barrister, strongly indicating that the offer of no costs may well be reconsidered if this matter was to be dragged on any longer. Sure enough, within 10 minutes he had collapsed and the entire business was dismissed.

Now, this is worthy of further understanding. What Doogle was REALLY trying to say with the mowing argument was that I had crossed the most sacred line any Fowl had even known. You see, in Fowl Language what you mowed, you owned. Because their entire property had no distinct boundaries each Fowl defined what was "his" according to the area they maintained. If you mowed it, you were telling the others "This is mine!"

Now it seemed to him that a Judge of the Courts had determined that his entire basis for ownership was nonsense. It deeply affected him, that a judge could not grasp this deep, sacred principle that had ruled his entire existence. Doogle had done extensive mowing to this point, but I noted a rather curious and strange thing occurred after this case was closed.

He started mowing erratically. Zigzag patterns appeared in random sequence. Tufts of grass were left in the middle of the field, and areas once mowed were ignored. Things became murky, disjointed and entirely random. Then an even stranger habit began: the Stone Stacking.

Doogle moved from mowing as a rational for ownership and started stacking stones to mark territory.

He started to be referred to as Stone Stacker Doogle. This alone has made the lad a laughing stock beyond imagination, but of course, no one said so to his face. In true Boringbar form, all gossip and whispers are done behind the back. They are sharpened up, honed to a fine point of sarcasm, and then planted firmly between the shoulder blades when you are not looking.

Yet I am the first to admit, they were impressive stacks of stone. One was spectacular! It was based on a particularly large boulder that had rested for years on the Crown Road near his dead parents house. This monument was stacked with the most extraordinary array of stone sculpture of the Doogle variety that you have ever seen. Small rocks counter pinned large ones, rocks on their edge balanced with other rocks on their edge. It was sheer art.

I guess that perhaps I should not have done it, but by now the way was clear to upgrade the road, and I had the dozers and excavators on site to start the clearing. I asked that the excavator driver collect the large "stacking" rock, now technically an obstruction on the road, and put it outside my front door.

After that, I made sure I stacked a small pile of stones upon it to announce to Doogle that this was MINE.

I would wake on the odd morning to find the stones removed and scattered and once I discovered the removed rocks carefully placed neatly in an upturned hat! I guess he wanted to make sure I did not think it was the wind at work.

Poor Doogle: He had lost the Rock of Ages, so what does he do? Easy! He takes his tractor into the bush and finds himself another stone, and this time makes sure it is placed just outside the road boundary. (In case I tried to sneak up and steal it, I guess.)

In the three years I have been away from Boringbar these stones stacks have multiplied to an insane degree. They are now all over the Fowl property, in every nook and cranny, on every ridge, at every boundary. Of course, it is Doogle way of saying "It's all MINE!"

What can you do? The poor lad really has gone for the long trip up his own orifice, with the analogy of being stuck up there at the end of the valley. He is now officially registered on the disability pension, even though he is 6'4" and healthy as a horse. No one knows how he managed that one, but put yourself in his shoes. No female relationship, ever. No friends beside your sisters, and they are not friends but co-conspirators. No one wants to know you. No one ever visits you except for the odd equally looney loser.

That was when I discovered another curious fact about our dear enemy-come-neighbour. A woman was looking for the drug dealing house at the "other" end of the valley, and happened to call by Doogle's house asking for some smoke, thinking it was the right place.

The woman was a friend of Spanner Shadbolt, another neighbour, and she told him that Doogle did in fact have a foil or three for sale, and she bought some off him. However, it was hydro, not bush weed. Given this, and given the fact that Doogle had set the Police onto Spanner for allegedly growing 50 plants on the Fowl Property, thus causing him a whole lot of grief: Well, Spanner had Doogle followed.

The results were curious. First the lad took off to a local beach and, taking all his clothes off, he started waving his willy around all over the place to all who had the sad benefit of this vision. He went DANCING naked along the sand, can you believe? His little dogs were yapping away, loving the sun and surf, and Doogle danced along with them is his birthday suit. Then it got interesting. He put on his clothes, got in the shit heap he calls a car, and carried on to a warehouse. This turns out to be his very own private hooch factory.

I suspect we may have found the source of Doogles never ending supply of funds for legal cases. As I said, I think I was just about the only person not growing a plant or two to pay the rates, but it seems that dear Doogle was getting somewhat more adventurous and ambitious than just paying a few bills. He had become a drug dealer.

This is not exactly an uncommon occupation in Boringbar. With the tourist markets of Bling Bling just down the road, there was an insatiable demand for good weed with virtually no risk because of the extraordinary lack of policing. If you kept things low key there was almost no chance of being caught. And even then, if you are picked up, just give the cops a foil or four and you generally can walk away free.

I don't think any police officer at the Bling Bling station ever quite grasped the irony of them drinking and smoking away at the shop, then booking people for exactly the same crimes. Or maybe they did and didn't give a shit. I suspect they just enjoyed the fringe benefits without too much brain power beyond the good fortune of working in Bling Bling.

IRONY

I always remember the term "Irony" because of the way it popped into my head. I was barely 8 years old and about to get the cane for not doing my religious homework at my private Catholic school. Getting the cane for not doing your religious homework? Sure, NOW it seems obvious that this is crazy, but I was just a kid. Even so, a WORD pops into my head, just as the good Brother is raising his cane to strike.

And what was this word that popped into my thoughts? Irony. I naturally enough asked the Brother as he raised the cane to strike me, "Excuse me Brother, but what does IRONY mean?"

I remember well his response. The good Brother caned me even harder, saying through his red, pinched face "Irony, I will show you bloody irony!" I think he may have been born in Boringbar.

The one thing I realised then and there is that people in power, people with authority, and people with a vested interest in controlling you: These people just do not appreciate humour that appears to ridicule them. Thus, many names are changed in this book to protect me from the guilty.

Poor Doogle. He so much wanted to control everything around him. Yet, because of his abject paranoia all he succeeded in doing was to create a sad life that contained absolutely no joy of living. He was tighter than a nun's butt, as they say, and twice as lonely. His strange form of self-interest had led him into the impossible situation where he was slowly, and certainly, destroying himself.

I did have the odd person call me up, and ask if it would be OK to kill him. I always said no, because for one, why ask MY permission? But the real reason was because I knew the cruellest fate he could suffer would be a long life.

MR MUM

There are some people who have an irrepressible urge to have a great time, and they just love to share it. One such Soul was Mr Mum.

Mr Mum was the drug baron's drug baron. He had the million dollar house, the million dollar property and a fine network of agents throughout the town. He was one of the five main growers in the district. What is more, he was an entirely decent fellow. He had helped me place the Tulip Oak floor onto the joists when I started building. He had a truck with a crane, and for a few dollars he agreed to come and lift the sections of floor I had collected some years before from a house that was being demolished. We lifted them up, and relocated them on the bearers. This created the floor of my future home.

Everything in the Boringbar house was recycled. I would find a house that was coming down, and negotiate with the demolisher to pick up what was left when he was finished. In the case of the floor, it was still in situ, so I paid for a forklift to move it onto a truck (using the perennial currency of the district, a carton of beer) and the man brought his machine down the road. We lifted the floor in four sections, directly off the bearers and onto a friends truck. He subsequently dropped it off at the property.

The floor had been under a tarp for 2 years while I gathered materials for the job, and finally the stumps were in. So, with the bearers levelled and everything aligned, the floor went down. It fitted perfectly. I paid Mr Mum his carton of beer and a little cash, and we all went our separate ways. I had no idea of his business at that point, but found him very agreeable so one day I decided, on impulse, to pay him a visit.

Well, wasn't I surprised!

The Mr Mum I met there was like a different person. He was veiled and guarded, asking what exactly it was that I might want. Now, I have lived long enough around people to know that when a person's nature appears to change radically, there is something causing it. So I said a pleasant goodbye, suggesting that it was probably not a good time to visit, and made my way to see some other friends who lived just up the way from him.

It was there that I had the network explained. Mr Mum was the local Drug Baron, and was the one who effectively supplied everyone in the district with a living. He never sold direct to the public, but had a series of "safe houses" which were used in rotation to sell to people who called by.

No one house was the focus for anything, and for all the world it looked like people paying a visit to friends in the country. These friends just happened to have a large supply of ounces and foils.

The way it worked was brilliant. Everyone in the end sale house was a farmer. No one in the network paid up front for anything. They had a chain of customers who would call ahead talking about what fruit they wanted to buy, and how many kilos they might want. Of course, they wanted organically grown. The farmer then trotted up to Mr Mum and withdrew from the locked shed (which was called the Smoke Bank) the allotted requirement for that day's projected sales. The buyers arrived, cash in hand for their "Fruit and Veg" and left with the goods. The farmer went back to the Smoke Bank, and deposited the cash into an old night safe.

Now the Smoke Bank itself was never approached directly by Mr Mum. He had a tunnel from his own property which he used to move the goods in, and later to take the money out. Thus he could never be photographed receiving money or trading drugs. It was enormously profitable, and at the end of every years trading Mr Mum put on a fabulous party to which all customers and clients were invited.

The fireworks were magnificent, and a good time was had by all.

This continued for many years, and I presume some arrangement had been made with the local constabulary because it appeared that Mr Mum was impregnable. Then things took a turn for the worse. Mr Mum was brought up on charges by the local "D's" for cultivating 49 plants.

Now: In the language of the valley, this was a simple message. This was one plant short of a Federal offence and what it meant was that the protection money you were paying had become inadequate. The locals were calling out for more, and you had better provide it. I presume a deal was struck, because all he received was a smack on the wrist and a $5000 fine. Considering there were over 200 plants growing at that point, that works out to a cost of $25 a plant.

Now, when you realise that each plant would make up to $5000 profit you may well understand that this fine was certainly no deterrent.

Now was it intended to be. It was just a signal to improve relations and cash flow. Business as usual was the message, and the next raid on the town and district found Mr Mum and the other four main Drug Lords sipping coffee at the local coffee shop. Their properties were not even flown over by the helicopter. However, things were soon to change in a curious way.

Do you remember when I was talking about Keith Knight earlier on? Josiah had decided to move up the hill to camp in his yard, behind his abandoned house that sat in the MO that was in the forest. This is a place lost in the wilderness with very restricted access, and NO access from public roads. We had discovered a pair of hippies up there. They were obviously growing hooch in an attempt to improve their lives and bank balance. Well, who cares. But these were odd people, weird vibe folk, and soon after things started going wrong with equipment around the farm.

No one liked them, in particular Josiah the Monk.

One day he saw them walking in the forest, looking furtive, so the Monk took action! He chased them off from where he was camping by taking up a large scythe, holding it over his head and uttering a primal scream of "Killllll kiiillllll!" while looking directly at the young would-be drug lords.

This put them in rather a panic, and later when Josiah accidentally starting burning down one of the houses they were in, they got extremely upset and just plain creepy.

They were becoming a real nuisance, so I called up one of the main police stations and explained what was happening up there. The next raid in the district encompassed the old abandoned MO and this was the first time I met the REAL drug cops. These are not the "nice polite type" you see in police stations. Three 4 wheel drives pummelled through the property unannounced one day, and roared up the hill.

I had no idea who it was, and later, I caught up with one of them, and waved them over. Looking at me were four face that were at the least hard, at the worst positively criminal. All were bald, all were mean. All looked like mercenaries, and as they slowed down, one of them waved a Federal Police badge at me.

I said "You know what, you went through my property without a warrant, without a request, and it was clearly to make your way up to the properties behind searching for drugs. You know that if I were called into a court, and your actions were made clear, any arrests you have made would be put into question?" The look I got was, shall we say, threatening.

"However," I continued "I am going to do no such thing and indeed I warmly invite you to call any time, unannounced, and look where ever you will, OK?" They just grunted at the snivelling civilian in front of them, put the foot down, and were gone. But I got the message. There were more than the local lads in town. These guys were Federal Police. and very obviously ex-army. Probably ex-SAS.

A year later I am chatting to Mr Mum in town. He was always very friendly away from his property, and returned to being jovial as it appeared I had gotten the message. His personal place was a No Go zone. We were once again getting on quite well. We chatted about this and that, about property values, about what I hoped to get for my place if it sold. It was all very amiable. This is when he pointed out that he was leaving the valley.

He was moving to larger acreage further out, I knew why, of course. Needless to say, I wrote down his new number, promising to call if I were ever out in that direction. He said he was intending to move away from Boringbar in the next month or so.

Now I really have no idea if it was the fact that his leaving would prove a loss of revenue to the local officers, or if it was the new drug squad fellows I saw up behind my place, or if it was the freaks that had been caught rattling the cage that were behind the story, but only weeks after our chance meeting poor Mr Mum was behind bars.

He had been busted with 200 plants under cultivation. Here is where the hard truth becomes apparent. When you are arrested and found guilty for major dealing such as this, everything you own is repossessed by the Government and sold at auction.

The million dollar house and property was gone, the new property was gone, the freedom was gone, the car was gone. Government advertises that this is a deterrent, but the truth is that for the government it is simply PROFITABLE to do business this way. You tell me what is worse, the drug dealer selling dope or the theft of his property by the State?

However, repossession of property is but one of the raft of new laws that have been brought in to control people and to raise revenue.

In the last decade, every single year that has passed the NSW Government has created approximately 10% of new law in that year. That is 10%, added to 10% added to 10%! Putting this into perspective, if you had a 1000 laws in 1995, you had 1100 in 1996, 1210 in 1997, 1331 in 1998, 1464 in 1999, 1610 in 2000, 1771 in 2001, 1948 in 2002, 2142 in 2003, 2356 in 2004 and come 2005 you will have 2591 laws … Or in other words 1591 new laws in ten years. That is an increase of law by 150%. Come back in another ten years and the increase in the number of laws will extrapolate to over 22000 new laws. That is an increase of 22 times the otherwise perfectly workable level of law that existed only 20 years earlier.

How can anyone even remotely hope to not do anything that will not in some way breach some law somewhere? It is becoming, nay it is already, ridiculous. Soon I will need to fill in a form to scratch my butt.

I do not blame people for becoming outlaws. In an ever increasing weight of law, only the paper shufflers seem to be able to rise to the top. It is becoming almost a civic duty to be an outlaw! We already have entire governments breaking international law and invading countries on the pretext of weapons of mass destruction, yes? In truth I do believe that World War Three has already begun: It is the war of the government against its people.

How did the Law help me? I was living next door to a terrorist, but was there a single legal recourse I could follow up to safeguard myself? Was there a single law that would protect me against a creature who knowingly and continuously attacked me in both the courts and threatened me by cutting power cords, cutting water supply, and even daft things like throwing rocks onto the roof of my home? With all of these new laws, my own basic rights were not being enhanced, they were being submerged.

Mr Mum was a decent fellow. He grew organic Marijuana, and made a healthy profit from the business BECAUSE it was against the law. However, he was a person with standards and his own ethics. He was not dealing Ice, or Smack, or GBH or Fantasy but old fashioned smoke. What is more he worked hard making his business profitable and efficient. It is just unfair, blatantly and deeply unfair that pieces of law can be enacted that take away his life's work.

The laws not only imprisoned him (we all know that this is part of the game) but they also bankrupted him.

He comes out of prison in a decade, and he will come out a pauper. Or so it would seem. What REALLY happened is that Mr Mum had arranged through his solicitors to pay someone somewhere the sum of Five Million Dollars, and was out of jail within the year. Crime must actually pay, when you think of it.

I think you could say it was the best justice money could buy.

On the other hand, I was trying my best to make it through with honest effort, and going nowhere. Now the NSW Government has enacted fire legislation that makes my property not only far more difficult to sell, it reduces its value. I broke no law, committed no crime, yet everything is being taken away from me as well.

Fortunately I am saved form insanity by understanding that it IS insanity. Life gives us warnings, and Mr Mum surely got his warning. I was warned before I purchased Boringbar about my mad neighbour, but we read the signs in the way we read them, and we always think we can beat the odds. I have simple proof of this fact, look at how many people buy lottery tickets, play the pokies, and bet on horses.

Life is a lottery, and you hedge the bets as best as you can, but in the end when you finally discover that you are looking down the barrel of a gun the only common sense thing to do is to DUCK.

Quack quack quack.

LOGICAL FALLACIES

"Out of the Frying Pan, Into the Fire" **Plato**

L OGICAL FALLACIES: When the same facts that add up differently for different people, clearly there is an indication that the logic being used is questionable. In Ancient Greece, the concepts of logic were demonstrated as the basis for rational decision making, and the concepts of illogic were also defined. This comes down to us as the Logical Fallacies.

As a race, we are supposed to be governed by the principles of logic and reason. Obviously, there was an exclusion if you lived in Boringbar.

When the final curtain is drawn on my life, I am sure I will see all the many occasions where I misread the opportunity, put the wrong foot forward, and made mistakes. Yet, in the final measure, what really counts is that we can earnestly look into the past and say that, at least, we did our best.

At one time I would have earnestly believed I could have said that, but now I see how belief itself is something that is forever changing. Some things that I believed were completely earnest have turned out to be a lie. Other things I believed true now simply appear ridiculous.

For example: At one point, I firmly believed that I not only had to have honey (rather than sugar) in my coffee, but that it was ALSO very important to add the honey AFTER the milk. Why? Well I had read somewhere that it was less acidic.

I am drinking a strong acid bath of double strength cappuccino and I am worrying about honey being slightly less acidic? No wonder 100 different waitresses all looked at me oddly, but hey! Give the customer what they want.

If the customer wants honey after the milk, fine. I now understand that it was a stupid belief, but at the time I BELIEVED it was right, and that belief helped me cope with my problems. So the paradox of the Logical Fallacy is that it is OK if it helps you get through the night, but eventually it must be addressed if sanity and commonsense will prevail.

I have finally come to understand why the first step of education with the Pythagoreans was to re-organized the muddy thinking of their students. Giving people a sense of proportional logic, giving people a set of measures, this helps FOCUS. Focus helps ATTAINMENT. It's a good thing, because it helps people build their lives on solid ground, and not the sand of opinion and belief.

The process is really one where poor foundations are washed away, to hopefully expose the rocks of reality as your new foundation stones. These practices and measures are still with us today. The terms we use have changed since those times, but the substance of what was taught remains with us today in a process called "The Logical Fallacies".

If schools would just go back to teaching the logical fallacies, so many of societies problems would vanish. Instead the curriculum often teaches what prove to effectively be lies, or things that are in an almost direct opposition to truth. Instead of teaching people what is logical, our schools currently teach student that the fallacies are truths, and they do this under the guise of politically correct thinking.

Logical Fallacies have been up on the net for all to see for years. When you understand these, it is usually pretty clear that we have all been guilty of practicing quite a few of these "falsehoods". Sad but true. Let's briefly go over them and with any luck you will see where they are inside you. We will make far more sense of the situation at Boringbar by using these as a study mirror. This is my rearranged "list" of Logical Fallacies downloaded from the web..

The LOGICAL FALLACIES:

Fallacies (falsehoods) that result from errors in induction

Dicto Simpliciter or Overstatement: An unqualified generalization. "The weather is never any good around here"

Hasty Generalization: Stating a conclusion based on too little evidence or based on ignoring some evidence. "You can't grow bananas on that slope, no one ever has and no on ever will."

Stereotyping: Giving the same characteristics to everyone in a group (related to overstatement and hasty generalization). "You just can't trust any mechanics around here."

Forced hypothesis: Reaching a conclusion that is not supported by the evidence or a conclusion that is more complicated than necessary. "Michael and Doogle live next door to each other, so they should be really good friends."

Non sequitur: From Latin, meaning "it does not follow"; this refers specifically to conclusions which are not logically derived from the reasoning that precedes them. "My Mother got sick, and passed away soon after he moved in next door. Therefore, he killed her."

Slippery slope: An argument in which we assert that X should not happen because it will inevitably be followed by consequences Y. (Y plus X = Z with Z being something which is terrible) "We should not allow this subdivision to go ahead, because once you get one, you get another, and soon the whole valley will be chopped up."

False dilemma: An argument asserting that only two (or a limited number of) options exist when there are actually more. "You are either a Mooball drinker, or you are a traitor." "I am a Ford Man, and everyone else is a fool."

False analogy: An argument based on a comparison of two things when the differences between the two are too great. "Everyone who has ever suffered a serious illness has breathed air, therefore it is clear there is something it the air that kills you." "I bought a Fiat tractor and had no end of trouble with it. I reckon it is the terrain around here, they were not built for it."

Post hoc: From the Latin "after this, therefore because of it," this means simply assigning a cause-effect relationship where none exists or where it is difficult to prove there is a cause-effect relation. "When they starting laying off people at the cane mill, the problems really got underway with the kids at the local school. That cane mill is causing the bad grades."

Fallacies that result from ignoring the issue:

Begging the question: To assume that part or all of your argument will be accepted as true without support. "The council should not subsidise development of alternative timber plantations because the existing camphor supplies are more than enough." "The report by the anti-corruption committee cleared the Tweed Council of wrong doing which proves how corrupt they are."

Red herring: To introduce an irrelevant side-issue and divert attention from the topic at hand. "There is no way that Doogle Fowl should be elected Mayor because it has been proven he scammed the government with his back injury."

Straw man: To accuse your opponents of holding erroneous or ridiculous view or attitudes and attacking those instead of attacking their arguments. "This damn developer is a con who wants to knock down the forest just to make himself some money."

Ad hominem: From the Latin meaning "to or towards the person." This is the strategy of attacking the proponent of an argument rather than the argument itself. "I fully expect that you would support that notion, because you have already demonstrated clearly that you are an idiot.

A special form of Ad Hominem arguments occur when someone attacks an argument by attacking the speaker before he or she speaks. It is called **"Poisoning the Well"**. "Jane Fonda is going to speak tonight about how we ought to give more to help Tsunami victims. Don't forget; this is the same Jane

Fonda that visited Hanoi and criticized the war when our G.I.'s. were dying in Vietnam. We should not listen to her."

Argument ad Miseriocordiam: "Argument to Pity": An emotional appeal to a logical issue. While pathos generally works to reinforce a reader's moral sense, if a writer relies on an appeal to emotion only to accept a conclusion, it is a fallacy. " I know I should not have said or done this thing, but I could not help it, I was sick with worry about what people would think of me if I failed."

Common practice: Sometimes called "bandwagon" fallacy. This is to argue that an action should be taken or an idea accepted because everyone is doing it. "Yeah … It's fine to clear that patch and put up a shed. Old Joe did the same last year and no one worried about him."

Argument ad populum: from the Latin "to the people"; appealing to the beliefs of the multitudes. "Real farmers believe in the need for poisons and rat baits." "It was good enough for my Daddy, so it's good enough for me." (A form of this called "snob appeal" is often used in advertising: "Holden is the choice of intelligent discerning Australian."; "Caring mothers choose Pampers."

Argumentum ad Baculum: Appeal to Force, bullying, or the "Might-Makes-Right" Fallacy. This argument uses force, the threat of force, or some other unpleasant backlash to make the audience accept a conclusion. It commonly appears as a last resort when evidence or rational arguments fail to convince (Most of us have mothers and fathers who used it with us.)

A local newspaper used to publish articles about development in the area being negative capitalism gone mad. However, their main advertising revenue came from the local estate agents. The estate agents got together, and advised the newspaper that there would be no more advertising while such articles continued to run. The articles stopped.

I can safely say that I have heard every single false argument listed here presented in one form or another as an absolute truth during my time at

Boringbar. What is most worrying is that virtually ALL decisions handed down by the local council are wrapped up in some way with one of more of these Logical Fallacies.

In the many solicitors letters between myself and the Fowls, I read again and again how their solicitors employed, and apparently believed, some of the most outrageous logical fallacies, yet even when this was pointed out in black and white, they refused to recognise or correct them.

Now here is the rub, the true irony of the matter: Because I had consciously worked for many years to keep my mind trained on what was clear and logical, and because I lived in an area where logical fallacies were the norm, when I put forward my arguments in clear language, no one could understand them.

When you twist up the logic in your head, you twist up communication. What this creates is a curious situation where you start to believe that only the people who share your logical fallacy can understand you.

I can put it a different way. My brother and his wife are avowed Catholics. When my Sister in Law had her seventh child, I asked her "Do you think this might be the last child?" What I was really asking was "Will you use contraception now?" yet what she heard was "Will you stop having Sex now?"

Her logical fallacy was her belief that whatever the Pope said was right, was right. It was an inversion of a Post Hoc fallacy: of believing infallibility exists in an imperfect world. No matter your religion, race or belief: Whatever aspect of life you look at, if you can apply the principles of pure logic to it, you will soon start to see the shaky ground on which most people's arguments are built.

The reason why I mention this is that I was of the firm belief prior my arrival at Boringbar that the world should, and could, be aligned along the principles of logic. I was of the belief that the courts were based on logic and that our laws were, broadly speaking, logical. And here is the core, the very reason for all my problems and concerns. People are NOT logical.

The simple truth is that the human experience of life is NOT logical. But it goes further, because the chain of events that follow on from people living in illogical patterns is that they think wrongly.

I think, therefore I am. If you think WRONG, what you ARE becomes wrong. Once any of these "false" logics become accepted as correct within the individual, everything becomes coloured by the lie. The dire reality of life is that once falsehood is accepted as truth, it becomes your truth.

And the curious consequence of this is that, as an individual, we will be misunderstood. This is a given in a confused world. Whether we are right or wrong is irrelevant, the truth is that, either way, we will be misunderstood.

You know this. Most of us do things that are really quite illogical. So often our actions are completely absurd, and looking back we realise that it makes little sense. What we do, and how we act often make no sense. For example: Because he meets a woman with nice breasts, a man may well destroy his marriage. He doesn't mean to, and it makes no sense to do it, but something in his emotions takes control, and he decides he prefers that woman to his wife.

.Even if his marriage survives, his wife hates him because he made that choice. Her pride can thus ruin what was left of the marriage, and financial chaos ensues. It is a Logical Fallacy to imagine our pride is more important than our life. Because our pride is important to us, we destroy our lives. Why? Because our passions rule us. Here I came to understand something very basic:

Our passions are NOT logical. If they were, they would not be passions.

Buddha cried out that we needed to relieve ourselves of our desires, and that this would lead to the faultless life. Yet the need to relieve ourselves of desire is a desire unto itself, thus we are destined for a state of imperfection.

When I finally grasped that the Fowls were not logical in their behaviour over the road and sheds, and nor were they ever going to be logical, then the tension inside myself eased. When I finally accepted that no matter what I did or didn't do, Doogle would hate me, then it ceased to bother me.

Why did he hate me? His passions dictated his actions. In the simplest of terms, I had bought the land "he" wanted and it was my fault.

The upshot of all this was that I learned to let go of a belief that people would act logically and/or act in their own interest. When we analyse what people BELIEVE is right and logical, it is often based on what they imagine will help them to survive. It is really some sort of Logical Fallacy that is running them, often to the point of blindness. I found release from the pain of seeking common sense and logic as an outcome by accepting that Doogle was mad. A step further, and I came to understand that his insanity was his reality. I can only presume that to HIM, my reality was evil, wicked and dangerous.

As mentioned earlier, I was warned about this by a magistrate many years earlier. I was in court trying to deal a fellow who had rammed my motor bike from the rear with his car, and absconded. There were some strange demands being made by the man, and I said "Your Honour, all I am looking for is common sense …" The Magistrate looked up over his glasses and said "If common sense were the issue, Mr. Wallace, no one would ever be here."

I have come, grudgingly, to realise this was a perfect truth. Specifically when it comes to dysfunctional situations: If common sense were the issue, no one would ever be here.

Remember the Dictum: Dysfunction has Five Principles:
1. **Low-heeled, two-faced bitchery that holds pretence as the ultimate sacrifice.**

2. **High notions of grandeur sloshing about in the sloth of human desires.**

3. **Badly repaired emotions sinking in an endless ocean of compromise.**

4. **Flotsam and Jetsam pretending to be Titanic's before the Iceberg**

5. **Paranoia of the fear we are paranoid of our fear**

The Fowls, Boringbar, most people I knew in fact, all shared at least two or more of the afore-mentioned Logical Fallacies, and not just as an ASPECT of their persona, but as the BASIS for their existence.

I was sincerely surprised when I realised this, and everything changed as a result. Now the blinkers were off, I began to see how my ex-wife, my brother's wife, the people I knew, they also shared these attributes. It is oddly disappointing when it starts to appear that you seem to be the only person seeing anything clearly.

The obvious here is that I, too, had the potential of living in a Logical Fallacy. Everything I believed was logical may well have been based around a false internal argument. And I cannot argue to the contrary, other than to say that at least I was aware of the possibility.

I suppose I had wanted SOMEONE to be free of this curse. However, the next stage of the journey, the stage where madness came and stayed at my house, was to prove the most painful. And yet oddly enough, this was also the most fruitful period of all.

Part Four

Love, Lust, Madness and Mayhem

"Whosoever is delighted in solitude, is either a wild beast or a god." **Plato**

Sometimes change comes into your life quietly, like a cat in the night, and at other times it is like a tornado hits. Miss Buzz was a tornado who walked in like a cat on silent feet. You got buffeted in one direction while at the same time she was rubbing up against your leg, purring. It has a name: Multiple Personality Disorder.

The fact is my whole life was disorder at that point. I had pieces of me all over the place. My consciousness was invested with a thought about that person from my past, a tool in that shed over there or a project on the computer that I would get to one day. I had no idea about mothering, though I was in a position of being father and mother, and as a result my little guy was starting to get out of hand with a deep and silent resistance.

Later I was to see how he was being tugged by his mother, and how he was essentially depressed and saw no way out. I was going the same way, and between being a father, raising a son, paying mortgages and all the other external issues, the house I had so proudly built had turned into a clothes basket. Stuff was everywhere except where it should be.

It is hard to imagine how badly I let things slip, but I promise you, it happens. It was clean, but all over the shop. But, this beautiful woman who looked 16 turns up. She is really in her 30's and basically just wants everything clean and tidy, and once organised, onto sex and sex and then sex some more!

Well, after several years of deprivation I was more than happy to oblige.

Ben, the little bugger was miffed. He had Dad under his thumb, and now this was getting shook up. Miss Buzz knew exactly where this particular little ten year old was at, because she had raised one just like it. The war of household supremacy had started, and the games he played are worthy of an entire book. But let us stop and quickly go back to the beginning, so that the story can unfold as it should.

I have to say, there is always something painful about Love. But don't let me put you off! It is just that when the tides turn from solitude to sharing, that the jumble of things and unfinished conclusions that have always been put under the rug invariably turn up, and are often well-dressed and expecting to be noticed. Old girlfriends, who had shown no interest in years, start wanting to call by, or write, or whatever. How did they know?

It would be wonderful if the wonder of the first embrace, the first kiss and everything else nice and sweet remained, but we are seasonal creatures. Our moods are like the coming and going of the tides. A faithful dog is my model of perfection. He bays at the moon, gets a pat, eats dinner, and loves you regardless of what you do. But people, no matter how much you care for them, will change. Mostly, with a change of mood, they will forget to remain appreciative of the simple things.

We humans usually have far too many thoughts about everything to remember the simplicity of kindness and affection. We seem to continually create hurdles inside and outside that we have to jump. I guess if nothing else it gets us emotionally more fit.

The Arrival of Miss Buzz

A new relationship is like a new pair of shoes. You have to walk around in it for a while to find out if it's really comfortable!   Susan Gale

There are moments, pivotal points in everyone's life where decisions are made that affect the course of your destiny. I met Miss Buzz at a party held by the wonderfully hedonistic Professor Anarchy. A gathering of assorted rascals, losers, winners, grinners, vixens and voxens (women who once were vixens) had assembled. A great announcement was made, and some loser got up to make a large announcement about a small rock. It was a very ordinary rock, something so worthless that not even Mad Doogle would have selected it for his standing stones. But we were told otherwise!

The Loser declared that this was a sacred rock, one which he had taken from Professor Anarchy's garden some years ago, and kept with him while he travelled the country, always dreaming of his return to this sacred place. Finally he was here, and with great flourish and suitable ambient applause, the rock was placed back in the garden. I cannot say that it made much of a difference to the garden, but obviously it had made a difference to our orator.

I muttered to myself, "Some people can succeed with inanity so well that they convince themselves it is important."

She was sitting beside me at that point, an attractive girl with a lovely smile. Earlier I had tried my charm, my wit and my wiles on her, but she seemed indelibly resistant to all forms of male embroidery. I had mentioned to the two gay men, who were on the porch with me at that time, and who were watching my efforts with amusement, "Don't think I did so well there, hey?"

One thing few people realise about gay men, often they are gay BECAUSE they understand women. They knew exactly what the girl was up to, and basically said "You got no chance sunshine" Yet here she was, a mere 40 minutes later, smiling at me. Perhaps something about the comment about the rock-man loser made her laugh? I asked if she wanted a drink, and got up to see what was about. Cordial seemed the best option, being better than water and not as cantankerous as cheap wine. I brought it back, and she seemed puzzled "You got CORDIAL?" she quizzed.

"You don't like it? I can get you water if you prefer?" I said. "No," she answered, "I really like cordial, but no one ever gets someone cordial. What got into your mind that I would want cordial?"

Now, dear reader, I find it never pays to tell a pretty woman who finds your action favourable that you actually didn't think about WHY you did a thing she seems to like. The truth of me arriving with cordial was simply that "it seemed a good idea at the time" but I know enough to never say these words to a woman. Why?

Because in their mind, ANYTHING could be a good idea at the time. These are not STABLE words, they are dangerous, "could be anything the next time I see him" words. So I stepped over the obstacle saying "You just seemed like the sort of person who liked cordial. In fact, I do as well."

Well, all my flattering and battering earlier had scored nothing, but this odd little comment brought forth a huge smile. Then someone said "Hey, Michael plays guitar! Get him to play us some music."

In retrospect I suppose it was meant to be, she was a singer, and she adored someone who could perform in public because at heart, under the hard-nosed exterior, she was very shy. But more than this, she really looked at what I was playing, she really listened. It seemed to me that she CARED about music.

This impressed me deeply at the time, because it is a rare thing indeed. I had this deep sense that I had to know this woman better. This is why, when she said she needed to go down to the shop to get some smokes, that I said I would be happy to drive her. Now, as a rule I can't stand people who smoke, but at this point all my ideals were tossed aside. You know why.

I drove her down to the shop, and as she got out of the car I felt I had to say something, but what? All that came was, "I want to go out with you."

"Where?" she asked, not really understanding what I was saying.

"Any where you like. There's a party at some friends this afternoon, but first I have to go show some people the place I am selling right now. But you can come along if you want."

"Sure"

That was it. All my attempts to charm her failed, but a simple "let's do something interesting" worked.

So we went back to the Professors, packed up her bag, and drove down to Boringbar. I showed people the property, we then went to the party, where I rather cleverly got the girl half-drunk on Chartreuse. Long story short: She pretty well moved in right away.

It was instant chemistry, a total high, a drug of ultimate choice. I was not to be fully aware of the side effects of this drug for a few months, such was the oblivion of common sense that our shared euphoria created.

Now to be fair, I did sense there was something wrong. I really did try to find her a flat away from where I lived because some part of me sensed trouble. But her enthusiasm for my bed somehow overcame my instinctual objections.

Not so with the ex-wife. When she saw Miss Buzz for the first time, she looked clearly put out. Buzz pulled me aside and whispered, "Have I come between something here, because if I have I don't want to." I assured her that the divorce was now five years old, and there was nothing to come between.

I then reminded her about something we rather forgot to note in the heat of passion the night before. My ex-wife was actually down stairs on her bed near Ben's room when we arrived home, and there was no doubt she heard us having it off through most of the night. And into the morning. "Oh!" she said "That's right, she might be a little miffed."

A little miffed? I was not to understand what an understatement this was for a number of years. The ex-wife was infuriated, incensed and abhorred the very breath Miss Buzz breathed. Not that she showed it, she never showed such emotions, but you could feel it and smell it like the burning of witches in the distance. As she was leaving, and I was not to know it would be the last time she would every stay over, my ex-wife gave me another forced hug, such as the type I was entirely used to, but then a surprise.

Looking towards Miss Buzz, she went over and pulled her in close and hugged her warmly, too warmly. EXTREMELY warmly, with her pelvis thrust forward. Buzz looked up and mouthed over her shoulder "Is she Gay?"

I did not fully grasp right at that moment how large a cat had just been put amongst the pigeons. Unfortunately for the ex-wife (who had always won against the little helpless birds that had arrived in my life prior to this) in this particular school yard fight she had met a right little tiger. It turned out that my dear, sweet, 16 year old looking Miss Buzz had fangs you could not believe. I know NOW, believe me I know. I still bear the scars on heart, mind and soul.

But not then. That was the thing with Miss Buzz. She looked cute, innocent, light and breezy, and on one level she was. Her blue eyes had an edge to them, however, that when fired up could turn ice to stone, then melt it.

People were offended, at first , when I turned up with what they thought was a teenager. A lot of women I had known grew instantly weird, thinking I was some sort of cradle snatcher. Truth is, come the next year Miss Buzz would be a grandmother, and her fully grown-up daughter lived just down the way. However, when Miss Buzz bounced into rooms, smiled her magical smile, and laughed her amazing laugh, the hardest hearts melted. But only if they were male. They would became INCREDIBLY bitchy if they were female.

Buzz Buzzed, and she had this extraordinary ability to perceive what another woman was thinking and how she would act. This upset women, not because she saw, but because she TOLD a male. Secret Women's Business is the rule, which means it is business for women only. They instinctively knew she was betraying the clan by revealing their thoughts and feelings to a mere male. And she was! The girl was an amazing education in the female species.

I learned so many secrets. For instance, I was taught how women put out the "scent". What I had experienced with Moigle was real, they actually do put out a psychic scent to attract a male, and it is done by imagining you fully soaked in their juices, and locked into their presence. It is a subtle art of casting fishing hooks out to snag passing males. I was taught how a woman will adjust her appearance and her posture in a hundred subtle ways to attract a male she fancies who is walking by. And of course, now that I was taken by another woman, I was instantly more desirable than when I was single.

Competition is the aphrodisiac most women cannot resist. Find a beautiful girlfriend and all her friends want to compete with her in getting your attention. It's an animal thing. Show up with an ugly, plain girl, and they are not interested because they already KNOW they are sexier then that one.

As an experiment I was asked to look at a woman sipping coffee in a café'. Nothing special I thought, nice straight back, good posture. When we walked past Miss Buzz suggested we look quietly back and see how the woman was sitting now. She had visibly slumped over, and I realised how moments ago she had taken a posture to make her tits stand out more. "Never forget," Miss Buzz instructed "Boobs are the main sexual organ for a woman. They are the visible sign she displays. You may want her fanny, but she will display her breasts in a hundred different ways in order to get your attention. Some men like feet, others like legs, most like butts, but ALL men are subconsciously drawn to erect perky tits."

How did she know?

She was right. The honesty was both refreshing and disconcerting. She had the most remarkable insight into the ways of women, but when I started to find out the reasons how and the process she went through to obtained this insight, I came to understand that I was dealing with a very tortured and damaged Soul.

Miss Buzz, for all her brightness, had a very dark undercurrent that ran through the subconscious. It was a monster that had grown as her last defence from her incredibly difficult circumstances. Not only had she suffered a loveless, brutal childhood, she also had survived a ruthless, vicious husband who had stolen two of her children from her. Why? Two Reasons: Spite - to hurt the bitch who dared walk away from him, and the Second was Greed. This meant that he, the millionaire's son, could now get a Government pension. But it was mostly done for the sheer spite that the frail little sparrow he had beaten up for 9 years had dared to leave him.

Now she was had a fully fledged multiple personality disorder, and if she for a moment believed that I was looking in any other direction but hers, the self defence monster would emerge as an attacking beast. I loved her, but also learned to keep the beast at arm's length. The monster usually only woke up for a few hours a week. At most a day or two of madness would be the worst attack. Then it fell back into slumber until something jarred it awake again. The frustrating thing was that, like the alcoholic on a binge, the next day Buzz never realised what she said or did.

MPD comes in many shapes and forms. Some affected have quite mild personas emerge, while others have extreme. Some people have several "people" running at the same time. Miss Buzz had numerous personas, which seemed to some like severe mood swings, tor the worst case of PMT you could imagine. But there was a physical cause, because the abuse she suffered had created a hormonal reaction. It was condition classed as a Shock Disorder, which occurred because of the brutality she had survived. The beatings had affected her endocrine system, her pituitary gland, and finally her adrenals. These gave out unbalance hormone production for extended periods. The common term from war is "Shell Shock". But I truly believed one thing was certain, even though her monster attacked, I believed that at heart she loved me.

I had said fairly early on in the relationship, (knowing how latent insecurity and paranoia could turn a person's thoughts to abject bitterness and jealousy) "Miss Buzz, the Yo-Yo existence you are in does no one any good. Eventually you will have to decide between me, and the tapes of your past that are running in your head." In the meantime, I battened down for the ride because, despite the problems, the sex was great! It is simply remarkable what a person will put up with when they know that, at the end of the dark tunnel, there is a warm body waiting.

In the end, I guess I always knew it was a dead end. To be fair I had all sorts of warning and should not have hoped for anything better. I had rationalised that the red flags I saw were areas to avoid, and that I could negotiate my way around them. But the truth is that the red flags advertised the problems you could NOT avoid. Do not swim between the flags, people. On one level it is sad, and certainly expensive, but on the other I learned a lot, and you always pay for your education.

The unfolding of this saga is best seen through the experiences and conflicts of the people we met along the way. The first and most significant of these was a family I had known for some years, some people who had been introduced to me by Skerick and Dealer: The Streets.

The Three Day Party

Some people you meet are just different. The Streets looked normal, but they just lived in a world not inhabited by any sanity that you or I might recognise. I have mentioned Lucifer Street in passing a few times in the book, and now it is time to take a closer inspection. Boggy and Lucifer Street believed they were the new beautiful people. I could see their upwardly mobile motivation, yet at heart I had always thought they were simple and nice people. Indeed they were country folk!

They were nice family people who only liked drugs on weekends. I visited quite often because I liked them, and they were not like others. There were several points of interest in the Street household, one being the marvellous way their 12 year old could fill a dress, and over the years as she became a 16 year old who filled a dress even better I found myself saying, "If only she were older" I said it only to myself of course, and I said it fully aware the mirror quite rudely demonstrated how much older I was. But the girl was just lovely.

They seemed such a NICE family, a good family, a family family where I felt comfortable and got on with everyone. Their house was a respite, an oasis away from the madness of Bling Bling. Over the years their humble, if quite large, brick home became transformed to a Spanish hacienda with rental rooms under, and they even collected their own private Japanese slave. (whom I suspect quite fancied myself - and several other fellows - as a passport opportunity) Then it all started to change. Boggy and Lucifer bought a block near the water, and proceeded to build this HUGE mansion.

To be fair it wasn't the house that changed them. It may have accentuated things, like how a lens shifts and enlarges your focus, but what was to come must have been inside the Streets from the start. However, there IS something magnificently ego magnifying about magnificence. The new place had walls of glass, waterfall fountains, sea views, marble floors and semi circular rooms with large gaping vistas that towered over the more common place residences surrounding them. These things do stir up our latent impressions of superiority.

A house like this changes things in your perception of self, which is exactly why palaces are built by kings. Yet it was more than just the Streets' house, the entire town of Bling Bling was changing. The mindset of the village was undergoing severe yuppification. In this part of the universe money didn't just talk, it shouted. Bling Bling was coming of Age as a Yuppie Paradise. The parties were getting flashier, the money was getting greedier, the people were getting shallower, and slowly but surely the old hippie culture, with its affordable rent, was being squeezed out of existence.

The Streets certainly did their part in extinguishing the flame of hippy-dom. They were at the vanguard of change, cavorting in the new while waltzing with the old. The money making plans and the exorbitant rip-off called the tourism industry squeezed and sqooze (as Winnie the Pooh did in the rabbit hole) the upper middle class mentality of "money for gods sake" into the light of day.

Slowly the Streets had eked out a better state of equity in the growing real estate market, and things were looking good when a large cash settlement was arranged on the old house. Profit and cash expands your possibilities and so, with hot cash in the hand, this new and very reasonably priced block came available quite close to the ocean. If you went up high enough, a Sea View!

Boggy was a builder, and so a great plan was launched to build the ultimate beach house, the Big House, the Millionaire Mansion. The banks OK'ed the finance, so with both confidence and power-saw in hand Boggy went at it!

Surreal as it may sound, Lucifer was at that point also accepted to join the cast of Survivor. I know that sounds odd, because they had two children under the age of five at the time. What mother leaves her kids to go on an 8 week jaunt with the Survivor crew? Well, Lucifer does.

The kids were given to their Japanese slave girl to maintain, and off Lucifer went with a plan to win a million dollars, while Boggy built the home to contain it all. Of course, she didn't win. No, Lucifer pissed everyone off so much with her bossy ways (I had never noticed how bossy she was before that) that she was the first person evicted. But she had to stay there for the 8 weeks anyway. Contest rules forbade anyone coming home, and when they did they were not allowed to talk about it.

While she was away, her now 15 year old daughter had a birthday. I dropped over and, with a bottle of Chartreuse, her step-dad and I initiated her into her first experience of alcohol poisoning. Seriously, no, we didn't do that, she only had a sip or two to taste and looked absolutely funny trying to walk. She was a good, bright Soul in a household that was suffering increasing degrees of Dark.

This started as a quiet realisation that the external surface of the Streets was not as it seemed. There was a darkness I started to feel in there. But you could not quite put a finger on what it was. But this is how it is with the dark.

Show dark the light, and it instantly hides behind someone as their shadow. It cleverly remains forever hidden, and the bearer of the light never realises it. Shadows always lean carefully away from you. They never challenge, but give in to the light even as they oppose it, appearing to be weak, and insubstantial. But dim the light, and the shadows reach out to swallow the room.

And tell me: What is the Speed of Dark? We all talk of the speed of light, but the Dark is instantaneous. It is a powerful monster that swallows you so swiftly that you hardly know you have been eaten.

The Dark was moving in to the Street Household. I turned up to visit on the day Survivor aired, which was shortly before the move to the new huge house. Boggy was home with the kids, alone. Lucifer was off at a Survivor function. Watching the show as it airs, it starts to form, this darkness. I see first-hand how Lucifer is cast adrift from the rest of the crew, booted on the first night, and I can feel Boggy is in a foul mood. I echo outwardly what seems to be his thoughts: "What, you are working your butt off creating a future while she is sunning herself and eating food on a holiday with the Survivor crew for eight weeks? Is that it?" He grunted, saying "Something like that."

Then the psychic door opened. I realised there was deep dissension in the background, and that he was thinking of leaving her. There was little I could say, so I asked, point blank. "Are the problems so serious that you are thinking of separating?" Boggy just grunted again.

I didn't know, or want to know, the details but I wished him the best whatever he chose. However, I pointed out the timing was pretty awkward. I also pointed out the obvious, that sometimes things get out of proportion when a big change of life is in the wind. That seemed to make sense, and he settled down. I heard no more of divorce. The house got completed, over budget and over time, but DONE. Next came the house warming, and in true Lucifer style, it had to be BIG. I and the new girlfriend, Miss Buzz, were invited.

Thus we arrive at the Three Day Party. Curious. It strikes me that in the middle of the Three Day Novel Quest I include the three day party. And there are more analogies than you might expect. It is hard to put this into clear words, but in both tales the underbelly of human nature become revealed unto itself. So many things emerged from the Dark during that party, just as the poison and venom of an entire decade emerged from my heart as I wrote this book.

But let's focus on the party for the present. The full cast of stars and extras were there. The marijuana wafted on the night breeze, encouraging the birds to fall from the trees, and various fashionable pills and potions circulated with careless abandon.

There were Belly Dancers doing insane things with pelvic thrusts, gay girls pulling strings on stupid men, movie producers pulling themselves, builders of the house, friends, family, relatives and the entourage of children that followed, and a bevy of older women with toy boys in tow: Everything and everyone.

And everywhere there were pure as the driven slush pretenders to the throne of desire. Miss Buzz came along with me, with a degree of trepidation because she had met Lucifer before and had experienced no great love for the woman. Indeed, when we arrived things seemed, well, different. I felt it, and wondered what it was. Buzz knew.

Miss Buzz said there was the ripe smell of an orgy in the making, which I scoffed at, saying the notion was absurd. It was to be the party to end all parties, and in the mind's eye of the hostess, that was certainly how Lucifer explained it. I hardly imagined this would go as far as a Roman Orgy. Yet, as time revealed and as the truth remains in that unholy, sad reality that constantly gnaws at my brain, something was up!

It slowly dawned on me that this was not just another party.

From the moment I arrived, from finding the now 16 year old daughter in a sexual gyration on the dance floor that looked obviously affected by Ecstasy (and not the natural kind) to realising that a blue eyed blond kept staring at me wherever I walked in the room, to the weird old woman who wanted to show me her etching while her 20 year younger boy friend made strange and cryptic comments, well I had guessed that something was amiss. The alarms were ringing, but was it a fire or a wake-up call?

Miss Buzz and I walk up the stairs and find Boggy Street passionately french kissing a women right in front of Lucifer. Then, around the corner two gay girls approach, and immediately they start trying to get Miss Buzz to get her clothes off and come with them. Lucifer comes up from behind, huffed and controlling her rage, and says, sweetly through clenched teeth, "I know you will want to stay so we have made sure there are clean sheet on the main downstairs bedroom for you both." There is a lingering scent hanging off the words. Something more is expected.

A man follows Miss Buzz around, staring at her from the shadows. No matter what room we go to, he is soon to be found there. The weird bells are getting louder and louder and slowly it occurs to me that there may indeed be the expectation of an orgy in the wind. Finally, after we share a number of useless conversations with drug affected fools, Lucifer starts to make a move on Miss Buzz, asking her to take her top off. Of course, Lucifer had just had a boob job, and she said she just wanted to compare. What was that that Miss Buzz had said about women and their tits?

But this Miss Buzz has lived in tougher, far tougher worlds than Lucifer could imagine, and knew the game. Miss Buzz laughs, then puts on her most wicked smile, and asks for Lucifer's shirt, which Lucifer whips off and hands over. Buzz smells it, licks it, looks Lucifer directly in the eye, and then tosses her shirt onto the floor. "I am not interested in your stupid little school girl games!" She says, clearly and deliberately.

I think this was the point that hell froze, and the party stopped in mid-flight. Lucifer BURNED with this. She burned, and finally I saw clearly the Dark that fuelled her. She somehow managed to contain her rage but I quickly took Miss Buzz by the arm and led her upstairs. This entire party had many undercurrents, and they were not just coincidence. This was a calculated series of games and one of them was called, "Split up the happy couple".

Upstairs we found Skerick barely able to stand, barely able to talk, and so under the influence of ecstasy it was starting to look like a health risk.

Meanwhile his wife, Dealer, was happily ensconced blowing some Ayurvedic power, cocaine-like, up the noses of all and sundry. Skerick was beyond conversation. Earlier he had mentioned that he had taken ecstasy for the first time, but that it had not appeared to have worked, so he took some more. Well, it was working now. "How are you coping, do you need help?" I asked "No man, it is totally cool. I mean, it is so TOTALLY cool." he answered.

We were later to discover that soon after this he went catatonic and rather than stop the party and call an ambulance, the Streets immersed him, naked, in a cold bath in an attempt to revive him. Apparently he had seen God, but for the present it would appear that he was having a long conversation with his son.

To her credit, Miss Buzz contained herself until we got to the car, then she exploded all over the windscreen. "How could you be so blind? How could you not have known? How could you have walked me into that trap?" and on it went like this for the next hour.

I explained that we men are simply idiots, and really do not notice these girl games. But at last the pieces started to fit. For years Lucifer had been playing a game of cat and mouse in her mind, shaping her marriage, shaping the men she knew, shaping up a situation so that she collected a menagerie of interesting energies to call up for her personal pleasure.

Her identical twin sister had once confided in me that they had both started their sexual lives at age eight, sexing the workers on their father's farm. I had asked the sister if she felt damaged by the experience at such a young age, and she said "Oh no, we loved it. The problem was adjusting to life without it."

Sex is a powerful magic, and sex, drugs and rock and roll were the fashion at Bling Bling. Boggy and Lucifer were merely new Bacchalians, and they had plenty of followers to worship at their Tantric Temple.

But it wasn't me, and it wasn't Miss Buzz, so we left that scene, and soon after this episode we were to leave the Bling Bling scenario and all the people I had known there behind forever. It had all just worn out its welcome.

YOGAHURTS

"Lust is the craving for salt of a man who is dying of thirst."
Frederick Buechner

And what my friends are the true passions that diminish the Soul ? I list them in the same order used by both Pope Gregory the Great in the 6th Century AD, and later by Dante Alighieri in his epic poem The Divine Comedy; the Seven deadly sins are as follows: Luxuria (extravagance, later lust), Gula (gluttony), Avaritia (greed), Acedia (sloth), Ira (wrath), Invidia (envy), and Superbia (pride).

Yogahurts **(who we had met earlier as Yoghurt) was the all-natural all-loving all fuck-me sort of girl.** She loved men, she loved sex, she loved getting naked at the beach, and when she saw me with Miss Buzz, she decide it was about time that she loved me as well.

It was a problem, because she kept ringing on the pretext of the Harmonics work I was doing, asking if I needed help with the next seminar, asking how she might put up posters, asking how she could help organising an introductory talk, asking whatever she could imagine to ask. Her calls were happening three and four times a day, and it was clearly a case of obsession. Her problem was trying to get around Miss Buzz

Yoghurt tried to sweet talk the girl, she tried to dominate her, she tried to ignore Miss Buzz. She tried anything and everything she could to get around the wall she imagined Miss Buzz had erected between her and I. Actually; I was the one building the wall. Yoghurt had become a royal pain in the butt.

I liked her a lot personally, but not sexually, and it was becoming clear that her desire for connection was a sexual one.

This sort of thing is often a problem for any would-be couple who get together. Energies from the past, the 'stuff' that hangs around the edges, feels a tug on the wires, and this wakes it up. Just like a slumbering spider is woken by an insect in the web, people wake up on the web of psychic connections.

Women will have a man as a friend for years, and as long as he remains single and unattached, she will leave him alone. But let him find romance, and suddenly all her own lost passions emerge, and she will project her lust all over him, now he has become unavailable.

Chaps, let me tell you a secret. If you want to sex any girl who is a friend, tell her in confidence that the girl you have just met is IT. You have fallen in love and it's marriage, babies, the whole nine yards. Make sure you talk about the future wife in the most glowing rapturous terms you can imagine. Several things will happen: Your woman friend will want to meet the woman, invite her over, get to know her. Next she will want to compare herself to the woman, and then she will want to prove to you that SHE is better, by sexing you.

It is a simple psychosis. Uncomplicated, as Paul Smart would have said, in its complication. Lust, desire and need are so easily activated by just taking the candy away from the baby. Offer yourself openly on the sexual plate, and not even a slut will want you. Take it away, and the slut inside every woman will awaken and want to know what they are missing.

I have never had so many beautiful woman make passes at me with their eyes than when I went out with Miss Buzz. It shocked me, surprised me, and delighted me. But it horrified poor Buzz. You see, any man she had ever gone out with was always busy succumbing to the pleasures of the flesh, and she was always left alone and betrayed.

Her internal tapes were saying that, for sure, it was all going to happen again, and her anger and resentment at my apparent stupidity grew and grew.

Well, it was difficult to deal with her anger on one side of things, but on the other hand, for me it was like being a kid in the candy store!

I had women bowing low before me just to make sure I saw their ample breasts. I had gay men making passes at me in the street, asking why I wanted to hang out with a woman. I had sweet little girls giving me google eyes as I walked along. Even complete strangers would come up and sit beside me, airing their sex in a way I find hard to explain, but which at the time was quite compelling. Older women, younger women, all women suddenly discovered they wanted me.

It got ridiculous. I am simply NOT that attractive.

Then I realised what it was that triggered it all off. It wasn't me at all! All this was triggered by the beautiful young woman I was with. It was all a competition by these creatures to see if they could win points by getting the attention of another man away from his girlfriend.

As if to prove the point, this all stopped as soon as Buzz moved out. You can't blame her, yet even so I am glad she left. After several years of back stabbing and gossip from an extraordinary array of people poor Miss Buzz became exhausted, and literally began to lose track of reality. Sadly, I had to move her out of the house as the relationship had degenerated to madness.

The side effect was that the looks from other women stopped. I had become a commoner once more, the prince had reverted to the froggy-self from whence he came, and the glass slipper had shattered.

However painful these things are, there are always benefits. Miss Buzz had helped Ben, and she also managed to break the hypnotic trance I had been held in by the ex-wife. I had not even known I had been trapped, but when the snip happened, when the strings were cut, I realise how much better it was.

But all this was a couple of years in the future of where we are at in the story. In the meantime, within mere months of our meeting at the good Professor Anarchy's house, the spark of passion we had ignited had turned into a firestorm, one that burned in the hearts of many who had known me.

The symptoms were many. Friends started acting oddly. I could feel the gossip wheels turning in the background. Something had set them off, some line had been tugged, and most were reacting to it with a dull resistance to change. A brush fire had been started and hearts were aflame as the animal within squealed and snarled at this unexpected shift in the wind.

Yet, no heart burned more fiercely, or snarled more cleverly, than that of the ex-wife.

I can honestly say that the next two years were some of the most educational of my life, in that I learned how the Dark can rise up and control people in ways we can barely imagine.

CATS and WOMEN

"Cats are the wildest of the tame and the tamest of the wild" - **Mark Twain.**

I had 2 cats in the house, and 2 women in my life. And both knew they would never get on. It was a simple equation. While we men like to think that one plus one equals two, in the world of women and the world of the cat, you only want ONE. One plus one equals only one thing: Argument!

The truth is, when these two met it was an instinctual hatred. Visceral and vicious, the snaps and snarls showed the colours that were really flying on the hidden mast. My two cats didn't get on all that well either!

Miss Buzz had arrived with Lynx, the 16 year old, wise to the world cat, in tow. She met CC, the much younger never-left-the-property cat. All would have been fine if CC had simply rolled over and allowed the older cat to rule, but she simply would not, and could not. Thus they could never come to a point of harmony between themselves.

It got absurd. Both cats would have pissing contests to mark their territory, which is fine but they did it IN the house. Lynx went fruity, and one day I woke up to a curious tinkling sound that was anything but the pipes of Pan. There was Lynx, legs spread apart as she had positioned herself over the face hole in the massage table. She watched herself pee with total fascination. I shouted at her, but she looked up with no sense of shame what-so-ever, as if to say "Now, wasn't THAT impressive? I am just like you people going to YOUR toilet!"

Another day I wake to a different deep tinkle, and this time it is Lynx sitting over a hole in the top floor, doing exactly the same thing. Now the pee is working through the boards and finding its way down into Ben's room. Thank God he was away that weekend with his Mum. But enough was enough, Lynx had lost the notion that there was shame and decency regarding her toilet. But clearly the cat saw nothing wrong with her actions. It seriously looked as if she was significantly impressed with her abilities, and certainly she showed no qualms sharing her intimate details of pissing, and WHY didn't I want to know? She got shooed out, but it just didn't stop there. She kept coming back in to piss all over the place.

Clearly she was marking territory in the same way a male tom cat does. Finally I had had enough. By now she knew it was wrong, and as she raced away one day I pinned her to the floor as she flew past and said, "ENOUGH! STOP IT!"

That was when I saw the fierce wild cat emerge. All the pats and kindness in the months since she had arrived now meant for nothing. Her claws were out, and it was a fight to the death. Now, something about cats. When the adrenalin hits they lose all notion of their size in relation to the rest of the world. She really thought she could beat me up and show me who was boss. It didn't quite happen that way. I bagged her, whacked her over the noggin with my open palm, and while she hissed and pissed and growled and snarled even more, I held her behind her neck, and at the base of her tail, so she could do nothing but glower at me. She had lost the game of control, and hated me. Out went Lynx. She didn't come back in for 3 months, so miffed was her pride.

Now I know what she was really doing is drawing her attention to the fact that she was unhappy. In her mind, she had come from being queen of her house, and been dragged into a world where she had to share a place with a real bitch. CC (the other cat) *was* being a bitch, and purposely cuddled up to Miss Buzz right in front of Lynx. Then she would gaze back, as if to say to Lynx, "Mine now!"

Lynx watched first hand as another cat had moved in on HER person, and so in revenge she smuggled up to me. It was a round robin of who got what, and how much, and when. Just like girls in the school yard. Finally it came down to attention and just getting it through whatever means worked.

Pissing, Crapping, Hissing, Snapping were all attention seeking patterns and it was fast becoming clear that the two cats would NOT get on.

When Ben's mother turned up to drop him off, she smiled sweetly and asked "How are the cats getting on with each other?" By this time I had started to understand the female double speak. This was a direct analogy between her and Buzz, and it was directed at Miss Buzz. I smiled and said "Fine, the odd spat, but what can you do with cats?" She smiled as she left, and I had the sense that in her mind, the hidden plan to get back the husband she never wanted was working out just fine.

Then the unexpected thing happened. I got inspired to finish the place. Cement went down in the garage, a new porch went on the front, an excavator came in and levelled whole areas around the house, clearing it up and creating acres of flat land. It looked like a dust bowl for a bit, but when the grass came through the whole property was starting to look like a million bucks.

I noted that every step up in appearance for the house was a step down for the ex-wife. Finally, she would not even drop Ben off at the house, but at the gate, and would make him walk in. It was clear that the two women were somewhat akin to the two cats.

Then the LONG phone conversation happened. the ex-wife, who hardly said boo on the phone, or even in person, now wanted to talk for almost 2 hours about "stuff". Miss Buzz knew EXACTLY what she was doing, and stupid me only thought she was trying to be nice.

Better everyone gets on, I had said to Buzz when I saw how my relating of what had just been spoken about was not going anywhere good. "Hurrumph" was the sum of her response. In the meantime I just kept busy. Then soon after, a curious thing occurs. We discover the deep, dark secret of Lynx.

I had started the painting of the house, getting a fellow in to help, and one day he came down to say "You won't believe this". I went up, and I had to believe it. For the last few months that Lynx had been sulking outside, no doubt due to my unfair and unreasonable treatment of her, she had made her mark. On the roof, right about where the "other" cat was fed was this HUGE mound of cat shit. It was all over that section of the roof, and nowhere else. Lynx was saying to CC, "I shit on you!"

Slowly I came to realise that the ex-wife was doing exactly the same thing to Miss Buzz. I took her to a meeting with a group of people I had known on and off for the last 20 years. These were not close friends, associates at best, but each one of them acted strange and completely snubbed us. That was when I discovered how Ben's mum had been hard at work, visiting all the important and potent gossips within that particular network. There was no way Buzz was going to get an easy time of it.

It got worse. The ex-wife had even travelled to Sydney to see another group of friends I had down there, and she went out of her way to sad-sack herself. In fact, anywhere I went and anyone I went to see, they all seemed to be well aware in advance of Miss Buzz. Now you really have to start asking yourself, who on earth would be so invested in this situation to even bother?

Even in Bling Bling, old Skerick and Dealer, she even got to them! We had visited and been informed of the dramas of the Three Day Party. Indeed, the orgy theory had been proven correct. The house was a Tantric Temple alrighty, and anything and everything went down. Lucifer had even put it on Skerick and Dealer for a fling with shared partners. Dealer really didn't seem to mind that so much. Earlier she had done a deal with Boggy and his workmates, where they had constructed a flat under their house for her Bum Flush clinic. In return for a good deal, she would give them all a good going over with her sacred bum flushing hose. What is a virile young fellow going to do when a stunning and elegant European woman offers him something kinky? They ALL went for it.

So as a professional Bum Flusher, Dealer had already flushed the butt of many men in the Lucifer group, and seen the obvious attraction and equipment that they might possess. I can only presume that she believed she was offered more at home, as apparently they did not feel drawn to the suggestion.

However, we certainly all heard about it.

Yet, as much as she was willing to quietly backstab her friend Lucifer, while we were there the woman herself turned up to visit! Obviously someone had placed a call, because she did not just turn up, Lucifer had dressed up to the Nines, and had even had plastic surgery. What is more, apart from the Nip and Tuck that withdrew lines from the bank of her visceral age, her entire styling had become an EXACT copy of how Miss Buzz dressed.

Granted, Bee was a stylish dresser. She had a fashion sense that was unique, but the whole point of a unique fashion sense was that it was YOURS. Lucifer had out rightly stolen her whole way of doing things. She came in as a tower of power, cold and indifferent, and walked straight up to me, ignoring Miss Buzz.

Looking me in the eye (I felt like a rat pinned in a science experiment) she started demanding answers. "How are you today?" was not a simple question, it was really saying "I hate that bitch beside you and I am going to PROVE who is top bitch here." That is, apparently, how some women live their entire lives. I suspect it was an overdose of Dynasty, or similar, when they were young?

There was little I could say, and Miss Buzz kept silent. I asked her how her brother was, knowing he had left in disgust after the three day party. She said between gritted teeth "Fine" which seemed to end the tennis match. However, I looked up and saw a look of pure bemusement on Dealer's face. She was loving it! Skerick avoided my gaze, and Lucifer went over to a group of women who seemed strangely attracted to her, and I honestly overheard her saying "Yes, I intend to be the new standard for women in Australia."

What is even more incredible than someone saying something like this is the fact that a throng of people sat about listening to the crap, and believing it!

There's not a lot to add to that, is there? I gathered up Miss Buzz, and we left. I never visited Skerick and Dealer again, but by chance I saw them at a festival in Brisbane. Now, they had both known my ex-wife in passing, however when we said hello she asked, warmly, "And HOW is your DEAR WIFE going, Michael? We saw her yesterday, and she seemed wonderful."

How Extraordinary. You know people for years, you talk about things that some might consider deep, you feel there may be a kindness shared, a friendship of sorts. Then they choose sides in a war they are not involved in, and you get the collateral damage from their snide asides. It would have been sad, except that it was happening to what I thought had been good people. This made it more poisonous than sad. Something in the mix with Miss Buzz was bringing the natural bitch out in a range of women that I had thought immune to such behaviour.

But maybe it was ME. An analogy between the bitch fight here, and the bun fight with the Fowls next door, was becoming apparent. The Fowls had gone all through the valley, seeking compatriots for their view of "No Road". In passing I had only recently been chatting to one of Mr Mum's erstwhile drug mules, and he asked about the "shed" and why I wanted to go to the courts to knock it down. I looked at the fellow, somewhat surprised because I had never mentioned the subject before. "Didn't you realise they are on the access to my property? The Shed I don't care about, it is simply that the Fowl's father put it smack in the middle of the Crown Road."

When he got the full story he seemed genuinely shocked. Of COURSE I wanted the shed out of the way, common sense told him that. But the fact of WHY he was shocked came back to the fact that he realised he had been lied to by people he had known for a very long time. The fellow had been an associate of the Fowls for over 20 years.

I instantly recognised the pattern, and knew without a shadow of a doubt that the human female cat who believed she had been kicked out of the house was now consciously crapping all over the top of anywhere we would be likely to go. What an incredible effort! However, now I knew where the problem and the difficulty was coming from. Here is where it got truly weird. A few days later a strange email arrived, sent to Ben from his mother.

It was all about a story where a woman lost her home, but before she left she put prawns in the curtain rods. No matter what the former husband and the new wife did, the smell was everywhere in the house. They changed the carpet, the furnishings, the curtains, but the SMELL remained. Finally he agreed to sell the house back to his ex-wife, and sold it cheaply. That was when she removed the curtain rods, and sent them to him as a parting gift.

Finally it dawned on me. All the trouble we had been having with Ben, and all the difficulties I had with getting him to do the simplest things, they were not just the child, or the events of his growing up. She had been planning to poison his nature ever since he made it clear that he preferred to live with me.

Once, some time ago, he was in the car and he let off this incredible stench of a fart. It was rank, and we all had to pile out of the car. Miss Buzz gagged, and was sick on the side of the road, it was that bad.

However, I had a sense of what it really was, because I had experienced this when Ben was a young fellow. "Did your Mum feed you a lot of eggs this weekend, Ben? " I asked. "Yeah" he answered. "I got eggs for the last three meals!" I guess the red flag was raised, because the only people in the world who knew how Ben's bowels reacting this way to too many eggs were myself and his mother. She had planned this little message, something she knew I would understand, and yet at the same time she would be sitting somewhere else, looking like an angel with an alibi. Like the cat licking the milk off her lips, saying, "What? Who? Not ME?"

Buzz did not hate the woman. But she had known from Day One the type of creature she was. She was no fool, and had bided her time. Now that I was waking up, she started speaking up. "When you were away on a business trip," she explained, "I called up your ex and baited her. I simply said, 'You cannot believe how he acts!' and that was enough. She spilled the beans, telling me all about how bad you were to her, how you ordered her to do everything, how she was your personal slave. She said she realised all this within the FIRST YEAR of your marriage, but that she could not escape. When she got away. she had to leave with NOTHING, and she was still suffering for it."

"She actually said this?" I asked, rather incredulously.

Miss Buzz nodded. "She made you sound like an absolute monster, and I found myself wondering what I had gotten mixed up with. I wanted to say something, because she was just so convincing, even though it seemed at odds with what I saw. But just now, when I saw how she treated her own son, using him as a weapon with the eggs and farting, it started becoming clearer. If she can do this sort of thing to their own child, use him as a tool to attack us like this, well, that is just cruel. This is a really calculated nastiness."

The ex-wife had been so convincing that even Miss Buzz had almost believed her story, and believe me Buzz was no fool. She was mad, but she was not stupid. However, she also knew she was the one who had baited the ex-wife for a response. She bided her time to ask about the details, and had chosen to wait until the opportunity arose to question this.

Buzz then asked me to detail exactly what happened with the divorce, and how it was the poor woman was left with nothing. I had to pause, because when Buzz left HER marriage from a man who really WAS brutal, who beat her up and regularly choked her to the point of death, she really ended up with next to nothing. Not even her children she had born him were allowed to be hers.

In a sense, she wanted to know if that she was entering a repeating pattern, so I stopped and explained to both Ben and she what the reality was. Like the so-called poison of "he wants to destroy my shed" that was spread about by the Fowls, the ex was doing the same thing to Miss Buzz.

It wasn't a hard story to disprove. I showed her the documents, THREE properties in the name of the ex-wife, all clearly dated around the time she left. One of them was the Federation house on the River at Uki that I had personally restored and then given to her. I explained that she sold all three properties, and spent the money. I had two properties, Boringbar and a share in another one.

I sold my share property for what I could get, and gave her most of the money. I ended up taking over one property of hers that was difficult to sell, adding it to the Boringbar mortgage, and detailed how I had personally ended up with just Twelve Thousand Dollars all up. This I used to built Ben and myself the house we were now in. The net result of our divorce was a very large mortgage against my name. She was free and clear.

Buzz was genuinely surprised. Shocked was more the word. Even she, who was so excellent a judge of the negatives within people was amazed. "But how COULD she? She KNEW I would ask. She KNEW you had these documents to prove your story!" Of course, the EX was gambling on driving the wedge in so firmly that Miss Buzz would never ask. Women can be vicious.

Now, here is where people make the big mistake. They tend to believe that other people will act in a similar way as to how they would. The ex-wife herself would never have bothered to question such a tale so carefully told with such deep and meaningful tears. What is more, no one else ever did, so she could get that axe into the back just a little more firmly with every retelling. The bastard would roll over and die ONE day, and she would be the victor.

I sigh at this point, dear reader. How could she have forgotten I was a writer? It is now Monday morning. Alonso won the Silverstone Grand Prix last night rather convincingly. Those finely tuned engines, and cars built for but one purpose had hurtled around the track at impossible speeds, and every single car out there is a miracle of fine engineering. Yet only one would win.

Winning signalled wealth and riches and accolades. It meant that one team stood supreme for that brief moment in time. Why the hell do you think we call ourselves the Human "Race"?

Now I find I have a strange race happening in my own life, a race with no winners. It is a horse race on a round oval with no beginning and no apparent end. There are three people in it, myself, Miss Buzz (who is as highly strung and highly tuned a thoroughbred you will ever meet) and the ex-wife.

Miss Buzz has spent an enormous amount of time in the garage inside her head, going over every possible move, looking at every outcome, building the motor of emotion and reason to drive her to wherever. She had gone mad, in simple truth, as a result of abuse. And I am talking REAL abuse. Her father that had been raised in the evil Bindoon orphanage, and had been raped, beaten and tortured every day of his young life.

He firmly believed that strapping his kids every day, not allowing them friends, and insulting them was in some way a very good upbringing. And in comparison to his own, it was! His fanatical belief in the Jehovah Witness faith, and his vicious temper are what drove Buzz from the family home and onto the streets of Kings Cross at the tender age of 13.

She had survived, getting raped and beaten up on occasions, but survived without prostitution. She was an exquisite young girl, a truly refined beauty that put tattoos over her arms thinking it would make her ugly to men, thus safer.

Her marriage, when it happened, was worse. He was a total head fuck as well. A manic depressive woman beater who had a rich family and a gift of over $20K every month from his insane mother. Buzz lived in three floors of marble with bathrooms and kitchens everywhere, but her life was hell. In the end she left with nothing, not even her clothes, and barely with her life.

Years later she discovers her EX has moved in with her former best friend, and that when he tired of that one, she was dosed with arsenic in an attempt to get rid of her. The former friends' now dead husband had also died showing the typical "cyanide" scales on his face before he committed (ahem) suicide.

Then we bumped into a hit man she knew through acquaintances in the valley. He told her that years ago he had rejected the money offered by her EX to have her done in, saying to her, "What a prick, and he took your fucking kids as well." It was clear to me that if she had merely asked he would have considered the removal of that scum a pleasure, not a job.

Buzz was the type to just let it go. Her only option at the time was the death of the EX because he had money, power and he would have killed her kids if she had taken them. He told her he would, and she believed him. He said if they didn't stay with him, then he would kill them, and make sure she stayed alive to suffer the pain she had created by leaving him. He said he would then get his biker friends to collect her, and take her out West, where she would be their sex slave for life.

Well, her EX used to work for one of the most violent criminals in Sydney, and the uncertainty of whether he would kill her kids was enough for her to just leave it. She cried every night for 7 years, and she still cries some nights from the grief, the sheer simple grief of not just her loss, but how her own children were now being slowly poisoned by his whispers.

I was quietly trying to bring her out of that loop, but with every step forward someone seemed to be trying to stick a knife in somewhere. People I had known for years would write in email, people from the other side of the world, and they would be saying sarcastic, cutting comments like "How's the little girl?" (Apparently they were told I was going out with a 16 year old)

Doogle Fowl next door now seemed like a cakewalk. His petty terrorism, the cutting of power lines and water pipes, seemed innocent and simple in comparison to the extraordinary back stabbing that the EX had embarked upon. And both seemed like babes in the wood compared to the incredible cruelty of Buzz's EX. But let us remember readers: HE wasn't around anymore.

MINE was even using her own child as a weapon in her whispering campaign, and doing the weirdest things. I was later to find out (as an example) that if Ben behaved well when he was visiting her, she walked around naked. If he was argumentative, she put on her clothes. It's like, Huh?

I had an inkling of this when he was 8, and suddenly got very shy and had to hide himself when having a shower. I asked, on instinct, if his mother still allowed him in the shower room when she was washing, and he said, quietly "Sometimes".

Now to Miss Buzz. After the loss of her own children she was having a difficult time accepting another, particularly as Ben was being a real brat, causing trouble wherever he could. Finally he said after a year of this "I want to live with Mum now!" And would you believe, a house came up for rent right around the corner. I said "Fine Ben. Tell you what, I will call your Mum up and tell her the good news, and that there is even a house around the corner. You want to go look?"

He said he did, so we drove around, looked at the house, and I spoke with the owner of the property. He was willing to rent me the place, so I called up the EX and said "OK, Ben wants to live with you now, and what's more I have found him and yourself a house to stay in, right around the corner." Ben glowed triumphant, he had WON! He was getting everything HIS way.

Or so he thought.

His mother duly arrived almost a week later. She called up and asked him to meet her at the gate and in this way she collected Ben for the weekend. He arrived back on the Monday, and I asked if she and he had gone to see the house for rent. She had driven by, apparently, but said nothing. Another week went by, I left a message for her to call, because there needed to be some sort of answer. Finally she picked up from the answer phone and said "Weeeellll… " I knew already what that meant. "Weeelll, you see, I am helping a friend here, and she is away, and I have to be here to look after her job, and I am getting paid, and weeeellll …" For the uninitiated, this is how my EX said "Fuck off"

"OK" I say cutting the chase. "Do you want the place, and are you going look after Ben. Yes or no." She knows she finally has to decide. Now keep in mind, I was going to pay the rent on her new house. I would have done just about ANYTHING to get this boy stabilized and away from the different house he was at every weekend. Ben was always in someone else's pocket, playing by some other child's house rules. Her answer, when she finally gave it, came with a drop of more than an octave in her usual vocal inflection. I had not heard that tone in a long time, it was the same tone she used when she said she was leaving. "No." Then she hung up. That was it.

Now came the really hard part, I had to tell Ben. I was thinking "She is vicious. Her own son, she doesn't want her own son." He came home from school, and I asked gently if he had any idea what his mother was intending to do. He said, slowly. "I don't think she wants the place around the corner." I asked how he guessed at that. "The way she screwed up her nose, and called you names under her breath." Did she go in, look about? "Yes, but I had to stay in the car."

Now came the hardest, and cruellest part. "Do you know what this means, Ben?" He nodded, fighting back tears. "Do you understand that your mother is not saying anything, but that her actions are speaking for her?" He started to cry. "Well, Ben, I think we also know that you just wanted to prove this to yourself. Do you think maybe this is what the last year was all about?"

He burst into tears. My big ten year old fell into my arms like a baby, needing a hug. I kept thinking to myself, she doesn't want this? She doesn't want to be loved like this? It just seemed incredible to me that a mother would reject her own child. Now, to be clear, she was rejecting the situation. She didn't want the inconvenience of an old house (I know, I had already rented one for her the year before and she walked away from that as well). She didn't want the inconvenience of having to look after a child full time. She didn't want to live in the same valley as me, and then finally it dawned on me! She had stuff she was hiding.

So I guessed at it. "Do you think that Mummy just wants to have her own boyfriend to herself?" He looked at me, wondering how I knew. "Maybe" he said with a quivering lip. Ah ha! That was it. "Do you know why you were not supposed to tell me about him?" I asked. "No" he answered, but relieved it was finally out in the open.

"Well, it doesn't matter. What matters is that you finally understand that you are here, you live in this house, you go to your own school, you have your own friends. You have your life here." Ben nodded, I could feel the crushing weight falling on his heart, but what else could I do. He knew as well as I did that his mother had basically told him to piss off.

That was the day when Miss Buzz changed. This was no longer just fun, a little boys heart was broken. I think all that she was unable to give to her own children she now gave to Ben, and I have to say, she was a magnificent mother.

Ben was slowly cajoled out of the brat hole he was hiding in, and started to help around the house, doing some dishes. He was fat and overweight, and I knew that in his case it was a form a self defence. Well, she took him swimming, she talked with him, she hugged him, she played with him, and slowly she pulled him from that black hole into which he was falling.

To know Ben today is to met a really decent Soul. But "today" was a long way off. This was way back then, and now the cat fight got started in earnest. NOW the EX had to defend the fact that somehow it might come out how she had rejected her own son. So she formed another plan. Her whispers and gossip got even more cruel, and odd things started happening. Little things, like people in Boringbar (that Buzz had never spoken to before) started asking her about why she left her children behind.

At the school play, Buzz and I sat together, and though the EX knew most parents in Ben's grade, she conspicuously sat off to one side, her shoulders hunched over more than normal, and refused to look up and see that we were there. For all the world, she looked like a battered, fearful housewife, and not at all like the jet setting world-travelled yacht-sailing daughter of a wealthy family who was educated at one of the best schools in England.

Buzz knew the game, she had lived it with HER ex many years before. He would play "poor me" to elicit sympathy, then beat her up when they got home. She was not falling for it, not one bit. This was a woman who had done the ultimate crime, she had rejected her own child and NOW she was projecting that the child had been stolen from her by the stereotypical nasty step mother.

Why is it that people are always SO willing to believe the stereotypes? The nasty evil stepmother had stolen Cinderella and was forcing her to suffer under the blows of harsh discipline, while working her fingers to the bone. The whispers and the backstabbing increased in tempo, but we had a child to sort out and paid little attention to it all. It took a year for Miss Buzz to pull Ben into line, and by this time the end of his primary school days was upon us.

The court cases with Doogle were still carrying on in the background, and I had more than had enough of Boringbar and its petty games. I decided that it was time to move on, and this was when I decided to move up to Brisbane.

I had found a really good school for Ben, and was looking for a suitable place to rent while I was trying to get the property sold. Little did I realise it, but this was absolutely counter to the secret plan the ex-wife had. She had an entirely different notion of how things were to go, but at the time she said nothing. Ben was much better behaved, yet he still had his wiggles and it was specifically when he returned from his mother's that they got worse. As I had suffered a woman taking my oldest son away from me, and refusing to let me see him for almost 6 years, there was no way I wanted to do this to another person, so I worked with the situation as best I could.

Then the right house turned up. It was a big place, on half an acre of land, extremely private and right on the water. The views were incredible, and the house was a huge step up from where we had been living. I could rent out the cottage at Boringbar to offset the rent and now that I was in town I would be able to find some work to bring in much needed extra cash.

Things were looking up. Even on the property, finance had been arranged that would allow me to complete the subdivision so the process of shifting, re-signing mortgages, and moving all the "stuff" was made far simpler. It felt like freedom after a long imprisonment. The property market was shooting up like a rocket, and the value of Boringbar had doubled in 6 months. Finally, all the hard work and tears and sweat would pay a dividend.

What is more, Buzz had the brilliant notion of converting all the Number and Pythagorean information I had already compiled, and to rework it into a form that was a game. I did the research, and came across the notion of a divination game using Polyhedral Dice. The Pythagoreans indeed DID use Polyhedral Dice, and in fact they introduced them to the West. What is more they used them to teach math as well as divination.

I was hot onto a new research venture, and one that looked like it may well pay off in a significant way. The concepts behind Divinity Dice were underway. (laddertothemoon.com.au)

The new arrangements meant that Ben was staying the last few weeks of the holidays with his Mum. It was convenient and allowed me to move everything up to the new house in time for the start of his school year, but there was a hiccup. Ben needed to come home a day early to get his school uniform and all that stuff sorted out. It is really important, that first day of school in a new town where you know no one. It is essential that you feel at ease and that you fit in. But the EX refused to drop Ben off. If you thought it was weird before, now the situation just got completely insane.

Instead of dropping Ben off, she wanted to have a three way conversation on the phone. Buzz hopped onto the second phone, both of us puzzled by what the concern might be. It transpires that the ex had booked Ben into a different school and that after seven years of living in other people's houses, she had gotten a job, rented a house, and was organizing for Ben to live with her.

I said "Have you asked Ben what he wants?" I could hear the air suck back in her throat. "Well, actually I thought it would be something that we could work out between ourselves." I asked her to put Ben on, and asked simply, "Do you want to go to the school your Mum has organised for you, or do you want to go to the one up here?" He said without hesitation. "I want to go to the new one up there."

His mother had been listening, of course. Her tone was icy, and she said "Fine, well it was all organized. I had booked this in advance 5 years ago, and this is a VERY difficult school to get into, but if HE wants to go to the other one I won't stop him." I swear I heard the ice falling in the background.

That's when I said, simply and clearly. "You call up, a day before Ben is to go to a new school in a new area, and when he has left all his friends behind. Then you say that you have decided that after rejecting him all this time that you want him now. You call up and think everyone is going to bend over backwards to fit in with your dreams? Really?" I found it completely absurd, and started laughing at the utter stupidity of it all.

She hung up. Ben was dropped off at the gate without any clothes other than what he wore, and we had to get him to school early so that we could find him a uniform for the first day. The cold shoulder and the strange vibes went on for another year and a half, and I was dragged into what is called "counselling". This entailed me listening to a barrage of abject crap being ejected from her mouth about all the evils that I had apparently done, but when I suggest that the woman who acted as the step mother should be part of these discussions, the tone freezes over. It is clear that in the mind of the ex there is just NO way Miss Buzz can be part of her world view.

When I finally get to have my say. I ask what any of the above has to do with the welfare of the child. The Counsellor then said "Well, in my earlier discussions with Mrs Booboo (I might add, Booboo is her first husbands name. All through our marriage, and to the present day, she still uses the married name of the former husband. He killed himself because he didn't think he was good enough for her, just to let you know.) Mrs BooBoo indicated that there never was a PROPERTY SETTLEMENT."

Oh, the penny finally dropped. All of this was about MONEY. Now that Boringbar was worth a million bucks, she wanted a slice of it. I then realised the WHOLE show about renting a house, finding a school, and being the new now perfect mother was all about the second bite at the cherry. She didn't give a shit about Ben, she wanted MAINTENANCE. Keep in mind, all the time I had been looking after Ben, she had not paid one red cent for his upkeep. I didn't care, I didn't have any money, but I certainly didn't want HER money.

Now she wanted to put the shoe on the other foot, and go for some CASH. Buzz was patiently waiting outside, and I need to point out, she was actually very sick. The years of suffering she had gone through had depleted her adrenals, and this was quite a serious illness. It triggered of a very bad case of rheumatoid arthritis which could leave her immobile for days at a time. She was pale when I called out to her, to see how she was doing.

I asked if it were OK for her to come in, so that I could get a female understanding on what was happening here.

Well, that instantly ended THAT session. Another was booked, and Buzz turned up yet again. Now here was the really odd part. The Ex didn't realise she was coming, and when she saw ME enter the room her face LIT UP. It was like her fanny has suddenly come alive and flushed all the way through to her smile. Then Buzz walked in the room, and she shut down completely, scowling.

We had a different counsellor this time, a smarter one, and she caught the look. This was an intelligent woman, and when the EX ran from the room, weeping: She knew it was a game. We had a chat, and finally she said directly to Buzz. "You are the one between the rock and the hard place here. But the child is happy with you two?" We said yes, but I added that if Ben wanted to live with his mother he was perfectly entitled to do so. It is just that he doesn't want to. She smiled, she had seen this before, but normally it was the male playing the martyr game.

"There is nothing I can do here," she said, "And from what I can see the child is not in any danger, or compromised. So in truth, there is also nothing I need to do here. I might suggest you see a divorce lawyer over the property issue, however."

Now, weird as it may seem, even though she had more property than myself at the time of separation, and even though she sold the houses and spent the money, if the child had gone to her, she would have had a claim on the value of MY property. I began to see how her own child was merely a bargaining chip, and Miss Buzz suggested her pride was now well and truly hurt. "A woman scorned," she said as we got into the car. "They are very dangerous."

Well, it was true. It was like the Iron Curtain and the Berlin Wall were re-erected over night. Behind the scenes the gossip got worse. Old friends would no longer speak to me, and the woman even made sure she visited my own father at least once a week, making him things, being nice. It was WAR, emotional war and she was using everyone I knew as ammunition.

It got worse when I went to a meeting with a group who knew the ex-wife and myself. I turned up with Miss Buzz, and more than twelve women all came up and snubbed her directly to our faces, making snide, unpleasant comments.

Every one of them had been connected to the EX in some way at some point.

Another even more Ex-Ex of mine turned up and started parading herself, saying how good the sex was when she was with me, saying this in front of people and in front of Miss Buzz. That was enough, we went outside, and Buzz vomited. It had gotten to an absurd level of the ridiculous. Human nature, while pretending to be so self-righteous is disgusting when it starts believing in the rumours and gossip of a whispering witch.

In African tribes, this sort of behaviour is well known and common place. The Shona call it "The Witch Dance" and it is the sum total of how a person who learns to pull psychic strings will bamboozle everyone in the village and turn them against innocent parties. It was their ancient equivalent of burning them at the stake.

Now, something you do not often read about, regarding witches. The reason for many of the witch burning that happened in the middle ages was for the same thing. Their property.

You get rid of someone by calling them a witch, and you steal their property. It was all about the MONEY. We both knew what she was up to. Basically she wanted to be bought out. If I had signed over a fat cheque there and then it would have all stopped.

And I would have, if I could have. However, the finances were not working well. The finance for the subdivision was drawn down at 12% and I was paying for this, but when I presented invoices from earthmoving people, the company refused to pay them. This was another part of the insanity of that time. I had thought I was doing it tough with Doogle Fowl. He was an absolute WHIMP when it came to the ex-wife and finance companies.

The nut of it was that I was cold stoney broke without a penny to my name. I was fighting prejudice and bitchery at every corner, and on top of this, the NSW Government was changing the rules for building and the new fire regulations were making bush properties like Boringbar much harder to sell. From looking good, it was looking pretty bad.

In truth, the relationship with Buzz had also changed and become one of an emotional minder. She was great with Ben, but as far as I was concerned, she was too emotionally damaged for any sort of real connection to be sustained. I would have preferred to end everything, and just go back to Ben and I, but she was too ill to be left on her own. So in a sense, I had two children to look after.

Worse, Ben was getting to go back to his Brat Nature. We could both see it happening, and we both knew it was his mother pulling emotional strings on him. How she did it was remarkable, she did NOTHING. She did absolutely nothing, and let him run wild. There was NO discipline. She even gave him the master bedroom with the en-suite in the flat she rented, while she stayed in a small side room. Every second weekend Ben knew he was being released from Daddy and Buzz and the discipline, and would able to go absolutely WILD. He was not even required to come back at night, and he often stayed out at friends' places. He was encouraged to be wild, and he loved it.

Then he started stealing money, because staying out all night meant you needed cash for hot dogs and the like. Well, he was just 12 years old and becoming uncontrollable. Finally Buzz said that it had to stop. Ben needed a break from his mother for at least 3 months while we pulled him back into line. Finally, I agreed. There was no other solution, so I mentioned to Ben that maybe it was time for a break, and that he needed to stop seeing his Mum for a few months. We had found out about the stealing, and other stuff, and we ALL knew it was time for a change.

However, before the big break I pointed out that he had to come clean and tell his mother that he had been stealing her money. Keep in mind, we are talking $70 a week here! He had claimed people were giving him work at $15 an hour when he was at his Mum's. Obviously he had been stealing it, and making up a story as to how he was getting so rich.

Well, he tried. He opened up, and tried to tell her the truth. He said that we all needed to sit down and talk. A reasonable request from a 12 year old, I thought. But it got a strange result; the ex said she needed to speak to her solicitor about it. Huh? Of course, she meant about a meeting, but Ben thought she was going to report him to the police, and that he was going to prison.

She had not said it nicely, and had in fact hung up on him, so he tried to call back. She had taken the phone off the hook. He tried her mobile, but it also was off the hook. Now he got angry. He hopped on the computer and sent her an email demanding to know what she meant. She refused to answer but called up the next day and said "You know little Mate. I love you so much. I know you don't understand, but I really really love you." The only thing was, Buzz had answered the phone.

Mrs BooBoo got the fright of her life when she realised who she was speaking to, and went to hang up, but this time Buzz caught her, and woman to woman asked her to come clean. She finally admitted that there were "issues" and that she was struggling to resolve them, and that she was doing her best, etc. ad nauseam, blah blah. And you know, if you listened long enough you would end up thinking that maybe the Pope wasn't a Catholic.

Buzz got off the phone and said quite categorically, "She is still in love with you, that's her real problem. She wants you, but she doesn't want you, and she sure as hell wants to make sure everyone else doesn't want you. All this crap has not been about Ben. It has been about YOU."

Blow me down, and call me stupid!

The year before, Eminem had made famous the following lines:

I tell ya Mama
I never meant to hurt you
I never meant to make you cry
But tonight, I'm cleaning out my closet.

The upshot of all of this is that Ben said to me in private, "Dad, does this mean I don't HAVE to go see Mum?" I said sure, if he didn't want to see his mother, he had that right. As he was almost 13 the courts would listen to what he wanted. Now here is the first time I get completely and totally shocked.

Ben was RELIEVED when I said he didn't have to visit his mother if he didn't want to. He was genuinely, and deeply RELIEVED. He wrote to her himself, in his own words, and said he didn't want to see her for a while. More to the point, could he please have his stuff back. Well, he certainly got his "stuff". It arrived over three days, at a rate of two boxes a day, delivered by the Australia Post courier service.

In all the boxes (and I looked carefully) there was not one card, not one note, not one word of goodbye. It was just so cold. Some months later I was looking for something in his room and saw a computer disc with "Ben" written on it in his mothers handwriting. I popped it in my computer to see what was there, and I saw it was all his "stuff" that had been on her computer. But there was something extra: A file labelled "ben" that contained ALL the letters she had been sending to her solicitor.

To this day I do not know if it was intentional or Freudian. Did she mean to put it in there as a final parting shot across the bows? However, it was just unbelievable. Absolutely everything she had said and done to ME had been inverted, switched and convoluted to appear that I was the aggressor. It was all there in black and white: stealing her son, making her poor, causing her grief, attacking her good name, insulting her in public, and baiting others with false rumours. What is more, she accused me of being a pornographer, teaching my son to abuse women, and worst of all, driving too fast thus making him an irresponsible citizen. OMG, I drove too fast?

By now, none of this surprised me, but at least I had confirmation of what I always suspected. But in there was some really nasty lies. Mrs BooBoo was telling her solicitor that Buzz had intentionally left her own children, and could not care what happened to them. She said Buzz had told her "Oh, if I want them back, I will just tell the judge I was temporarily insane! They always give kids back to the mother."

That chilled me, more than any of the other stuff, and this was the thing that really hurt Buzz. Now she knew why so many women had been so vindictive, but what could we do about it? The damage had been done, the rumours had been spread. Buzz typed a brief letter to the same solicitor, enclosing a copy of the letters, saying that if these slanders continued Mrs BooBoo would find herself in court. I have not heard a word since.

Oh, but Ben was angry. He really wanted to have some sort of showdown with his mother. He started telling us how two-faced she was, how she could be really quite nasty and vicious when she wanted to be, but that other people only saw the angel face. I asked him who may have been in the back-biting and gossip loop his mother had developed, and he named quite a number of people. They were all on email, so here I figured a little open honesty was what this child needed to learn. I suggested that he attach the letters his mother had written, and send them ALL to everyone involved, with a note explaining why he didn't want to see her again.

Out of ALL those people, one responded. Just ONE, and their response was "We want nothing to do with this." I would have thought "Fair enough" if they had not stuck their beaks into my business in the first place. Eighteen months later, a number of these same people call me up to apologise, saying that they never were really a part of anything in the first place, but that they knew how awful it must have been for us. Blah blah blah …

Even though they had stabbed me in the back, I was grateful that at least they finally stopped, and begun to recognise the game. You feel a little less alone, but the damage had already been done.

It was a little like when my Grandmother died. My uncle had called my Dad asking "What should we do, send some flowers or something to the funeral?" Dad's answer was very simple, and wise. He said "She probably would have preferred them while she was alive."

Poor Buzz. The viciousness of that calculated onslaught was the final nail. She was very ill, very weak, and very fragile. She looked strong, because like a wounded animal in the jungle you HAD to look strong or else the piranha would attack, the hyena would slaughter you, and the circling vultures would pick up the pieces. Buzz, she slowly went mad, and started imagining things that were simply not there.

Buzz was absolutely certain there was something up, but the real problem now was that everything had stopped. In the emptiness that followed, all the echoes of insult and injury now came back like phantoms to haunt her. A drum beats powerfully because there is nothing inside. Shadows seem far stronger than light when the heart is beating too fast for our common sense to catch up.

A few people had apologised, but they never said what for and it was already too late. We think we shed light with an apology, but really, these things can create larger shadows than the pain you hope to cure. What good is an apology? It doesn't help feuding cats to agree.

I might add the cats get along OK now. Lynx is now over 18, and CC is getting up a little courage of her own convictions. They will still hiss, and carry on like sisters will do, but they are overall accepting of each other. Acceptance cures, apologies aggravate.

Lynx has spent a good part of this weekend on my lap, purring away. She is like my psychic guardian for all the dangerous rumours that have been flying through these stories of madness and mayhem. As I am writing this, she looks up at me with her sweet eyes, as if to say "You didn't really tell them about the poo on the roof, did you?"

Miss Buzz is gone for good, and sad to say, quite honestly I am glad of it. The truth of the matter was that I was hoping that her damaged psyche would somehow repair itself, but the reality was it was getting worse. It boiled down to myself becoming the unpaid carer for a mental patient. She was one of the few true cases of Multiple Personality Disorder you would see. In one persona, she would put on 2 stone in minutes, and sit for a week playing x-box. Then she would flip to the next person, and drop the two stone in under ten minutes. The dark rings under the eyes vanish, and she would become a 16 year old again.

Or perhaps it would be the vixen, followed by a bitch. She had become a very difficult wreck to live with, and I had to get her moved on, because now my own health was suffering. Yes, it was the stress that caused it, and she deserved better, but I had found my limits of endurance were done.

Today I wake up to a house devoid of stress and tension, and I am deeply relieved to have it all over and done with. I am finally free of the baggage and personal conflicts of some twelve years of war.

So, the telling of this story brings to a conclusion my tale of the Boringbar War. Do you recall how, way up the front of this book (some three days ago, almost) that I discovered the theme of this tale? Well, all these randomly plucked stories we have ploughed through (It hasn't been too arduous has it?) are all connected. They all carry a theme of:

A/ Waste of Money and Time

B/ Karma and Difficulty, and

C/ Getting rid of the subsequent wrecks.

Every time I had made a small gain in life, one of these would rear up and bite. I got married, starting raising a family, and started developing financial stability, and something would come along to shake it down. Success in relationship for myself, it would seem, is a red rag to the dragons of this world, and all sorts of "stuff" started charging at me because of the small modicum of success that I had stumbled across.

So much was wasted in these last 12 years. So much karma was burned, and by karma I mean the pictures that float about in our heads and which direct our actions in the small and minute details of our lives. And now, it is all about getting rid of the wrecks. I am sticking everything that is extraneous on Ebay, and seeing what someone will pay for it.

PURPOSE

L ast night I had an interesting meeting. The local Porsche fellows had a member setting off for overseas. They wanted to bid him farewell, so I popped out (I needed a break, I can tell you after being hunched over this keyboard for so long). Ben's broken collar bone was now settling down and able to move without abject pain, and he was up to coming along for a meal.

They are a very decent bunch, and eventually I get to chat with Dave, and I ask how long he is going to be gone for. He indicates that it may be permanent, because he has found he finally has a place where his talents can be put to use.

I ask what he does, and he explains that he designs public transport systems. He explains: "In Australia, you make the recommendation, you prove your point, and if implemented, everything will work better. But the reality is that it gets filed and never looked at. In New Zealand, you do the same but at least they read it before saying there is no point because there is no money.

"Now, I am going to Dubai because they really WANT a decent public transport system. They WANT to see what I come up with, they WANT to put it into practice, and money is no object. I will have a purpose there. It is somewhere I can make a difference, where I can really contribute."

This is music to my ears, and a fellow I barely know suddenly feels like a brother. Someone who would like to make a difference, not with war, not with winning, but by just helping others to have a better life. That's a real man. On one hand it's a shame that I won't know him better. On the other, it is good because he is off living his dream.

I come home and I think of how Life could have been led differently. Things could have been done so very differently. I could have sold the damn place at Boringbar when Doogle wanted it and the ex and myself would both have had quite nice places free and clear by now. But instead, it became a WAR. What is more, when I asked my solicitor recently about the whole divorce thing, he looked at me and asked if I really wanted the truth. I did.

He then explained, quite simply, that it is WAR. All legal battles are war, where the best strategy wins. You need to align the best force to be employed in the best time and place to determine the best outcome.

It is never about right or wrong, he emphasized, and all about winning. And of course, for the solicitors it was all about getting paid no matter which way the dice rolled.

Through it all, I can safely say that by Fowl standards I am a winner. Everyone has lost, and despite me winning every round, the war was lost. However, I lost less than the others. The reality is, I took a beating and can still walk. That's it.

There's no glory in it, no victory march, no great spoils of war to spend.

Sad, but true.

War: What is it good for?

War is good for a whole batch of people. My war with the Fowls paid a lot of solicitors mortgages for some time. In regards the war my Ex waged, well Ben was the winner, because he had grown and KNOWS he has a loving parent in his life. He has also learned the importance of making decisions at an early age. It will stand him in good stead, I am sure, just as I am sure that somewhere down the track he will get on with his mother.

She, despite the way it appears here, is not a bad person. Does that surprise you? The truth is that she got lost in a war zone and accordingly her behaviour became absolutely abominable. Nazi's were not bad people by nature, they became that way through circumstance. "Fog of War" as McNamara said.

The mystery of it all is this, the person who is the murderer and the thug actually believes what they are doing is OK. The rational is simple: If they didn't think it was OK, then they wouldn't do it! Dale Carnegie in his famous book "How to win friends and influence people" gave a whole chapter over to this subject. People's view of themselves, what they see in the mirror of their thoughts, is simply not what other people see.

In fact, the mirror shows you the complete REVERSE of what you are. What you see in the mirror looks like you, but it is, in fact, your opposite. The Fowls saw me as a greedy developer wanting to destroy their world. There was no basis in the belief, but it is what they believed. It does not matter what evidence you present, because even the most open minded of people can see that there is something wrong with the way THEY process their world view.

The Fowls are hardly classed in the category of the best of people, and like most they will project BLAME, and refuse to accept CONSEQUENCES.

Moslem terrorists believe they are doing God's work by killing innocent people. And we have all heard the story that 9/11 was a military hoax to stir up the populace. What you believe is what you choose to believe. In the end it all comes down to this one simple truth: Shit happens. It really does not matter if the Pentagon was hit with a military missile (And let's face it, the footage released looks like a missile, not a plane) the fact is, it happened, and the consequences will be: What?

Two months before the Twin Towers came down I was talking with a fellow about setting up the Boringbar property for a festival by the Rainbow People. I mentioned in passing some of the difficulties I was having with the neighbour, and he said an odd thing, "If by November you are still paying a mortgage, or council rates, then we have failed."

I thought little off it, until the towers came down in November of that year. Somehow the dots connected. The fellow had been making trips to New Guinea on what seemed mysterious business. He was talking about new world orders, and generally speaking in "end of times" terms. So what? It happened, and what are we going to do about it now? Everyone has a conspiracy.

People, especially in Bling Bling, are all mad with conspiracy theories.

However, worldwide there had been a network of people who truly believed they were to catch the falling pieces of Western Society as it rained down. But did they really believe all of this was going to come from blowing up a couple of buildings? I find that a difficult thing to accept.

I personally think there was a whole lot more to it, and that there are a whole BATCH of reasons why we really ended up in this war in Iraq. But we are never going to be told in any official statement about this. Keep 'em in the dark and feed 'em on bullshit is an old saying.

I humbly suggest, and I suspect many people believe, that this is what is happening to us right at this moment. That's MY conspiracy. But no matter, things will be as they will be in Iraq. Yet I cannot help but imagine a different scenario, one taken from one of the most clever, but least known generals in history, Cornelius Sulla.

Do I really have a chance of stitching together this patchwork quilt of scenes and sequences in this three day quest? Do I still have your interest? Close the book dear reader if you are done, but I promise you, there is more to come that will amaze, delight and incinerate your imagination. It is time to look at an altogether different war, but one that is exactly the same.

The war in Iraq is the same type of war that raged at Boringbar. It is easy to get into it, and very hard to get out of. Terrorists control the events and the law is being ridiculed and abused every day of the week with impunity.

The names had been changed, the stakes are different, but the war is the same. No matter where you go, Iraq is a macrocosm of Boringbar and everything we have spoken of in this book. Yet to marry this statement up to the written word drags us through more pages. I just hope I can make it interesting enough for you, and that my aching back holds out long enough. Time to reach for the Chartreuse!

Let's do it! It is currently 1.15pm on Monday the 12th June 2006, and I have under seven hours left. At a page every 2 minute I can easily get in another 60 pages, but honestly, I will try to keep it short because I am in serious need of R&R.

My back really hurts, I have no idea if anything I have written is any good, and right now I am running on blind instinct as to where the words must go next. Truth is, this book is unfolding itself, and I am merely following the muse as she dances through my mind.

Time for the next Page!

Don't mention the War

"All bad precedents begin as justifiable measures." **Julius Caesar**

Years ago I was flying to London, and decided to fly via Sri Lanka. People warned me that a war was going on and to avoid the place. Little did they know I was more at risk staying at Boringbar that facing any mild mannered Tamil separatists.

I met an interesting woman in a group of people when I got off the plane at Colombo airport. I had seen her earlier on the plane, and had been struck with an odd recognition, and perhaps I also noted her rather large and well formed breasts. She was sitting in her air plane seat, and looked up me as I walked past in a "please help me" sort of way.

An Asian man had been harassing her, trying to feel her up, and she was obviously extremely annoyed by him. So I stopped and looked the guy in the eyes, stating that classic phrase of the Western Superiority."Piss off." He didn't speak English but understood he was being ordered to take his hands away from that woman's breasts. Mind you, they were breasts that had that sort of effect on you. She said "Thanks" and went back to reading her magazine while the Asian fellow cringed in his window seat.

If I were not married at the time something may have come of it, but as it stood Cherie (her name) and I and a batch of malingerers were all disembarking at Colombo. We formed a gaggle of Europeans in a foreign country. The single uniting feature of our group was that none of us have booked a room for the night, which in most capital cities of the world does not pose a problem, unless it is Sri Lanka. Despite the wonders of misdirection provided by the Lonely Planet Guide (The owner of which lives in Boringbar, BTW) we managed to finally find our way to a hostel. I must add, it's RIGHT as you go out of the airport, not left. RIGHT.

Needless to say, at the hostel it was a case of camping in bunk beds, and I discovered to my extreme discomfort and very late in the night, that my bed was full of bed bugs. And it seems, so too was Cherie's. We got to talking and discovered we were both heading in the same direction, so agreed to mutual company. That's the backpacker way.

Sri Lanka aside, I kept the connection and over the years we had many interesting chats. My study of ancient ruins and other areas of interest had no matching interest with Cherie, but we got on well, which she said was surprising because most men were scared of her. I asked why, and she said "Because I tell them the truth"

"The truth?"

"Yes, the truth. As in, if they want me to moan while they fuck me, I don't do it. Nor do I do anal, nor do I want to hear about their wives. Nor do I want to know about their personal problems. Nor am I concerned if they are transsexual faggots with two noses. Nor do I want lectures about leaving lights on, as my step father was a founder of Greenpeace and FUCK HIM, I will leave lights on to spite that obnoxious prick…"

No wonder men were scared of her. But this is not the point of this tale, even though I promise you, Cherie, a woman of three nationalities and several residency stamps, deserves a book of her own. The real reason for introducing her is the War in Iraq.

Once, when visiting her in London, she happened to relate to me an extraordinary story about the real reason behind the Gulf War, one that I have been able to verify as true from a number of sources. Now, as my story of marriage, divorce, war and Boringbar coincides with the occurrence of BOTH the Gulf Wars it seems to fit into this tale.

These wars are also a story of a bad marriage, the subsequent divorce, and the bitchery, witchery, betrayal, cunning lies, and good old fashioned deceit. Iraq became an odd analogy to my own twelve years of war.

Cherie worked at the time for the US embassy. I have already mentioned her breasts and how they had a power? Well their power seemed to cause grown men to blather in her presence, often saying things they later wished they never mentioned. In this case, a few different CIA operatives gave her pieces of a puzzle regarding the whole Iraq War, and putting these together I will now attempt to explain this.

Bear with me, as it takes a little time to piece together the scenario, but I promise, when you get to the end of this you will never look at a TV report or a politician saying anything every again with anything but the most suspicious and jaded of views.

MONEY is DOPE?

This tale starts after WW2 and is connected to the most curious fact that the US currency is printed on HEMP PAPER. The good citizens of the US are often ignorant of the fact that the banned, evil drug called marijuana is in fact the very stuff their money is made from, and more importantly, their money is printed on hemp with a very special type of press, called an Intaglio Press. Yes, like Boringbar, dope is the source of currency.

Originally, before the invention of a harvesting machine for Hemp threatened the cotton industry, all the US money was made in mills in the United States. However, a harvesting machine made Hemp a lot cheaper. This threatened the new nylon industry of Dupont and also the cotton industry, both of which were a major source of funds for many US Senators. This meant that hemp had to be banned.

That is a story unto itself, however this legal reality created a need for a new arrangement to get the hemp paper for the US Currency. Of course, this could no longer be grown in the US, so the basic material for creating money had to be imported, and so it was that the Shah of Iran became a friendly supplier of a VERY essential product for the US. It is a little known historical fact that the source for ALL the paper used for printing money in the 1950's, through to him being deposed, was the then very friendly Shah of Iran. (The use of hemp paper for currency also applied to the UK and many countries throughout the world)

This meant that **Mohammad Reza Shah Pahlavi,** commonly called the Shah of Iran, became a most important person. It is not clear how this came about exactly, but not only was the Shah the SOLE producer of the unique and specialized paper the US currency was printed on, he also was made a gift of an **Intaglio printing press**. This was the exactly same type of press used in the US treasury at Fort Knox.

It is unique in that it prints with a "raised edge" and it is this that gives US currency the immediate FEEL of money. Try it, take any US bill and FEEL the printing. It is slightly raised. Now FEEL the paper. It is not like normal paper at all. OK then. Once you have the paper, and the press, all you need is the plates.

Now, as I mentioned, the reasons are unclear as to why and how this happened. From all accounts it was the ultimate sign of good faith from the US administration. It cemented the Shah and the US Government alliance, and it also secured cheap oil for the US for many decades. The two countries were inextricably bound until 1979 when a revolution led by the Ayatollah Khomeini took control of Iran, and he also took charge of the Shah's intaglio printing press. It was soon after this that the infamous "Superbills" started to emerge.

This had become a significant and pressing concern for the US government, and it was becoming an increasing concern for many banks throughout the world, who were getting their debts paid in fake US currency. Now laundering money from drug revenues or blood diamonds is one thing, but when it is also counterfeit, something has to be done. US Senate records show the consternation in Washington, and the push to create a new $100 bill is clearly noted in Senate discussions.

By the end of the 1970's the US desperately wanted to get this press back, because Iran was reproducing an almost perfect copy of the US currency. How to stop the Iranians? To this end, they enlisted the aid of someone we all know, Saddam Hussein. Obviously a new source of paper was needed for money. At first, Iraq was used as the new supplier for the US paper, and the weave was changed to differentiate the new from the old. Then it went to another level.

In return for arms and military support Saddam Hussein was directed to get this printing press away from the Iranians. Why? As we all know, a lack of belief in the US Dollar would depress the world's economy. If you want to defeat a country, destroy their currency. This is all historically documented and it was a fact that the new "Superbill" counterfeit that was now being used around the world was threatening the world economy.

The "Superbill" was the ULTIMATE forgery. You had to burn it, and use a spectrometer to analyse the smoke to discover if it was a forgery or not. Now, think of what Saddam is thinking. He already is the new money-paper supplier to the US. If he had the press, and the plates, then HE had all the necessary tools to create his own money. Obviously, he was happy to receive US support in order to attack Iran. The nut of the story is that all this becomes an international game of "Chase the Press".

Anyway, a long drawn-out war ensued, one that sent Saddam and Iraq into HUGE debt. When he finally got the press AND the plates you can understand what happened next. He didn't give the press back. Going to war with Iran had entailed war loans. These large amounts of cash he had borrowed from the Kuwaiti Royal Family at interest and, honestly, wouldn't YOU love to pay your bills with counterfeit? That's exactly what Saddam did.

By 1990 the world was awash with fake US currency. (and, I might add it still is!) The effect on the Kuwaiti Royal Family was simple and obvious. They decided to move away from the US dollar as their currency of choice. The simple plan was to move their "pivotal" currency to the German Deutsche Mark and, as a State policy, they would remove US dollars from their bourse, and no longer accept US dollars for payments of loans. It seems a simple solution, but in the untold trillions of dollars involved with international money transfers, it also requires a sign of faith. The Germans required that SIX BILLION dollars that was lodged with the Chase Manhattan be transferred to Europe.

Now, that is a LOT of money. It indicates just how DAMN rich these oil states really are, but it also tells us that they are under the heel on international banking if they want to trade. Because the US Government had done nothing to stem the tide of the Superbill, the Kuwaiti Royal family, who knew they were putting their hand into the hornets' nest, decided that despite the risk they would have to act. Saddam was legally paying back their millions and millions of dollars with currency everyone knew to be counterfeit.

Saddam had not even tried to disguise it, or provide money transfers to justify his receipt of this huge amount of cash. He simply said "This is the contract I have signed, here in the money. If you don't like it, take it to the US treasury" It was poker on a grand scale, and the bluff worked. Saddam knew the US treasury would not issue any statement that would have caused a worldwide currency collapse. He had everyone just where he needed to have them. He had their financial balls in his hands, and he wasn't letting go.

Everyone knew he had the press and the near perfect plates. Everyone knew he was creating money with it. Everyone knew he was fobbing off his international debts with counterfeit. But what was the Kuwaiti Royal family going to do? Demand he pay them with a cheque?

They were hardly in a position to ENFORCE their mortgage and now that the war was over he didn't need the vast sums of money they could provide. The only option was to convert Kuwait to a currency standard other than the US dollar. They needed to avoid having to receive these DAMN superbills as payment for their loans.

Now, if the word got out that there was a perfect counterfeit flooding international markets what do you think would have happened to the US economy? If you recall, just prior to the Gulf War the US dollar was not looking good. Internationally, it was at risk because word had spread about Kuwait and the counterfeit superbill. More and more people were drifting over to the German Deutsche Mark. This may have even been behind the REAL motivation to create the Euro.

Look at this from the US government point of view. Any official admission of what all international currency traders knew, that the perfect counterfeit was already out there, and in amounts of BILLIONS of dollar, was not likely to happen. Memories of the Great Depression came forward. A huge devaluation of the US currency would threaten the ENTIRE world economy. No one wanted that, and Saddam Hussein knew it. He angled for a deal and got it.

The US could have the press if the bill for the cost of his war against Iran was waived. He wanted the Kuwaiti Royal family to wipe the debt. It would have been simple if the Kuwaiti Royal Family agreed to it, but they didn't. As far as they were concerned, they had already put in their application for the transfer of SIX BILLION DOLLARS into German Deutsche Mark, and that was that. The six month transfer period would soon be up and so, Fuck YOU Saddam! And what if the world economy fell over as a result? That can only be good for the Middle East, because they had LOTS of cash to pick up the bargains AND the price of oil would go sky high.

Now, clearly the US administration needed to sort this out. It wasn't just their skins on the line, it was the world's economy. Oil producers would be the only winners, and the entire balance of power would shift towards the Oil Producing Middle East. Where there is money there is power.

From out the blue a solution presented itself. In this international game of chess a small fry (who shall not be named) in the CIA came up with a remarkably elegant and simple solution. Look at who was heavily promoted to his level of incompetence around this time if you want to know more, but let's stay with the Iraq story for now.

The solution was simple, elegant, and it solved so many problems. There were only two ways at this point to stop the transfer of Kuwaiti funds to Deutsche Mark and remove the threat to the the US economy. By US Law, you have to be a convicted drug runner, or your country of origin need to be invaded. And that was the deal: Invade, lock it up for a bit. Cancel the debts.

So! Saddam Invades Kuwait, removes all the documents relating to his debts, thus there is no debt. No debt means he can give the printing press and the plates back to the US. Then Saddam goes home after suitable threats are made, and everyone but the Kuwaiti's are happy.

Simple indeed, but it is like running a doping scam at the horse races. People drug the horse, bribe the jockey and cajole the stewards but everyone forgets one important detail. They forget to tell the horse! Well, Saddam may be totally manic depressive but HE had horse sense.

Saddam, most people would accept, was a totally paranoid Bi-Polar schizoid freak, and as such we discover a link back to Boringbar. He is remarkably similar to my neighbour Doogle Fowl:

1. *He is a pathological liar who will say anything and say it with total conviction.*

2. *He loves to play war games with neighbours*

3. *He is ugly as sin and has a bad haircut*

4. *His fashion sense stinks.*

Doogle's brother once came up to me and said "Doogle just told me a story that I know is completely false, but in the end I agreed that he was right! I even started to believe it myself! How can he do this to me? I know he is lying, but I believed him."

That is exactly how pathological liars work. Of course, Saddam promised faithfully to follow the steps of the plan! You could imagine how he felt, he could hardly believe it! The US Administration was GIVING him the door through which he could walk into Kuwait, grab their oil fields, and get incredibly, amazingly, absolutely, blindingly RICH. How could they have possibly imagined he was going to just walk out of the place once he got in there? But of course he agreed. What is more, the US Administration had no option, they guessed what Saddam might do, but they could do nothing else.

They absolutely HAD to stop this money transfer from happening. As we mentioned, there are but TWO exceptions, and only two. ONE: You are an accused drug dealer (Add accused Terrorist to it now, and please feel a little sorry for Mr Mum) TWO: Your country is INVADED.

The mandatory six months notice the Kuwaiti Royal Family had given to transfer their SIX BILLION DOLLARS into the German currency was almost up. The US had to ACT, and ACT NOW. Their only possible solution was an invasion of Kuwait, and so this insane plan was enacted. Saddam took a stroll South with his army, went through all the banks and removed all records of his debts as agreed, (and was assisted in this by the many bank owners who had chosen to side with the US rather than their own rather unpleasant ruling family) However, once there what was the hurry to leave? Kuwait, after all, had an awful lot of oil he could sell.

Here the allegory fits Boringbar. Doogle Fowl coveted MY land. He would invade at regular intervals, seeking to push me out in any way he could. He invented lies and spread seeds of poison all over town, he even threw weeds on the road I had just upgraded, seeking to make it break up with their seeds sprouting in the spring. He would do ANYTHING to get my property.

What to do?

Soon enough the situation became clear to the US and the World. Saddam had decided to stay. He had firmly decided to set the cat amongst the pigeons.

WHAT TO DO?

"WHAT TO DO WHEN DOCTOR'S DISAGREE?"
PARACELSUS (15TH CENTURY)

S addam's intention to stay was now perfectly clear. The alarm bells started ringing, and George Bush Senior was dragged into this mess, and had to make hard decisions. Clearly this matter had to be resolved.

The Kuwaiti Royal Family were now between a rock and a hard place. In front of them was a document that would require them to leave their Six Billion Dollars in the US for an extended period, or else Saddam would stay. By now they also knew all their loan records with the Iraqis were torn up and were by all accounts a gift to Saddam Hussein. What could they do? They signed it, knowing they were caught like flies in a trap.

However, then it was made clear that Saddam had changed the game plan and this meant that US forces would have to force him out. By report, as a result of this great expense, a further Three Billion Dollars would have to be plucked from where it was lodged all over the world, and the new document required that this also be put into US currency.

Do you remember the three days it took to sort out the response to the Invasion of Kuwait? That is EXACTLY how long it took to get those papers signed. The Royal Family knew they were already kissing away a few billion dollars to Saddam Hussein, and that their gambit to move to German currency had failed. They were trapped, all that money, all that power, all that prestige and they were trapped like rats. In the end, their home was worth more to them, and so they agreed to pay the bribe.

Of course, Saddam was supposed to walk peacefully away, hand over the press and everyone was going to be friends again. However, he decided to play the game out a little further. He figured that the Germans would be miffed to lose all that money, and he was sure that the US would not be able to get everyone to agree to disagree with him staying in Kuwait. Already there were negotiations underway to sell oil to France, who could put a Veto up at the United Nations should the US try to evict him via the UN.

Saddam may have been mad, but he was not stupid. And I suspect he also loved the big stage, this ultimate game of big boys poker.

Now the weird little guy with the bad hair day was an international STAR! Saddam decided to stay, AND keep the press. What did he care if he drove the world's economy into ruin? He had all the oil he needed and HE would be OK. Saddam said "Fuck Off!" to the world, and that is the REAL reason why the West was so vindictive in enforcing sanctions the way they did.

Look at it this way. Do you remember how the Iraqi army was apparently a threat to the entire world, and how Saddam was another Hitler? Now look at how easily he was beaten in two rounds with the US. The reality was that his so called army was a cakewalk to defeat. He, personally, was never a threat, but the Printing Press was.

As we all now know, the UN agreed to resist Saddam Hussein. Even though the Germans had lost out, even though the French had been likely to make huge money out of sole rights to Iraqi Oil, they ALL knew the world economy was more important, so they did the deal. Thus we had the First Gulf War.

When Saddam realised he lost the gambit, and that the US was really going to come in and squash him, he finally agreed to hand over the press. Why else do you think the US military didn't destroy his army? The whole game was just about the US getting back the Intaglio Printing Press, and stopping Superbills.

The US got the press. They stopped the Superbill. They started the sanctions as sheer vindictive punishment, and to also make sure they kept this nutter called Saddam in check. Well, predictably in the Middle East, Saddam became a hero. He had stood up to the US and survived! He was a Golden Boy all through the Arab world. Sure some people suffered as a result, but who cares?

At no time in modern history had someone stood up to the US like this and survived. Of course, that was a situation to be rectified, to ensure that the bad example did not spread.

Now there is a really curious side bar to all of this. The Australian Wheat Board was intimate with ALL the dealings that were going on. They were very significant trade partners with Iraq. The board knew the FULL story well in advance and the directors were fully aware of what international bastardry was at play behind the scenes. They were main players in sanction bending deals.

Of course when the trade deal came up as a way around the sanctions they were happy to play along. Sure Australia will provide the wheat, and you (Saddam) get the extra 10%. That's just the cost of doing business. It was good for the Australian Wheat farmers and who cares if a few dollars went back into Saddam's pockets. It simply meant more business, that's all. Let's face it, the US had created this situation by giving away the damn press in the first place.

But Saddam was severely weakened militarily. All through the South, the leaning of the Iraqi Shiite locals was for the Iranians to run the place, so he developed some clear, simple messages designed to stop any invasion. He gassed millions. In other words, Iran, try to come in here and I will gas you. That was the real reason for the so called weapons of mass destruction.

And what of the rest of his "Weapons of Mass Destruction?" What about those so called "Tubes" that were designed as rocket shells for nuclear warheads? The CIA knew, and had documented, that Doctor Gerard Bull, a New Zealander, had been using these in an attempt to do a cannon-launched satellite into space. What is more, some suggested he was well on the way to succeeding, and guess what THAT would do to the entire shuttle program?

Imagine being able to launch satellites for what amounted to 1% of the normal cost? Soon every single penny-ante country would have their own spy networks up in the sky, and the US would be under threat from any one who cared to use Sat-Nav guidance systems to launch weapons against it.

Type "Gerry Bull" into Google and see how easy it was to discover the real reason behind some of these "Weapons of Mass Destruction". It was all bullshit, and the intelligence agencies KNEW that a lot of what they were putting forward was crap, but at the same time, they ALSO didn't know exactly what Saddam was up to. That was the whole point: He really was unpredictable.

All international diplomatic efforts failed for a very simple reason: The Law of the Jungle. If you are weak and vulnerable, then the very last thing you do is to shout this to the world. As long as your opponents think you can destroy them, they leave you alone. But the problem is that further negotiation becomes a double edged sword. Because you have proven yourself a pathological liar and broken your agreements in the past, you will do it again.

Ask Saddam: Do you have any WMD left? (of course not) Are you bluffing? (absolutely not) Are you lying? (What, me lie?) As you can see, any answer he or his administration gave was suspect.

What is more, when you are sitting on top of the world's most significant oil reserves, people who need that oil get very jittery. Extra extra jittery. But does that mean jittery enough to maybe walk in and just find out for yourself? It was a waiting game, a cat and mouse tactic where Saddam was stalling for time.

And here was the master stroke. Saddam had another string to his bow, he struck a deal with the Germans and the French to give them exclusive rights to Iraqi Oil IF the sanctions were lifted. That would surely stop the UN from agreeing to ANYTHING, and thus keep the US outside his country. It was the perfect plan except for two disconnected factors. The Twin Towers and George W Bush Junior.

Here it was again. Money, Karma and getting rid of the subsequent wrecks. The US had plenty of money to waste and all the time in the world. The karma of the Christians' versus the Moslems, well that was too perfect. Getting rid of the Wrecks? Well it certainly was time to try and tidy up this mess called the Middle East. And, by George, we had the right fellow to do it!

Stage One was closed. The initial rebuff, the pulling back by George Senior, the removal of the printing press. All done, and done successfully. I might add, George Senior was criticised for NOT invading Iraq the first time, and his response was very simple "I do not need a civil war on my hands". True, this is what he said!

Stage TWO was now opening, which was the reintroduction of imperialist intentions and get a foot print in a very volatile part of the world. Thus the REAL reasons for the invasion were quite obviously never mentioned in the lead up to the event. Let's review them:

Reason One: Saddam was about to get his Sanctions lifted by simply doing a deal with the French and the Russians for EXCLUSIVE rights of management and supply for Iraqi Oil. What do you reckon the US administration would have thought of that?

Yes, good old Imperialism reared its armoured head, and said "What, you want to cut US out of the deal? No way, Jose."

Reason TWO: This is more subtle. What is more, this shows the REAL purpose beyond merely controlling oil fields. And potentially this reason is CHINA. China is a run-a-way train economically speaking. It's labour costs are so low, and its efficiency so high that it poses a real and significant threat to the production base of the West. It has but one weak point. It has to IMPORT materials, and specifically oil, to feed the ever increasing appetite of the industrial monster now running the country.

Labour costs are insignificant in China. The REAL costs is in raw materials, and the Chinese boom had already seen the price of raw metals rise, but this was still not a huge factor for end price. What was needed was a wedge to drive up costs inside the country, forcing labour and production costs up. There is a tried and true formula: Increase the cost of OIL.

In a society of teeming millions moving towards cars at an incredible rate, the higher price of OIL all by itself would drive up wages, drive up production costs, and help address the balance of payments. In turn, this drives up Chinese prices, and makes the West a little more competitive.

We have already seen the US courting India, seeking to embrace that once rejected economy. This is but one of the prongs of the attack to stymie China. A competitor is being groomed.

But real and immediate action was required. The Bible says we are born of dust? Well the Bush family is born of oil and they have many powerful allies and friends who are steeped in oil. Can you imagine a better way to drive up oil prices than to invade the country that has 1/3 of the worlds supply?

So the game was played out: France and Russia are stopped in their tracks (did you wonder why France opposed the invasion so vehemently?) and China is driven to higher prices. Sure it may cost a billion dollars a day, but to the overall economy and the increased revenues from OIL, this figure is paid for many times over. By the US citizens, of course.

Here is the real Catch 22. The US Public are paying for the war AND they are paying for the huge leap in petrol price. We are ALL paying for the price rise in Oil. Think about it, 500 million people are ALL paying $40 more every week. Let's do the Math: 500,000,000 x $40 x 52 = $1,040,000,000,000 per annum EXTRA. That is a LOT of money. Is this over a Gazillion Dollars? And these are CONSERVATIVE figures. And people think Bush is stupid?

You want stupid? Look in the mirror for stupid, folks.

Even so, and even though the entire Iraq War is really a charade for other diverse purposes, some of which perhaps were necessary, the question I ask is simple: "Could it have been done differently?"

How would a more compassionate and understanding Administration looked after things? Was there a way to go about this quietly without ruffling the feathers of the world and the oil price so completely? Of course there was. What's more, it is what "I" should have done at Boringbar. 20/20 vision in hindsight, everything being clear in retrospect, and all of that. It is always easy looking back.

ALTERNATIVES:

If Iraq had no oil, there would be no war. Does anyone dispute this simple argument? We also all know that if there had been no Twin Towers, there would not have been the galvanising of public opinion necessary to ignore the UN and to just go do it. I am specifically avoiding the "9/11 being a set-up" question for the very simple reason that I just don't know. But we DO know a lot about Iraq because it is a matter of public record.

A lot of factors came together to create this war in Iraq, but what I am looking at NOW is what ALTERNATIVES there were in how it was executed. Could most of this needless bloodshed been avoided?

I say YES! I state, emphatically, that it could have been done far more easily, and I will point to history as to one of the possible scenarios.

I look to the past, and in particular to Cornelius Sulla, the first Dictator of Rome. Oh, you thought that was Julius Caesar? Well, lesson one; Julius learned his trade from studying his older cousin. Sulla was a brilliant General who was noted for many remarkable achievements, but specifically what some consider his greatest victory where no one died. This was his treaty with the Persians. (Known as the Parthians at that time)

Do you know what we call Persia today? **Iraq.** Since ancient times it has been common knowledge that to attack the Persians on home turf would at best be a Pyrrhic victory and at worst, a disaster.

Yet equally so, you could not stand by and let them attack you, gnaw away at your trade routes, and encourage piracy by giving free port to renegades, as long as they pay a share of the booty. This is exactly the situation Sulla faced, and it was the SAME story with modern Iraq. It is history repeating itself.

Invasion was NOT the key. Sulla knew he had to thoroughly beat a few armies to show the Persians that Rome had teeth, and then bluff them into a deal that Rome wanted, by giving them a better deal than invasion. This is EXACTLY what he did, and the Parthians grabbed the chance to avoid war.

However, his cessation of war and agreement with the enemy met with a curious reaction in Rome. He acted unilaterally for the good of Rome, and in doing so had ignored the Senate. Because of this he was ordered to disband his army and hand in a "please explain" letter to his so-called superiors. Sulla had effectively secured 50 years of peace on that frontier for Rome, and now the good senators wanted to play politics?

He was going to do no such thing, yet this was, in effect, a declaration of war against his own country. And here is the real mastery. Sulla knew Rome would be weakened by the inevitable civil war his natural reaction to their demands would have evoked, so he took a different, more considered course.

He presented Rome with the greatest scare they had since Hannibal. Sulla knew the Senate was going to label him a traitor and order his death because of his Peace Treaty, done as it was without their approval. He knew EXACTLY how they would react, but they had no idea what he would do. This was, as always, his winning card.

He took his army back to home soil, an army that anyone with any military sense in Rome knew they had no chance of defeating, but he makes sure he arrived just as winter was closing in. Now the clever fox played the cards close to his chest, and not even his own officers knew the game he played. He knew no Roman likes to fight in winter, so he makes an armistice, a suggestion that he and his opposing generals can agree to disagree yet keep their distance during the Winter months. He promised faithfully to stay on HIS side of the river during winter, and not invade Rome. Come spring they will all get to it.

The suggestion was a relief to most of the opposing camp, because they all knew they had little chance against Sulla's hardened warriors. Now they had some time to build up an army and possibly have a chance of stopping him. How could they refuse such a God sent offer? So it was happily agreed by all.

Sulla set up camp, and what a camp it was. All the glory and fanciful dreams of the Orient were brought to the Romans. Sulla put on grand shows, and provided women, wine and bread for his men unstintingly. He also agreed NOT to raid fields, but provided high payment for all goods brought to camp, so now the locals were more than happy for him to be there. In fact, his presence started a mini boom in the entire Roman economy.

People came from Rome welcoming the returning veterans with goods and wares they could buy, and his soldiers and retinue (rich with years of plundering) had a wonderful time.

But here is where his trap was REALLY set. The Roman soldiers on the other side of the river, Sulla's erstwhile opponents, wanted a slice of the good times their brothers were having. Suggestions and representations were made that perhaps, as they were all Roman, maybe they could come over and enjoy the festivities as well?

Sulla knew how Roman's thought and had counted on this very thing. He knew from the start that no Roman wants to miss a good time. "Of course," he cried. "We are all Romans! Of course you are welcome, but equally, let us not forget that come spring, we must all have at it in war. As long as you remember this, you are welcome in my camp."

The officers were treated particularly well, and each evening they were invited to listen to the marvellous exploits of their brothers in the many and various wars that had been fought against barbarian foes. The opponent's officers paid for nothing, and were given women, wine, and song as repayment for the simple pleasure of their Roman company. After all, being away so long on those damn expeditions made you appreciate what was fine and wonderful about home, yes?

Come Spring, and you already know it. Could you find a single soldier who wanted to rally against Sulla? Not a one. They were BROTHERS now. Friends who had shared food and good times. The Politicians, fearing for their lives, ordered the attack but these orders were in the hands of Sulla's spies well before they got to the opposing officers. He personally handed them to the "enemy" officers who were at that moment revelling in his own camp and he said "Oh well, I guess the party is over. We have to get to war now."

The look of shock on their faces was enough to tell Sulla his plan had succeeded. "Of course, if you do not want to wastefully shed Roman blood, I could only praise you for your wisdom. But it is up to you. You know I will win, and it is just a question of how quickly, and how many will die in the process. I would be saddened if it had to be you."

In a nutshell: The entire opposing army effectively stood aside, a virtual swapping of sides. Sulla strolled into Rome, executed all who still opposed him, and forthwith instituted a reign of terror that effectively reduced all opposition to Zero. It took two years, and during this time he reset the finances of Rome, and reorganised the government so that it functioned once more.

He already had the Senate pass a dictate that he could not be charged for anything he did while officially designated Dictator, and then two years after he took control of the place, he left for his villa in the country. Kissing his favourite boy friends in front of the Senators as he paraded out of Rome, he made a promise to never set foot inside her boundaries again. He never did.

What a way to win a war! Sulla kept his friends close, and his enemies even closer. Consider, now, if you will, that the Iraqi War was waged in such a similar fashion to Sulla's war on Rome. Instead of charging like the bull at the gate, imagine there had been no "shock and awe" bombing and the US Army simply moved in and occupied an area in the South. Enough troops to say they were there to stay, but not enough to say "Let's fight!"

One thing that the West seems to completely misunderstand is the Iraqi principle of hospitality. If you are invited into an Iraqi home, the owner of the house is honour bound to protect you. If you invade his house, he in honour bound to kill you. It is not rocket science to realise it is better to be invited in.

SO! Imagine if the US troops had only gone so far as Basra, where they knew they would be welcomed. Not only this, the army camps outside of the town, apologise for the necessary intrusion, and then the Generals speak the TRUTH. They explain that they just want to protect the oil fields, so please, go about your business. And when the locals ask: What if there is war? Please, if Saddam sends an army, we will meet him outside of town and deal with it then.

The whole point is that when you have already have complete and total military dominion over your enemy, why rush? It is a given that you will win, and so the question is more HOW will you win, and subsequently, how do you keep the peace afterwards.

So, copy Sulla. Set up a camp in a nice spot near the river, maybe build a casino, create a few places of interest to the local population such as free rides in Humvee's. Fun things. Hell, get Michael Jackson over to build an amazing amusement park that gives free admission for all Iraqi's!

However: Put your camp close enough to the city to make sure that any gas attack on YOU is an attack against THEM, and then issue the locals free gas masks. In other words, create some FUN but let them know there is a THREAT. Build a scene where you are WELCOME. Bring in lots of money, give away lots of treats, and for god's sake, don't bomb ANYTHING.

Leave the entire infrastructure in place, leave the oil pipelines there, and leave the water pipes there. Just move in and camp, giving the clear intention that you are not about to start this war. You are just there, camping out under the stars until it all starts, which may be in the autumn, or next year. Certainly, if there are any soldiers sent to fight you, point out that they are all going to die, and that maybe they would prefer a nice pipe of hashish?

Soon enough, the local Mullah's will realise that your side is the better side to play with, and you get INVITED to stay. Think about it; what's Saddam going to do? He knows he doesn't have a chance against the army, and by now the word is out, the Americans are good fun!

They give away toys, offer free amusement parks for the kids, and everyone is happy. Lots of money, good times, and fun. Saddam will start to panic, make stupid decisions, and his own staff would begin to see that they are on the wrong side. Your bureaucracy really runs the show, and the real goal is to turn them away from Saddam, and towards yourself.

The Kurds would be BEGGING the US to come in and occupy their land, so given this, Turkey agrees and another force is moved into the North. Saddam is surrounded, and people are deserting him in droves because it is much better to be with the Americans than him.

The US can start setting up their democratic state in the north and south, and soon the people in the middle start saying "Hey, this is way better than what Saddam offers!" and so his own support base starts to crumble. It doesn't matter what he does or says from that point on, he has already lost. You win the war without raising a gun or shooting anyone.

What's more, Iran sees this clever move as a way of destroying their hegemony with the Shiite in Iraq as well. They get less cocky about nuclear weapons, because now they know the US understands how to work with Arabs, defeat their leadership by appealing to the people. The Great Satan becomes Santa Clause. So what happens? They start to want to get on with their neighbour, who has proven they can be trusted with the Shiite people in the South of Iraq.

You DO win hearts by winning the wallet. Bring in truckloads of "stuff" so everyone who would have gone raiding and looting can come over to your place and you just GIVE them things, but in return you ask for favours.

This is key to understanding the Semitic people. Bargains are seen as intelligent and clever. Gifts that come with strings attached are smart! Giving people stuff without requesting a return favour means you are arrogant, and you would be insulting them. So what would these favours be?

Easy things, things that are natural to the Iraqi. "Get your brothers up in Baghdad to give us information" "Can you let us know where Saddam's sons might be?" etc. etc. etc. The entire country becomes your spy.

More importantly, by this time the US troops start to both like and understand the Iraqi people. Who, by the way, are a wonderful people. They are really an extraordinarily kind and generous race. By now the US soldiers realise that when Iraqi men are shooting guns in the air, it is a sign of WELCOME. So they don't shoot them, and therefore they don't create the so called insurgency we have today.

How many people realise one of the main reasons for the insurgency is directly a result of US troops shooting people who were welcoming them? They heard guns being fired and thought they were being attacked and shot their friends when in fact they were being welcomed!

It's the same thing as Sulla. "Look we are here for the war, but it is coming on summer and no one like to fight in summer. It's too hot. So tell you what we do, if that's OK with you. We will camp here by this river, and come autumn we can all get to it, ok?"

Even now, all the bloodshed would stop for the US if they simply withdrew to a safe haven, protected their oil pipelines, and just protected the borders from the Syrians and Iranians. Leave it to the Iraqi's to sort it out, and keep everyone else out of it. Give it three months of bloodletting, and the need for a balance would appear, and the Americans would then be slightly welcome, because everyone would start realising that living is preferable to dying.

Our old friend Josiah Joash would have done a much better job at fighting the war in Iraq than all the brilliant generals they sent over. Why? Because Josiah understood a really simple truth. Something his Grandfather the head of the Toe Cutter gang taught him. **Keep your friends close, and your enemies even closer.**

That was why I had to fight the useless, pointless war at Boringbar. It was all because I didn't do this. Mea Culpa.

If I had done the same at Boringbar, made Doogle the friend instead of the enemy, if I had appeared to have chosen HIS side rather than his brothers, would it have been different? Josiah would have taken this course, and the fact is that things would have gone far more smoothly if he had been in charge.

But the reality of the Sister's having their own agenda, and how we both missed it with Uncouth Tooth suggests that courts may well have happened regardless. The thing is, we can never know if the future could have been different if we had played the cards better in our past. I don't know if the war could have been avoided. Perhaps the COST of the war could have been lessened, but when you are dealing with Madness there really is no solution.

But, and this is a large BUT, by feeding the dog it learns to welcome you. This is still not to say that, in the end, the courts would not have been called in to decide the matter. In the end we would have arrived at the point where "common sense does not apply" no matter which direction we came at things.

However it is fair to say that by taking the side of reason and commonsense, I lost. By not ACCEPTING the madness and working with it, I paid a lot more in time, money and energy than I might have otherwise.

The same goes for Saddam Hussein. If the US Administration had accepted his madness, and not tried to superimpose their own beliefs over what he was doing they could have worked with the elements SURROUNDING the Dictator more effectively. But of course, they didn't want to.

The cold hard reality behind the war in Iraq is very simple. The only logical conclusion is that the then US Administration WANTED to push up the price of Oil, and who really cared who died in the process.

You think?

Epilogue

Keep your friends close, and you enemies even closer.

I almost cannot believe I have gotten through this irreverent and oftentimes irrelevant monologue in just under three days. It is now 4.14 pm Monday the 12th of June, 2006. Who could believe it? Almost 5 hours to spare. It really is extraordinary what can be done when we can move without distraction and with a sense of purpose. I will spend the rest of the time editing.

As always, it is still a case of "What to do?" Some ask me now-a-days what I would wish upon Doogle and my nasty ex-wife. Now you have read this story you may well imagine I would be vindictive and possibly curse them, but I do not. Not one little bit. In fact, long ago I realised that the only thing I would wish on them is a very, very long, long life.

And if you think about it, you would come to understand how truly wicked that this wish is.

What is there left to say other than to recap the simple truths of the Human Condition as I have discovered it in my sojourn at Boringbar?

One final time: The Rules of Dysfunction.

Boringbar Equals:

1. **Low-heeled two-faced bitchery that holds pretence as the ultimate sacrifice.**

2. **High notions of grandeur sloshing about in the sloth of human desires.**

3. **Badly repaired emotions sinking in an endless ocean of compromise.**

4. Flotsam and Jetsam pretending to be Titanic's before the Iceberg

5. Paranoia of the fear we are paranoid of our fear

Let me run through it, now you have the backdrop firmly planted in your mind.

1: People will happily pretend. As a rule, they pretend to be something socially acceptable in order to get what they want. They will consider their own lies and deceits to be a worthy effort to a greater cause.

2: In the process, people will read books, listen to societies memes and possibly accept these values. Subsequently, we garner concepts of what it means to be noble, important, great, etc. We then act out these concepts as we interpret them in our day to day life. But the truth is, most people are self-serving creatures who care not a whit for their fellows. Still, there are always some who choose to give rather than take.

3: The Givers help you to learn how to give. If this is the process you have brought into your life, you are breaking down the process of dysfunction, and will not likely proceed any further down that path. Even so, you can still get damaged by other self-serving individuals. Society as a rule is a process of Gossip and Backbiting, and this will eventually take its toll. You will know you are on the Slippery Slope when you start to join in with them.

Even the best givers can wear down. By this time, in order to survive, you start to compromise your ideals, making such tradeoffs as will please you enough so as to want to continue. Thus we arrive at Step Four:

4: All the compromise and tradeoffs, you start to realise they just do not work. In your heart you feel adrift, and you dream to be something greater than you presently experience. It could all be better, but how? Then like the silent cats creeping about. Middle age comes and the only thing that remains is your imagined memories of what you might have been. Waves of life push you where they will, and you become the alcoholic of circumstance, drinking in whatever opportunity arises to your taste.

5: FINALLY you realise your entire existence has been based on lies, and by now you recognise that all your friends are in the same (lack of a) boat. You are jiggling down the river, hanging onto whatever keeps you afloat, yet now you realise you are heading towards the thunderous waterfall. It is the sum of your fears that awaits, yet oddly you realise deep inside that this is the most logical conclusion to your life, and then comes Number 6

6: You Fall. You fall down into the well of desire, and you will eventually hit the bottom. To your surprise, it is never as far as you fear, or as desperate as you believe, or as important as you imagined. Then you look up, and see the stars shining brightly. Only at the bottom of the well do you realise they have been there all along.

7: Finally you make your choice: You live or you die.

This seven step process usually happens like a tragedy. It moves in incremental steps towards an oblivious goal. Small steps: You go through a small cycle, and you either live it up, or die it down. In the end it is simply the end you fear, or the beginning that you desire. You either move upwards in strength, or downwards in despair.

Often, some aspect moves up, while another moves down. Your finances may go up, but your ethics may suffer, as an example. It's a "Question of Balance", as the Moody Blues once said.

Descartes states in an apparent wisdom: *I think therefore I am.*

I say that's horse shit. We like to "think" we can run our lives with our thoughts., But we don't. We are a train wreck rolling towards a collision, for the most part. However, sitting on a beach at Manly Sydney many, many years ago (tears ago?) a sincere fellow by the name of Mika said a far greater truth: *I sink, therefore I swim.* And perhaps that is the only real truth we humans grasp.

My Message? Forget the message and enjoy your Chartreuse. I did.

RHUBARB (AUTHORS COMMENT)

This has been a Truth Story: Names have been changed to protect the guilty. Two cats have been patted and I faithfully promise that absolutely no animals have been harmed in the writing of this tale.

Three hours to go. I have had a few nips of the Chartreuse and the pain is significantly less now. I am urged from somewhere deep inside to just go one step more, possibly because as much as I understand that the Boringbar War is a tragic comedy, it is also a comedic tragedy.

The deepest tragedies are always incremental. It is that stuff in our life that hurts slowly, the experience which eats away our sense of worth a piece at a time, leaving us with only empty promises to fill the dark empty space that slowly, inexorably overtakes our imagination, our dreams and our hopes

I once believed, unquestioningly, that the negative was but a passing shadow. The positive, that depth of love and kindness we all experience as babies, I believed was the true reality. This is how it starts and this is how it should finish. Mea Maxima Culpa: Forgive me for my hesitation dear reader; forgive me for questioning my faith. Forgive me father for I have sinned and indeed, I have become human, all too human.

Paranoia, suspicion and regret are the new poster children for the legions of lost lovers. Are we truly made in the image of God? Perhaps some small un-recognized pieces of the jigsaw belong to something higher, but for the most part, who can look at the world and what we do to each other with anything more than acute suspicion that somewhere, somehow, someone is out to get us.

The incredibly stupid War in Iraq, or the war in the family, or the war in our head: They are all one and the same. What puzzles me is the paranoia.

The paranoia, and the propaganda, politics and pretence that go along with it. Why do we, or more correctly HOW can we, ignore the obvious as we do?

Most people are barely surviving their life. How do we keep smiling and pretending everything is fine? So many inside are falling to pieces. We are all swimming neck deep in horse crap, we are all floating on a sea of compromise. That's when we discover the truest faith, "*I sink therefore I swim*".

What is the similarity between communism, fascism and capitalism? All systems have vastly different realities to the theory they espouse, yet all these systems count on you finding someone else's shoulders to stand on in order to get you out of the crap.

There is the good side to our human nature, of course. Yet it seems to me we have to die to hear it! Does that sound odd? Think about funerals. We always eulogize the finer points of even the most despised humans we know at a funeral. It seems to me that when they die, we are far happier to know them.

Whether you were important or otherwise in life, even those who hated you will now laud your sacrifice of whatever. There is one thing that is certain, when you leave this earthly veil, it all changes. The odd way you wore sandals to social occasions, or the manner in which you committed other fashion crimes becomes quaint, curious, and positively lovable! Yet in life, it was gauche, oblivious and seen as just sad.

The simple truth is this: We do NOT love our neighbour. If they do not bother us, we let sleeping dogs lie, but we do not love them. In the course of our life we organize ways to not be bothered quite effectively.

In real life, we put old people into homes, put down old dogs, bury the hatchet in the back of someone with gossip, or conversely wrap our remorse with barbed thoughts around the reputations of former friends as they walk away. Generally we exist only to suffice enough for our comforts. If this is to be at the cost of another's comfort, so be it.

Really, I now look in the mirror and see a thousand traits in myself that tend towards the lowest, most vicious and uncaring side to human nature. Of course,

I might also be looking at the cat on my lap! ("Not I!" said the little blue duck.) What is worse, like the alcoholic grasping the bottle of Metholated Spirits, I know the poison I offer you in these words will not cure, but I long for you to grasp it, and drink it anyway.

The message is really one of choice. You can choose to be your own part in your own play. You can be the bad guy in the movie as well as the hero. What is that thing about the Heroin? We can choose to be oblivious, we can choose to act, we can choose to avoid. We can choose between good and bad, and the very choice we make will alter our view of what these are.

Evil? What is evil? Perhaps it is that whisper in our head telling us that we are better than someone else. That can be a very great evil. Give a person a servant, and they are a God. As a God, they have the right of life or death over those under them. Life can be given with a kindness, or death can be delivered with a conceit.

Out here in the "real world" the truth hurts. Sensitive hearts are dying in plague proportions, and being replaced by robotic machines wearing the latest fashions. We go where we imagine we should. And what we IMAGINE is what determines what we are, how we act, and how we see things.

In the years I have spent on this planet I have learned one thing. Our imagination is what rules us. Now, despite the fact that this imagination is generally abused and left to run around the wheels of circumstance inventing and reinventing circles to fit the ruts it finds itself in: Despite this, it is in truth our one sole possession. You may claim "Nay the SOUL is our greatest possession!" but I reply in the negative. We ARE Soul, we cannot possess it.

But our IMAGINATION is like Soul's Thought, free to run like the river. It is a wild, unchained thing to every child, the star to every wandering bark that Shakespeare makes passing mention of. The door of Imagination is what opens us to a higher place, a wonderful land where we never grow old, but we are generally too stuck in our religion of self to notice.

We are indulged, dear reader. We are indulged and poisoned and drunk on our own thoughts and feelings and beliefs and prejudices, and these things have submerged our imaginations into the petty, inconsequential and demeaning half lies we call our truth.

"The price the Gods exact for song? To become what we sing." Pythagoras said that.

The expense of this personal indulging in ourselves (the indulgence being what we loosely term the passions of vanity, lust, anger, greed and attachment) is quite beyond belief. The cost outweighs the singular reward of anything we experience in this lifetime. Why do we do it to ourselves? That is overt and obvious when you understand, and a long, trailing tale of confusion, mayhem, and just downright human ornery selfishness when you don't. You read the book now: Have you worked out the answer?

BIG CLUE: Saddam Hussein convinced his troops how evil the US was, how totally corrupt the entire system of the Americans was, by showing them footage of old people's homes. How could anyone cast out their parents into a home? What total barbarity was this? Mind you, the tug on the other side of the vision was the lure of Coca Cola and naked lustful women. Terribly evil, yet rather nice, which of course only makes it MORE evil.

Yet even as Iraqis hated America for what they did to old people, they were prepared to gas their neighbours and fellow Iraqi's with poison? As I say, we humans are a dichotomy.

I have met but ONE man who seemed truly above it all. He was my Spiritual Father, and in the 19 years I knew him not a single spiteful or hurtful word passed his lips. Even so, he was acutely observant. He knew when someone walked in a room what sort of baggage they were carrying, but rather than critique their fashion sense, he had compassion for what they could not let go.

Erwin Baudzus had fought in the Great War on Germany's side, and been sunk at sea three times. Hardly anyone survived a single sinking, he survived three, yet he said the hardest part was the five years AFTER the war. It was incredibly difficult, with everyone starving. Europe was wrung dry, financially, physically and emotionally.

So he came to Australia, expecting a very hard time because he was one of the soldiers that caused the world so much grief. Yet he arrived with his beautiful wife, Eva, and he was welcomed, given work, food, a place to live. He had expected to be beaten, chastised, and possibly even murdered, but hoped his wife would have a better life. None of that happened, he was brought into the arms of the Australian family, and just accepted for what he was.

He had a tear in his eye when he told me, and that was when he told me his secret: "I learned humility, I deeply learned it. As a race we Germans had wanted to conquer the world, but the kindness of these men and women who were once my enemy, just a few years earlier, this is what conquered me. I am free of myself, and thus I am now able to be myself."

And so I wish you this: I trust that, one day, you too will be conquered.

But the tale is not quite ended. This matter of the sheds and access was heard by the retiring Chief Justice of Equity, and he picked this case to be the very last one he heard. His judgement in ordering the sheds off the road was curious, in that It was only done, despite them being on public lands, because access was needed for a subdivision.

I ran this past no less than three Queens Counsels, who volunteered their time to inspect the judgement. I said to them, "The way I read this, Justice Hodgson is essentially saying that Public Lands can be used to build on by the public. In simple terms, I can build a house in the State forest, and as long as I am not obstructing anyone, this is perfectly legal now."

All three of the QC's agreed that this was how they, too, read the judgement.

It would appear that the retiring judge wanted to create a legal precedent that future generations here in Australia may need to take up. In this way, I walked away from Boringbar knowing that, perhaps, it had all served a greater purpose.

Perhaps.

I trust that, one day, you too will be conquered.

Overall, I know am not alone in any or all of the aforementioned dramas. Who has lived that has not known suffering? Most people's lives are a case study of the experience of loss. Each person's world is a series of gain, then loss, then regret. Some move past the passing "stuff" while others never get on top of things. Why? I am not certain. I do know the decisions we make are often guided by the depth of the Lies we tell ourselves.

So many false dreams! We earnestly believe these false things are real and it is in our very honesty of belief in a lie that creates the dysfunction.

So, here is the crux of the Boringbar War. What is a Dysfunction? It all boils down to a curious truth: It is the inability to see the obvious.

Think carefully on these words: The INABILITY to see the Obvious. Try as we might, we can't see the wood because of the trees. The Trees are all our "would be if could be" beliefs. All our hopes and aspirations, our dreams and our confusions are all rolled into a gestalt of perfectly imperfect faults.

The Truth? You want the Truth? Wouldn't you prefer something nicer? The truth is simply that the processes of most people's lives are surrounded in rings and veils of such glorious and insatiable dysfunction that we generally fail to recognise anything of true value until it is too late.

Because of the lies we believe are truth, we die not knowing ourselves, or at least we cannot admit to what we see in the mirror. But beyond all this philosophy of great and noble thoughts that we embellish and place on the portal of our personal wisdom, a stark soft centre remains.

The nut of it, the core of this rotten apple is a rude truth. I have learned in these last ten years plus two that beyond the waste, the difficulty and the process we endure, far past the things the lies we tell ourselves and each other, there is but one single result.

We either surmount the moment or else it drowns us. And in all of this the Tsunami of change awaits.

Yet though it all there is a constant mantra. *Yes: Life can be tragic. The Tides and changing fortunes of our lives can bring grief, but also joy.*

Life can serve up great loss. Whether this is losing money, grace, face, friends, support or whatever, it is a tragic thing. To discover the one you believed to be your friend was anything but, this is a very real tragedy. To discover that everything you believed to be right and proper is really just hand me down beliefs is tragic, not for the false beliefs, but for all the wasted time invested in these beliefs.

Look deeper in the mirror and we soon realise that all our fears and cravings and lonely nights have all just been just ourselves not in charge of our own imagination. That is the comic tragedy, the Divine Comedy.

Tragedy and loss. Perhaps this is the ring that binds them all. Look at Tolkien! His tales are a pure, unlimited tragedy, and yet by surviving same you are made glorious. But what does this mean to you and I? The answer can be found in an acceptance of tragedy.

It is, in fact, inevitable that we will suffer loss. The Tibetans tell us that we must contemplate our own death before we can appreciate our life. They are probably right. Certainly when I accept tragedy as a norm, it becomes less tragic. I am not sure if it ever becomes merely inconvenient, but the blow is lessened. Yet this is just one side of the coin.

Life can, and MUST, also be laughter as well. We all have our moments of triumph and joy that make life worthwhile, but really it is with our suffering that we learn the truths about ourselves. This truth the Buddha stated: That our tragedy, our pain, is the result of our passions and desires. And yet we learn more about ourselves BECAUSE of our petty human passions. (or not, as the case may be)

Envy, jealousy, etc. these PASSIONS are what set up the props for the One Act tragedy. These are what build our personal Towers of Babel. Our vanity sets us up, and our hubris takes us down. And it happens piecemeal, brick by brick. While the dramatic turns and events can shatter lives, for the most part we suffer slowly with a minor, inch by inch tragedy. Look at most every marriage if you don't believe me.

Like a rat gnawing through a wall to get to the meat, this state of reaching the tragic is incremental. It moves in small, certain steps towards a variety of uncertain fates. Then it opens! The Divorce falls on you like a guillotine, you lose your job, the shares you bought collapse in value, the money you invested gets stolen. The results of your personal termites decompose the floor under the rug where you have swept everything, and through the bottom of your experience you go! The heights you have created in your own mind become the very basis for the pain you suffer.

But then you recover, and build again. Hopefully this time it is not on sand, and in the rebuilding life reawakens in our veins. We see life anew, and spring lights the Cherry Blossom.

The Bard has been there way before me, and said it better. *Life is a Stage,* and the actors upon it are represented by the twin masks of Comedy and Tragedy. Yet each night the applause shifts, the moments differ and the results we experience will be what they will be. Sometimes, it is a glad event, a Midsummer's Nights Dream, and at other times pre-destined like Macbeth to its own sad end. We may pen an introduction, but really, life writes the script. And now I rewrite it so that others can understand.

So dear reader, it is settled. What we had here in the Boringbar War is a tragedy. I initially asked myself: Where do you start to paint such a thing? What colour do you use that is not completely black and white? And at what point did this horribly painful story turn into being just so damn weird that it became funny? You're the reader. You tell me if I managed to make it work, or not.

My personal travail arrived in the form of a twelve year saga of divorce, law courts, diabolical neighbours, human pettiness and extraordinary backstabbing on as grand a scale as the minds of any soap opera writer could imagine. The singular pivot to all of this, that moment when the specific choice was made which determined what road the fates would have me walk during the next 12

---

years, began with buying 250 acres at Boringbar. You too will have a pivot point, somewhere, sometime, so choose well.

In all, sad to say, this decision of mine extinguished the bright, easy going child within and burned a brand onto my Soul. Even now I can feel how it glows like a lighthouse, warning me of the rocks that lay ahead. The rocks which are the hard reality we term the Human Condition.

But let us not get morose! There is joy as well. And perhaps there is some freedom to be experienced? The precipice of purposelessness I have put you upon will hopefully give you, if nothing else, a vision of some horizon to avoid. This is a Travel brochure to tell you where you do NOT want to go, and which maybe will help you appreciate your own destiny a little more.

Allow me to apologise for the piecemeal pattern of words and stories I have presented to you. Usually you read a book and see the internal movie of it flash in front of your imagination. However, all you have met here is a series of jigsaw puzzles. This is a book of pieces, a TV Soap Opera rather than a novel. It's a remnant bin of things you throw out, not what you keep.

It is to be hoped that as you sorted through this personal rubbish bin from the last twelve years of my life that there was at least something to amuse you, some little titbit to put a smile on your face.

At the very least, if one day it seems to be a good idea to buy a large acreage in the backwoods. Well, think of "Greenacres" meets "Deliverance" and consider the next move very carefully.

So there we have it: The Boringbar War: A story about how I survived the War and had to pick up the Pieces.

It is 7:41 pm on Monday 13th June, 2006. My three days are up.

DONE!

HELLO PLANET EARTH

AVAILABLE ON AMAZON

Did this story brighten your day?

By the same author, you can also buy another book based around a series of short stories. This is a truly endearing book about a young man who goes into the wild to escape a society he doesn't understand, and discovers an extraordinarily wise child. Together, they sort out the purpose of each others life.

HELLO PLANET EARTH is an exquisite journey into a world of myth and fascination. It is story telling at its best. The disenchanted young man goes into the wild to find solace, and instead meets an amazing child, who teaches him about the real values he needs to grasp, through the stories of people he has met.

This book will leave you with a sense of joy and happiness.

Are you ready for something different?

From the same writer, we bring you the Divinity Dice Series. This series introduces a series of games that cast dice to give clear answers to questions you ask. It is remarkably accurate, and part of the Pythagorean Tradition made available for the modern person.

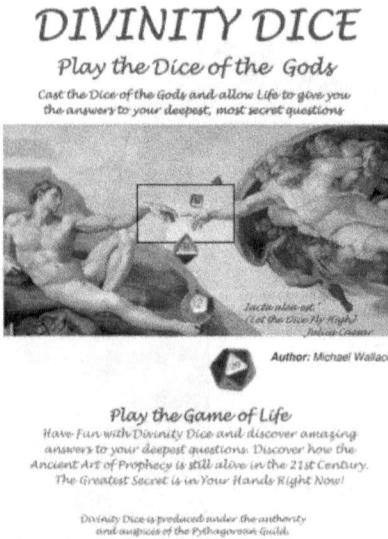

DIVINITY DICE
Play the Dice of the Gods

Cast the Dice of the Gods and allow Life to give you
the answers to your deepest, most secret questions

*Jacta alea est
(Let the Dice Fly High)
Julius Caesar*

Author: Michael Wallace

Play the Game of Life
Have fun with Divinity Dice and discover amazing
answers to your deepest questions. Discover how the
Ancient Art of Prophecy is still alive in the 21st Century.
The Greatest Secret is in Your Hands Right Now!

Divinity Dice is produced under the authority
and auspices of the Pythagorean Guild.

These books were written to help the individual grasp how number combinations worked. They provide an easy, practical way to give a natural "Oracular" readings, based on the various castings of the polyhedral dice.

Go to divinitydice.com.au for more information and pricing.

There is also a series of fun workshops available, which allow an individual to grasp the power of the Dice in a group atmosphere.

Absolutely ground breaking stuff!

Without doubt, the most comprehensive books on Dice Divination on the planet.
George Cockcroft, writer of "The Diceman"

Michael Wallace (Raven)

Michael Wallace is a remarkable individual. He is a Master Musician, Master Body Worker, Master Numerologist, Dice Master, Recording Artist, Songwriter, and Publisher. On top of all this he is also a prolific writer with over seventeen titles in print.

Known as "Raven", or what the Hopi describe as the Storm Bringer, he is a catalyst for change and renewal.

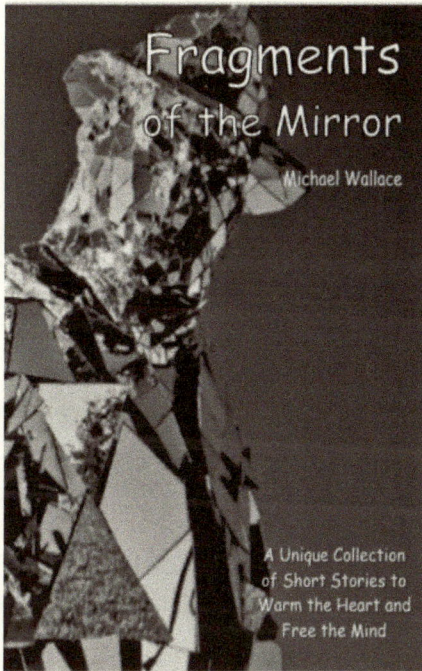

Fragments of the Mirror

Author: Michael Wallace

Available on Amazon

If you loved "The Boringbar War" then please go to Amazon and buy "Fragments of the Mirror". These are short stories that came from an earlier and far less jaded period in the authors life. These tales have a sweet resonance that restores kindness and love to the heart.

Alternatively: order from www.laddertothemoon.com.au

Other Books by this author:

The Book of Number Series

Jermimiah Versus the Grabblesnatch

The Divinity Dice Series

Ratology: Way of the Un-Dammed

Hello Planet Earth

Fragments of the Mirror

Water: More Precious than Gold

Enquiries should be made to the publishers at this Email Address.
Info.numberharmonics@gmail.com

ISBN: 978-0-9941798-0-7
Copyright 2015 Michael Wallace

www.ingramcontent.com/pod-product-compliance
Lightning Source LLC
Chambersburg PA
CBHW021137090426
42740CB00008B/825